SIGNIFICANT
ZERO

SIGNIFICANT ZERO

HEROES, VILLAINS, AND THE FIGHT FOR ART AND SOUL IN VIDEO GAMES

WALT WILLIAMS

ATRIA PAPERBACK

New York London Toronto Sydney New Delhi

ATRIA
PAPERBACK

An Imprint of Simon & Schuster, Inc.
1230 Avenue of the Americas
New York, NY 10020

Copyright © 2017 by Walter Williams

First Atria Paperback edition July 2018

ATRIA PAPERBACK and colophon are trademarks of Simon & Schuster, Inc.

For information about special discounts for bulk purchases, please contact Simon & Schuster Special Sales at 1-866-506-1949 or business@simonandschuster.com.

The Simon & Schuster Speakers Bureau can bring authors to your live event. For more information or to book an event, contact the Simon & Schuster Speakers Bureau at 1-866-248-3049 or visit our website at www.simonspeakers.com.

Interior design by Silverglass Design

Manufactured in the United States of America

10 9 8 7 6 5 4 3 2 1

The Library of Congress has cataloged the hardcover edition as follows:

Names: Williams, Walt, author.
Title: Significant zero : heroes, villains, and the fight for art and soul in video games / Walt Williams.
Description: New York : Atria Books, 2017.
Identifiers: LCCN 2017018270 (print) | LCCN 2017037552 (ebook) |
ISBN 9781501129971 (ebook) | ISBN 9781501129957 (hardback) |
ISBN 9781501129964 (paperback)
Subjects: LCSH: Williams, Walt. | Video games industry. | Video games—Design. |
Violence in video games. | Video game designers—United States—Biography. |
BISAC: GAMES / Video & Electronic. | BIOGRAPHY & AUTOBIOGRAPHY /
Entertainment & Performing Arts.
Classification: LCC GV1469.3 (ebook) | LCC GV1469.3 .W57 2017 (print) |
DDC 794.8—dc23
LC record available at https://lccn.loc.gov/2017018270

ISBN 978-1-5011-2995-7
ISBN 978-1-5011-2996-4 (pbk)
ISBN 978-1-5011-2997-1 (ebook)

Dedicated to K & P

Zero: *noun*; a digit or number lacking either positive or negative value.

Significant Zero: *noun*; a zero located between significant digits; that which on its own has no value, yet alters the value of whatever it touches.

CONTENTS

AUTHOR'S NOTE

In telling this story, I have made some adjustments. Some names and characteristics have been changed, and some composite characters have been created. Certain events have been combined and/or reordered. For the sake of anonymity, one situation has been retold from my perspective, with the permission of those involved.

1

TUTORIAL

My first video-game console was a cardboard box.

They called it the Nintendo Cereal System, and it was gifted to our world in 1988 by Ralston, a purveyor of fine license-based cereals. Unlike their other brands, such as Donkey Kong, Gremlins, and Ghostbusters, the NCS wasn't inspired by an intellectual property but rather a piece of hardware—the Nintendo Entertainment System, an actual honest-to-God video-game console and the one thing I wanted more than anything else in the world.

I'll admit, the Nintendo Cereal System was a poor substitute. As food, it lacked the impossible flavor profiles of modern, cutting-edge breakfast treats like Waffle Stix, Go-Gurt, and Ice Cream Shoppe Frosted Rainbow Cookie Sandwich Pop-Tarts. Its selection of playable games was limited to exactly zero. And yet, without a doubt, the Nintendo Cereal System was the best console I have ever owned.

To gaze upon the NCS was to see true innovation: one box containing two different cereals, each representing a different game—*Super Mario Bros.* and *The Legend of Zelda*. It promised "two different natural & artificial flavors." Mario was fruity. Zelda was berry. Both tasted like sweetened sawdust. Their shaped pieces bore no resemblance to the source material. There was nothing good about the cereal, and that was fine, because I didn't buy the Nintendo Cereal System for the cereal. I bought it for the box. And oh, what a box it was.

Across the top, in beautiful red letters, was the Nintendo logo. Beneath it sat a large square, its corners rounded to mimic those of a TV screen. On the left side was a poorly drawn interpretation of *Super Mario Bros.*, and on the right, *The Legend of Zelda*. I cut a rectangle out of cardboard, just big enough to hold in both hands. With crayons, I added buttons—Up, Down, Left, Right, B, A, Select, and Start. A shoelace stolen from my sister's shoe connected it to the cardboard console.

I would play that box for hours. My fingers mashed imaginary buttons as my imagination projected action onto that unmoving cardboard screen. I was Mario, flinging turtle shells like cannonballs, and Link, kicking lizard-men into dust. None of it was real, but it was perfect in every way. Reality never stood a chance.

That Christmas, I received a real Nintendo Entertainment System. It was the Action Set—the one that came with the two-in-one *Super Mario Bros.* and *Duck Hunt* cartridge and the NES Zapper, a light gun used to shoot down digital ducks. While my father plugged it into the TV, I read the manual from cover to cover. This is what it told me:

One day the kingdom of the peaceful Mushroom People was invaded by the Koopa, a tribe of turtles famous for their black magic. The quiet, peace-loving Mushroom People were turning into mere stones, bricks, and even field horsehair plants, and the Mushroom Kingdom fell into ruin.

The only one who can undo the magic spell on the Mushroom People and return them to their normal selves is the Princess Toadstool, the daughter of the Mushroom King. Unfortunately, she is presently in the hands of the great Koopa turtle king.

Mario, the hero of the story (maybe) hears about the Mushroom People's plight and sets out on a quest to free the Mushroom Princess from the evil Koopa and restore the fallen kingdom of the Mushroom People.

You are Mario! It's up to you to save the Mushroom People from the black magic of the Koopa!

It was nonsense, but my eight-year-old brain latched onto it like a Bloober, a squid the game warned me was "a guy to look out for." I was Mario; the manual said so. It was up to me to save the Mushroom People. This was my story.

Except it wasn't. This real, playable version of *Super Mario Bros.* was nothing like the game I'd been playing in my head for months. Instead of punching turtles and flying through the air, I mostly fell down holes and got mauled by Goombas, sentient shiitake mushrooms that have sprouted feet and fangs. My excitement turned to frustration as each death brought me closer to tears. This wasn't a game. Games were meant to be fun.

That was the angriest Christmas of my life. The longer I played, the sloppier I got. My deaths piled up, my blood boiled. All that pressure needed a release, and jumping on evil turtles wasn't doing the trick. I screamed and cried and swore off video games forever, which never lasts long when you're eight years old. Little by little, I progressed through the game, until late that evening I stood on a bridge across from my enemy—Bowser, king of the Koopa—a fire-breathing, spike-backed dragon turtle.

My fingers jerked wildly across the controller. On the screen, Mario leapt over fireballs, then sprinted beneath Bowser's legs to grab an axe someone had carelessly left on the far side of the bridge. With one smooth motion—so smooth you didn't even see it—Mario brought the axe down, severing the bridge's cables. It fell into fire, and Bowser followed. The king was dead. Long live me.

"Mom! Dad!" I shouted. "Come here! Bring the camera!"

I had accomplished the impossible and needed proof. No one in the history of video games could have beaten *Super Mario Bros.* in a single day. Was I the greatest video-game player alive? Yes. Yes, I was.

On-screen, Mario ran ahead to the next room, where Princess Toadstool was waiting to be rescued. When I saw her, my heart stopped.

This was not the princess I'd been expecting. She was short; shorter than Mario. On her head sat an oversize helmet covered in red-and-white polka dots. Strangest of all, she appeared to be wearing a diaper. Ten words appeared above her head.

THANK YOU MARIO!
BUT OUR PRINCESS IS IN ANOTHER CASTLE!

The game wasn't over; there were twenty-eight more levels to go. Our princess had not been saved. Mario, that mustachioed shit-weasel, had lied to me. This wasn't my story at all.

TWENTY-THREE YEARS LATER, I was in Santa Monica, directing voice recordings for *Spec Ops: The Line*, the tenth installment in the long-running military game franchise. It was May. Or maybe it was April. I could be wrong. For all I know, it was August. The year was definitely 2011, that much I'm sure of; but the rest is hazy.

This is not uncommon. The days and months blur when you're locked in a crunch cycle. Faced with a steady rhythm of day-in, day-out shit-work, the human brain has a number of safety mechanisms designed to keep you from going insane. Losing your sense of time is just one. Emotional dampening is another. They're good for a week or two, but the longer you crunch, the less effective they become. To hold off your inevitable implosion, you bolster your willpower with caffeine, alcohol, or substances more illicit; whatever sees you through to the other side, where you'll come out wondering who you are and where you've been and why the world seems to have moved on without you. It feels as if you've traveled through time, the only evidence to the contrary being your pale, bloated body, which has somehow aged faster than should be possible, and so you stumble blinkingly into the sun, hoping to find the person you were before this started, and maybe—just maybe—feel whole again.

Which is all to say, I don't remember what month it was.

Here's what I do know: the world was gone. Everything except for the one mile between my hotel and the recording studio had been erased. From 9:00 a.m. to 6:00 p.m., I directed audio sessions for *Spec Ops*. From 7:00 p.m. to midnight, I wrote scripts for a second game being recorded down the hall. The only thing keeping me upright was a diet of Adderall, Red Bull, and cheap red wine, which was necessary to numb the pain of a bulging disc at the base of my neck. Sitting, standing, typing—they all brought pain. Since I spent most of my time doing two of those at once, it usually felt like fire was coursing through my veins. Thank God I was living my dream, or else I'd have really felt like shit.

Pain had no place in the studio. Inside, there was no suffering—only work. This was our final recording session with Nolan North, Christopher Reid, and Omid Abtahi, our three main actors. We'd been working together for nearly four years, and this would be the last time we were all in the same room. I had four hours to get everything I needed. There wasn't even time to feel sad.

Halfway through the session, my BlackBerry blinked red. I had mail. My heart rate jumped well above its normal 121. A sudden layer of sweat burst across my skin, soaking my clothes and drawing them tight. Everyone knew I was recording. If they were emailing me, something was wrong.

SUBJECT: Hey

They're starting the game with the helicopter chase.

The surface temperature of my body dropped two degrees.

"They" were Yager, the Berlin game studio making *Spec Ops*. The helicopter chase was a scene in the game that took place around the fifth or sixth hour. In it, the main characters steal an enemy helicopter, only to be struck down by a sandstorm. It was a big moment, the climax of our second act, and it had no place at the start of the story.

Flash-forwards are a cheap trick: instead of hooking your audience with a smart, enticing opener, you jump ahead to something exciting and action packed. It's shameless, and I wanted no part of it. In fact, I'd already killed the idea a year before. We'd put months of work into the opening hour of *Spec Ops*. It was slow by design. Undercutting that with a flash-forward would reek of self-doubt. It would say to the player, "We don't think you're mature enough to handle a video game that isn't all action, all the time. Have some explosions, you mouth-breathing yokel. Please don't sell us back to GameStop."

A change of this magnitude required an executive decision. Only three people had that kind of power. The first two were the creative directors, Cory Davis and François Coulon, neither of whom would make the decision without consulting the other. Since Cory was sitting beside me in the recording studio, I knew they weren't to blame. That left only my boss, the Fox. Only he would have the gall to try this while I was stuck in recording, unable to push back. This was outright betrayal. Even worse, it was sloppy. The Fox should have known better.

I scribbled a quick scene on the back of my script.

We're back at the HELICOPTER CHASE from the PROLOGUE.
Walker can sense something is wrong.

WALKER
Wait! This isn't right!

LUGO
Well, it's too late now!

WALKER
No—I mean we've done this already!

ADAMS
What?!

WALKER

Fuck it! Never mind! Just shake these assholes!

Not my best work, but it did the trick.

I explained the situation to my actors. "We need to revisit the helicopter chase at the end of chapter 12 so we can grab some alternate lines. The scene will play out exactly the same as before, except for five new lines at the beginning. Nolan, after the chopper takes off, you're overcome with a crazy sense of déjà vu. You try explaining it to Chris and Omid, but nothing you're saying makes sense to them, so you shake it off, grab the Gatling gun, and start shooting down enemy choppers."

That was all Nolan, Chris, and Omid needed. I fed them the lines, one by one, and three takes later we were done. Afterward, Nolan gave me a look. Like his character, he could tell something was wrong. He was right to feel suspicious.

There was no way I could reverse the Fox's decision. *Spec Ops: The Line* would open with a helicopter chase, whether I liked it or not. But it wouldn't be a flash-forward. The lines we had just recorded would only play during the chase at the end of act 2. By changing those lines, we were changing the story.

I grabbed my BlackBerry and responded to the email that had started this whole ordeal. "Everyone dies in the helicopter crash at the start of the game. Everything after that is a hallucination as we lie dying in the wreckage."

This was my story, and I'd burn it all down before I let anyone take it away.

2

GOD, LIES, AND VIDEO GAMES

I never wanted to make video games.

Growing up in Louisiana, I didn't know it was an option. Games were made by Nintendo, Nintendo was in Japan, and Japan was a long ways away from Bossier City. Even if I'd known, it wouldn't have made a difference. Growing up, the only thing I wanted to be was Rainbow Brite. R. B. was a 1980s cartoon character who controlled all the color in the world and rode around on a talking stallion named Starlite. As badass as she was, this was not a practical career choice. Ignoring that she's a fictional character, Rainbow Brite just didn't have the staying power of her contemporaries. If I'd been smart, I would have picked a character from the Transformers, Ghostbusters, or even My Little Pony. But the heart wants what it wants.

I wish I could tell you there was a straight line from rainbow-powered pony princess to moderately successful video-game writer. The truth is, as much as we like to romanticize the idea of fate, there is never one thing that determines who we will become. Most of us don't have a Batman moment, where watching our parents get gunned down in Crime Alley sets us on a path to our one true destiny. And thank God for that, because in reality, those moments are more crippling than empowering. For the most part, we get by moment to moment, our experiences nudging us toward a future we can't see.

My first nudge was Sara, the student helper in Mrs. Green's kindergarten class. She was an older woman, a fifth grader at least, with cherry-brown hair and crystal-green eyes. It was my first taste of puppy love. I was dumbstruck whenever she walked into the room. Literally. When Mrs. Green taught us the alphabet, Sara and the kids who could read would go to the hallway for story time. So when our teacher asked those who could read to raise their hands, mine shot straight up. I'd never read a word in my life, but if it meant following Sara into the hall, I would have claimed mastery of any skill they asked. It never occurred to me that I'd have to back it up.

In the hallway, we sat in a circle and took turns reading a page from the book *Fun with Dick and Jane.* I knew that when it came my turn to read, my lie would be exposed. The other kids would laugh, but that was fine; they'd laughed at me before. What scared me was the idea of Sara casting me out of the circle forever. I thought about running, pretending to be sick, anything to escape that circle, but there was no time. The book landed in my lap. I looked down, expecting to see gibberish. Instead, I saw salvation—eight words forever seared into my memory.

See Spot. See Spot run.
Run, Spot.
Run.

Hot damn. I could read.

This was a teachable moment. Had anyone else been aware of what had transpired, they could have set me straight. Instead, the drama played out inside my head, leaving me to find my own moral to the story. Being a kindergartener, I latched onto the most obvious one.

Lying was magic.

Remember that one kid in elementary school who claimed to have an uncle who worked for Nintendo? I was that kid. In my version of the story, I swapped the uncle for my older brother. All it took was convincing a few kids, who in turn told others, and suddenly I was transformed from Walt, the nerdy kid, to Walt, the nerdy kid other kids pretended to like so they could come over and play top secret Nintendo games sent from my brother in Japan. It was amazing. I could be anyone, have anything, so long as I was brave enough to lie about it.

I hit all the classics: "At my last school, I was totally the cool kid. Don't believe me? You can ask my girlfriend when she comes to visit, *from Canada*. We met at summer camp. After she discovered my secret identity, she made me promise to be her boyfriend or else she'd tell everyone who I really am. She's pretty fine, though, so it's okay. Secret identity? Oh, it's nothing. Just, you know, I'M SPIDER-MAN!!!" (That last one might be unique to me.)

It's easy to convince people you have top secret Nintendo games at your house, so long as they never come over to play. But all it takes is falling off the jungle gym for everyone to realize you weren't bitten by a radioactive arachnid. Just like that, I was back at the bottom of the grade school social ladder. At least I still had video games to keep me company.

Super Mario Bros. may have disappointed me, but my faith in Nintendo was strong. I begged my mom to let me rent something new. At the video store, one game stood out among all the rest—*Marble Madness*. Marbles were great. I loved their whorls of color suspended in three dimensions and hoarded them in leather pouches hidden around my house. Without a doubt, this was the game for me.

To this day, I have never beaten the second level.

From there, it was nothing but more heartache. *Bubble Bobble, Blaster Master, Castlevania II: Simon's Quest, Ghosts 'n Goblins, Teenage Mutant Ninja Turtles, Who Framed Roger Rabbit*: when it came to picking brutal, unforgiving games, my record was 100 percent. These games weren't just hard; they practically cheated the player. In *Castlevania II*, characters would tell you where to go and what to do—and they'd be lying. To beat *Bubble Bobble*, you had to defeat the final boss in two-player mode *and* pick up a magic crystal which only appears for a few seconds; none of which the game ever tells you. If you managed to defeat the final boss of *Ghosts 'n Goblins*, you had to play through the entire game again, on a much harder difficulty level, because—surprise!—that wasn't actually the final boss. The only game I showed any skill at was *Duck Hunt*. Place an NES Zapper light gun in my hand, and suddenly I was Wild Bill Hickok, so long as I held the barrel of the gun directly against the TV screen.

If it weren't for my friend Jono, I might have given up on games and spent the rest of my childhood looking into those "sports" I'd heard so much about. Instead, on his recommendation, I rented a game called *Final Fantasy*.

Developed and published by Square in 1987, *Final Fantasy* wasn't released in North America until 1990. It was an RPG, or role-playing game, a term mostly associated with *Dungeons & Dragons* at the time. What made *Final Fantasy* different from other video games was the structure. Instead of playing as a single, predefined character, I got to play as four characters of my own creation. Each character was defined by a class, or skill set. They could be warriors and thieves, black belts and mages. Choosing a character's skill was exciting, but getting to name them was the real attraction. The game only gave you four letters, but that's all I needed. Walt was the perfect fit.

For the first time in my life, I didn't have to play as Mario or Samus or Link. I could be me, only better. *Final Fantasy*'s Walt was a thief, stealthy and swift. The other three characters were idealized versions of my friends. Jono was a black mage, master of dark magic. My friend Phillip was a black belt, mainly because he was the strongest kid I knew, but also because Phil fit the game's four-letter limit. The final party member was a white mage healer named Sara, Alli, Katy, or whoever else I had a crush on at the time. My history of unrequited love is written across old video-game save files. These girls didn't know I existed in the real world, but on my TV screen, they fought by my side against the forces of evil.

After *Final Fantasy*, the only games I played were those that let me change my character's name. Next was *The Legend of Zelda*, which closed the loop on my Nintendo Cereal System fantasies. After that was

Dragon Warrior, which I quickly wrote off as a cheap *Final Fantasy* clone, even though it had been released a year earlier. Then came the wonderfully silly *StarTropics*, which brought the experience into the real world by including a paper map I had to dampen to reveal a secret code necessary to complete the game. When I played these games, I didn't have to be Walt with the big ears and Coke-bottle glasses. I could be strong, capable, and most of all, important. That was the real fantasy, I think—not power or heroism but relevancy. In those games, I mattered.

WHEN I WAS A kid, my gaming was limited strictly to consoles, like the Nintendo Entertainment System. Our house wasn't what you'd call technologically advanced. My parents weren't the type to throw out something that still worked. When everyone else in our neighborhood was going crazy over cordless phones, we were still rocking rotary classic.

I knew people played games on their computers, I just didn't know how. My computer couldn't run anything more complex than solitaire. I'd visit my local game store, Babbage's, and stare longingly at PC games like *The 7th Guest*, *Alone in the Dark*, *Phantasmagoria*, and *The Beast Within*. Their box art was dark and disturbing, like something you'd find in the horror aisle of a video store. It screamed, "This is for adults." I was intrigued. What kid wouldn't be? But I'd never find out what those boxes contained, because PC games are evil.

Here's what happens when you buy a PC game:

You convince your mom to drive you to the mall. Not your dad, because he already thinks you spend too much time playing Super Nintendo. If he finds out the computer can also play games, he's likely to throw it out. At the mall, you run ahead of your mom, making sure you're outside her shouting range when she passes through the young men's section of JCPenney, otherwise you'll be trying on slacks for the next hour. Also, no one wants their mom looming over them at the game store. The cool kids would laugh at you. Everyone knows cool kids don't have moms. At the store, you agonize over which game to buy. Nothing you see is familiar. There are no mustachioed plumbers or blue-finned hedgehogs; those are kid's games. At thirteen, you're practically a grown-up. Using your adult intellect, you select the game most likely to show you some boobs, then make your purchase, being careful not to look the cashier in the eye. Afterward, you meet your mom in the food court, where you eat a corn dog because corn dogs are delicious. You lie to her about the game you bought, keeping it carefully wrapped in its bag so she can't see it. If she sees it, she'll know about the boobs. On your way out of the mall, you stick by your mother's side. You're almost in the clear; you just have to play it cool. Too late, you realize your mistake—JCPenney is having a sale on slacks, and you're just growing so gosh-darn fast. An hour later, you finally head home. Alone in your room, you unbox your latest treasure and load its disc into the CD-ROM drive, at which point the computer looks you square in the face and says, "Eat a bowl of dicks." Oh, did you want to play the game you just bought? Well, you can't, because the application wasn't able to start correctly, or the cabinet file had an invalid digital signature, or the VC++ runtime redistributable package wasn't installed successfully. What do these things mean? The computer isn't going to tell you. Ha ha. The end.

After the third time, I decided PC gaming wasn't for me.

Once more, Jono stepped in to save me from my foolish ways. At his house, he introduced me to a PC game called *Quest for Glory: So You Want to Be a Hero*. Like *Final Fantasy*, it was a role-playing game that allowed me to create my own character. Again, I played as a thief. When I was a kid, I got picked on a lot. Thieves had an uncanny ability to avoid detection. That appealed to me.

The best part of being a thief was the Thieves Guild. Hidden under the floorboards of the Aces and Eights Tavern, the guild was a place where thieves could be thieves. You could fence stolen goods, play a game of Dag-Nab-It with the Chief, or just hang out with Crusher, the Guild's Orc bodyguard. It was like being in a club. It was so much fun,

I began to wonder why it couldn't carry over to the real world. Stealing wasn't magic; it was a real thing people did all the time. If my friends and I could establish our own Thieves Guild, we'd be rich. I even knew exactly what we could steal—adult magazines. We'd all seen them sitting on the top magazine rack of the bookstore in our local mall: *Playboy*, *Penthouse*, *Hustler*, taunting us from behind their black wrappers. For a group of adolescent boys in a pre-Internet world, these magazines were more valuable than gold.

We met in the mall's food court after school. It was far enough away from the bookstore that none of the employees would see us together. It was also near the corn dog stand.

The Fixer entered the store first. He found a book of which there was only one copy, hid it somewhere in the store, and then returned to the food court. Next came the Lookout. That was me. My job was to browse books and keep an eye out for trouble. If things went south, I'd leave the store, signaling everyone else to abort the operation.

Once I was in position, the Decoy, Flipper, and Bagman entered in quick succession. The Decoy went straight to the counter and asked for help locating the book our Fixer had hidden. One of the two clerks followed the Decoy to the back of the store, at which point the Bagman approached the counter, ready to purchase some comics. While this took place, our Flipper subtly grabbed an adult magazine off the top rack and placed it on a lower shelf, inside a copy of *Sports Illustrated*.

The Bagman, now holding a bag of newly acquired comics, headed for the exit. On his way out, he spotted something on a table and stopped to look. At the same time, the Flipper took a magazine to the counter and paid for it. While the clerk was distracted, the Bagman picked up the *Sports Illustrated*, casually dropped the adult magazine into his bag of comics, then exited the store. The plan went off without a hitch. I wish I could say the same for Phase Two.

My idea was to rip out the pages of the magazine and sell them at school. That's how it worked in *Quest for Glory*: you stole something so you could sell it. Before the dawn of dial-up, porn was in high demand and low supply, so we could charge whatever we wanted. The price was set at twenty dollars a page. We were going to be rich—at least, we would have been, if there were such a thing as honor among thieves.

In the end, our Flipper was overcome with guilt. He ratted us out to our parents. We were grounded and banned from the mall; all fair punishments. But it didn't stop there. Faced with the knowledge that their children had become perverted criminals, they did what any parent in the South would do. They sent us to church.

IN THE BIBLE BELT, religion is a way of life—less of a doctrine, more of a social obligation. You can opt out, but you can't escape it.

South Louisiana is historically Catholic, due to its large French and Creole communities. North Louisiana, where I'm from, leans more to the Evangelical side of things. We like our preachers loud, our sex post-marital, and our choruses praiseworthy. It's an intoxicating mixture of theatrical drama and real-world peril. Impressionable teenager that I was, I couldn't resist.

First off, the Evangelical narrative was fantastic. With its emphasis on the book of Revelation, it interpreted nearly anything as a sign of the End Times. The world around me was a battlefield where angels and demons fought for the greatest prize of all—my very soul. It was like living in an action movie only I was aware of, and it was all building to the show-stopping climax, when I'd be whisked away to Heaven to watch the apocalyptic extravaganza from the safety of my cloud-cushioned box seats, bought and paid for by the blood of Jesus Christ, hallelujah A-men.

Another great thing was the sinning. As Evangelicals, we wanted to dance and drink and fornicate—we just weren't allowed. I was taught to fight temptation, and I did. But that never stopped it from building up in my chest like a balloon until I couldn't take it anymore and would finally just give in. Afterward, it took only a prayer for forgiveness to wash away my shame and start the cycle all over again. Honestly, there was nothing better. Candy is always sweeter when you know you shouldn't eat it.

The best part was that everything happened for a reason. This wasn't a trite, half-assed sentiment. Everything literally happened for a reason, good or bad, and the reason was always me. If my mom died in a tragic car accident, it was because God wanted to make me stronger. If mom left me a million dollars in her will, God was rewarding my faith. If I blew Mom's millions on cocaine and hookers, it was because God wanted me to fall so He could lift me back up. The Evangelical universe revolved around me, and I thought that was grand.

High-stakes adventure with no real risk, a reward loop driven by delayed gratification, and the emotional security of socially acceptable narcissism: no wonder I was drawn to organized religion. It was structured just like a video game.

IT WAS MY LOVE of the Lord that led me to Baylor University in Waco, Texas, the largest Baptist university in the world. I come from a military family, so it was understood that I'd attend college on an air force scholarship. In exchange for tuition, I agreed to four years of active service, to be completed upon graduation.

My plan was to study religion and become a military chaplain. But college has a way of shifting your priorities. There's something about the unsupervised freedom found within an idealized coed environment that makes you question everything you once believed. That something is called casual sex. Let's be honest: God is great, but He's not much of a cuddler. He and I didn't even make it to the end of freshman orientation before deciding to see other people.

Our breakup was made official when I switched majors to telecommunications, the closet thing available to a film degree. The way I saw it, when I graduated college, the air force would slot me into whatever role they wished, regardless of my major. I might as well study something I enjoyed. It was in Baylor's communications school, the Castellaw Communications Center, that I learned of the NoZe Brothers, a secret society of gadflies and thieves. The NoZe had plagued Baylor for almost eighty years. The administration desperately wanted to expel them from campus, but no one knew who they were. Aside from their very rare public appearances, the only proof the NoZe existed was a newspaper called *The Rope*. Every so often, a new issue would appear on campus, tackling topical issues through the use of satire, story, and fat jokes.

Everything I had wanted as a kid was right there in front of me. I had to join.

According to *The Rope*, the application process was simple. All I had to do was write a humorous article. I chose to analyze a nonexistent book, *Itty Bitty Bang Bang: The Soft & Seedy World of Midget Pornography*, including quotes and works cited. The instructions said to print it out, wait until nightfall on a given date, locate a certain church, go around back, find the bearded man carrying a flaming torch, and throw my article in a nearby garbage can. If my submission was deemed worthy, the NoZe would contact me. I did as I was told. Around 3:00 a.m., I received a call. What happened after that I can't really say. I remember being rolled down an assembly line in an abandoned industrial building while watching a fat, shirtless man pretend to smoke cigarettes through his belly button. Aside from that, the memories are hazy.

BEING A MEMBER OF a secret society isn't something you broadcast to the world, especially if it includes a regular schedule of vandalism, breaking and entering, and theft. But since the statutes of limitations have surely expired on any alleged crimes, I don't mind saying that yes, I was a NoZe Brother.

Unsurprisingly, the military didn't look kindly on my membership in an antiauthoritarian group dedicated to the humiliation of Baylor's leadership and principles. A semester before graduation, my scholarship was pulled and my commission was canceled. It was entirely my fault. If I'd kept my mouth shut, the air force never would have known about me and the NoZe. I just didn't see a point in joining a secret society if I couldn't brag about it.

I'd been banking on that guaranteed four-year job. Now that it was gone, I had nothing but a degree in telecommunications, a 45 percent attendance rate, and a 2.4 GPA. It was the best thing that ever happened to me.

You see, working on *The Rope* had kindled something inside of me. I'd spent many late nights composing articles and stories, and through them discovered a true passion for writing. It was a compulsion. If I wasn't writing *The Rope*, I was writing screenplays, short stories, anything that put words on paper.

It hit me fast. One moment, I was looking at words, simple tools of communication and expression. The next, I blinked, so fast my brain didn't register the action, but when my eyes opened, everything had changed. Those words, once simple letters, had allowed me to see them for what they truly were—ancient runes, almost alchemical in power and potential. I knew then exactly what I wanted to do with my life. There was no more confusion. I didn't want to be a cartoon, a preacher, an officer, or even a thief. The rest of my life would be lived in service to those goddamned unassuming words.

That's exactly what I told my parents when I called to tell them I'd been kicked out of the air force. "Don't worry," I said. "Everything will be fine.

"I'm going to be a writer."

3

BREAKING IN

BREAKING IN

There is an upside to desperation.

Creating art is hard, even painful. Writing in particular can require days, if not months, of solitude, doubt, and struggle against your better judgment. To be good, you have to put in the time and the effort. You have to consume the work of others, both good and bad. You have to write, then revise and revise and revise and revise until you can accept it is time to let go. Most importantly, you have to sit down every day and punch yourself in the face repeatedly, hoping in the end you will come out the winner in a fight against no one but yourself. You can teach yourself to live this way, but it does not come naturally.

Contentment, comfort, financial security—these are the natural enemies of the aspiring writer. Humans instinctually flee from suffering; it is hardwired into our DNA. When that suffering is emotional, writing can serve as an act of retreat. This is why it's important for writers to suffer, in one form or another. The good must be driven out until only the negative remains: jealousy, pettiness, desperation. And the greatest of these is desperation.

A year after graduation, I was living in New York, subleasing a ten-by-twelve room in Alphabet City. All I had was a laptop, a suitcase full of clothes, a broken futon I'd found on the curb, and a metal end table with wire baskets and a wooden top, which served as both my desk and dresser. It was June; my rent was paid to the end of August. I had around two thousand dollars I'd managed to save up by slinging CDs at a mall in Austin, Texas. It was just enough money to see me through the summer. That gave me three months to figure shit out, find a job, sign a lease, and start a life in New York City, a place where I knew next to no one.

Just because I was unemployed doesn't mean I was without work. While living in Austin, I had connected with a pair of aspiring producers working with a director who lived in Hell's Kitchen. For the life of me, I can't remember the guy's name, so Guy is what we'll call him. Guy directed rap videos but was looking to move into feature films. He had a script: a 1980s true-crime story about Jamaican drug dealers in Brooklyn. It was in rough shape. The man who penned it had lived through the events, so he knew them firsthand, but he wasn't a screenwriter. The producers suggested I could take a few passes at the script. I suggested they pay me.

"Get it to a filmable state," they said. "Something we can sell. Then we'll talk money."

It sounded shady, but no one else was banging on my door. By July, the script was finished and sent to everyone involved. The next day, I awoke to two text messages. The first was from one of the producers: "This is great. I think we're officially in the movie business"—which was surprising, as I thought he already was in the movie business.

I texted back, "Glad you like it. Let's draw up a contract."

Response: "I like that you're serious about your career, but this kind of talk can scare away good opportunities."

I knew it was bullshit, but part of me held out hope. I wanted to believe this could be my big break. Unfortunately, the summer was halfway over, and money was getting tight. I didn't have the luxury of waiting around for them. I needed to find a way to turn words into cash. If screenwriting was the highest rung on the professional-writing ladder, I would go a few steps lower and try again.

Comic books seemed like a viable path. I'd been a fan my whole life, ever since my older brother left me a box of *Swamp Thing* and *Marvel Age* issues, but what really got me hooked was reading my first

Spider-Man comics while home sick with the flu. Peter Parker, the man behind Spider-Man's mask, was a lot like me: smart, socially awkward, and picked on by others. In other words, we were nerds. I'd always been drawn to characters like Peter. Donatello from *Teenage Mutant Ninja Turtles* and Egon Spengler from *Ghostbusters* were great fictional role models. Their bookishness didn't exclude them from groups; rather, it made their inclusion vital. Spider-Man, however, was not a team player. He and his secret identity, Peter Parker, were both outcasts, shunned no matter what they did. Not a great example for a budding young mind, but certainly more relatable. Reading Spider-Man comics didn't make me any less nerdy, but the inspiration I found in them made me confident enough not to care. When I ended up an aspiring writer in Manhattan, it seemed only natural for me to get a job at Marvel, work my way up the ladder, and repay the favor by writing *The Amazing Spider-Man*.

This was 2004, four years before Marvel would release the first Iron Man movie, beginning their transformation into a multibillion-dollar cinematic juggernaut. They had the X-Men and Spider-Man franchises at Sony Pictures but were still mostly known for their comics. Even so, I knew they had to receive hundreds of CVs every day. If I was going to stand out, I'd needed to do something drastic, like walk straight into their office and ask for a job.

You'd be surprised how easy it was to do that.

With a freshly printed résumé in hand, I hailed a cab to Midtown. On my dad's advice, I wore a suit—slightly wrinkled, but nothing too horrendous. All my life, he'd told me to always wear a suit when meeting a potential employer. He should know, having worked a few summers at his brother's suit store. In the fifties. I'd have bet good money no one at Marvel wore a suit to work. It seemed wrong to show up in one, but no more wrong than showing up at their door unannounced, without an appointment.

After what felt like the longest elevator ride of my life, I found myself standing outside the Marvel office. I tested the door: locked. I rang the bell. A moment later, the door opened just enough for a very tall, very muscular man to peer out. He was wearing a T-shirt and jeans. I silently cursed my father.

"Can I help you?" the man asked. His tone made it clear this was just a figure of speech.

I launched into the speech I'd practiced on the ride up. "Hi! I'm Walt Williams. I was wondering about any job openings you might have. I recently graduated from college and have always wanted to work at Marvel, so I thought I'd stop by and introduce myself. I'm a hard worker and a fast learner, and I'm willing to do whatever it takes to learn the ropes, even if it means starting in the mail room." That's right; my entire plan amounted to working my way up from the mail room. Why? Because that's what I'd seen people do on the tee-vee.

The man stood up straighter. "I'm the mail room."

I got the hint; I just didn't take it. I had paid for the cab ride there, so I was damn sure going to see it through. "Well, like I said, I'm willing to do any job. Whatever it takes to be part of the Marvel family. Is there anyone here I can talk to?"

"Everyone's at lunch."

"That's okay." I pushed my résumé through the cracked door. "If you could just pass on my résumé, I'd really appreciate it."

"Yeah, uh-huh." Okay, he was done. He shut the door in my face.

I still haven't heard back from them.

Over the next couple of weeks, I crept further down the writing ladder. I was too long-winded for short stories, but didn't have enough to say for a book. Essays and articles were too dry for my taste and left me wanting to shove a pencil in my eye. I submitted reviews for restaurants, plays, books, and films. Not a single one earned a response, and with good reason—I was a terrible critic. If I hated a play or a restaurant, it was easy to rip it apart with words, but I lacked the thoughtfulness to analyze and celebrate the things I loved. It's a good thing there was no market for clickbait and hot takes back then, or else I never would have learned there is a big difference between being a writer and being an asshole.

My writing options were exhausted, my bank account nearly depleted. I needed to make something happen soon, or the whole adventure would have been for nothing. I was now desperate enough to do what I should have done from the beginning.

IT IS A TRUTH universally acknowledged that wherever hangs a Lone Star flag, Texans will gather beneath it. I consider myself a Louisianan, but the truth is I'm one-quarter shit-kicker on my father's side, which was enough to draw me to the Lone Star Bar in Midtown one July night.

Having exhausted all avenues, I had chosen to deploy my nuclear option. There were two fellow NoZe Brothers living in Manhattan—Saltzman and Groverfield—both of whom had graduated from Baylor a decade before I arrived. We had never met, but I knew them by reputation. Saltzman was a screenwriter; Groverfield was an editor at a publishing house. If anyone could help me, it would be them. I knew a job offer, or even a recommendation, wasn't guaranteed. Our shared brotherhood bought me a few rounds at the bar and the chance to state my case, nothing more.

If this were a story, now would be the point where the hero is granted a vision of his or her possible future, as personified in an older, more successful acquaintance. Our hero would then express bright-eyed eagerness, along with moral flexibility, signaling his or her willingness to do whatever it takes to succeed. This would be enough for the elder statesmen to take a shine to our hero, having recognized they are the same on some primal level.

None of that happened, because this isn't a story; it's my life. I am not a hero so much as I am a collection of insecurities and paranoid delusions molded into the shape of a pudgy doughboy. Saltzman and Groverfield were polite, generous with their bar tabs, and willing to answer any and all questions. I was utterly intimidated by their niceness. Unable to engage with me on any meaningful level, they broke off into their own conversation, leaving me to get acquainted with their friend Wayne.

"What do you do?" he asked.

"At the moment? Jack shit." I hated that question—not because it was small talk but because answering it felt like a lie. "Though theoretically I'm a writer."

"That's cool. Working on anything?"

"Nothing worth talking about."

"Well, if you're looking for a job, I might be able to help. Ever heard of Take-Two?"

Not even once. Wayne wasn't surprised. Take-Two Interactive was the third largest video-game publisher in the world. The name didn't ring a bell, but they owned Rockstar Games, makers of the wildly popular Grand Theft Auto series. Things weren't going great for Take-Two. They were embroiled in a scandal dubbed "Hot Coffee." Someone had dug into the code for *Grand Theft Auto: San Andreas* and discovered assets for an unfinished sexual minigame in which players could have clothed sex with their in-game girlfriend after she invited them in for coffee. This content wasn't accessible to players; Rockstar had cut it from the game. But the code and assets still existed on the disc, and sophisticated programmers combing through the code had found it. They created an unsanctioned modification, or mod, that activated the unfinished code and replaced clothed characters with naked models. That's what mods do: alter a game's content so it functions differently than the developers intended. Mods can swap out art, introduce new gameplay systems, or, in the case of Hot Coffee, unlock an unfinished minigame that was never meant to be seen by the public. When the Hot

Coffee mod was released, nongamers who had never heard of mods misunderstood what had happened, and the company got unfairly raked over the coals.

"You can probably guess things are tense right now. It's still a great place to work, though. And we just opened a new publishing label, 2K Games. I know they're hiring for some entry-level positions. You should send me your résumé. Who knows? There might be a match."

Two weeks later, I stood in Take-Two's lobby, dressed in my best and glistening with sweat. I was interviewing for a game analyst position. The job would require me to play games currently in production and provide feedback on how to make them better.

When Wayne arrived in the lobby, he took one look at me and stopped. "You wore a suit." It wasn't a question or statement; more of an involuntary expression of disbelief.

"Is that a bad thing?"

"It is if you want the job. Listen, just take off your jacket and tie, untuck your shirt, and roll up your sleeves. No one will hire you in games if you wear a suit to your interview. It shows you don't know anything about the industry."

"I don't know anything about the industry."

"Please don't tell them that."

I followed him into the building, shedding my clothes as we went. "Are you sure about this? I'm really, really sweaty." August in New York was brutal. Summer had turned the city into a giant brick pizza oven. Everything carried the familiar, sickly-sweet scent of rat death. The smell didn't bother me, but the heat was unbearable. Growing up in the South had done nothing to prepare me for summer in the city. I would sweat all the time; not profusely, but enough to look eternally moist. That's a great look for a cake, but terrible for an interview.

"Maybe they won't notice."

We stopped outside the conference room where my interview would take place. I was sweaty and disheveled, and I had a red tie sticking out of my pants pocket. "I look like I'm stumbling home hungover after senior prom."

Wayne refrained from giving me a reassuring pat on the back or even a handshake—a valid call on his part—but he gave me a sincere smile. "Just be yourself. You'll do fine." Then, he opened the conference room door and introduced me to the Fox.

I knew nothing about the man who now stood directly in front of me. He was small in both height and frame, but also lean and strong. He dressed in a style best described as Victorian sailor chic. His eyes were two different colors: one blue, one brown. When he spoke, it was with a thick French accent, making it hard to parse his words.

I later tracked him down online and learned he began working at Ubisoft in 1997, where he was credited as part of the Internet team for a driving game called *POD*. Four years later, he was a vice president with a slew of hit titles under his belt—*Rayman*, *Splinter Cell*, *Prince of Persia: The Sands of Time*. It's impossible to know how much the Fox contributed to the success of those games, but it appears to have been a substantial amount.

In the years since we met, I've heard many rumors: He was once a stand-up comedian. He was either a secretly devout Buddhist or he abhorred all religion because, as a child, he witnessed a murder committed by a holy man. He's Italian but claims to be French, simply because he likes France more. He's an American pretending to be French because it lets him get away with saying outrageous things. Based only on my personal experience, I am willing to believe any of them.

"So, this is a QA job?" QA stands for quality assurance, denoting testers who play in-development games, finding and logging bugs for the team to fix.

The Fox shook his head and tutted. "No no no no no. The game analyst is a creative job. You would be comparing our games against those of our competitors and coming up with ideas on how to make them better.

"We make games for every platform," said the Fox. "To do this job, you will need to be familiar with PlayStation, Xbox, PC—all of those. Which ones do you own?"

"Oh, I don't own any video-game systems."

He recoiled at that. "What do you mean you don't have any?"

"I have a laptop, but it's kind of old. I'm not even sure it could play a game."

"You do realize you're applying for a job at a video-game company." Any interest he had in me was quickly fading. He was looking for someone with an understanding of modern games—what was good, what was new, what people enjoyed. "Well, I used to own an Xbox and a PlayStation, but I sold them when I moved here. Now that I'm out of college, I kind of thought I was supposed to stop playing games and get a job."

He laughed. My quaint naïveté had won him back. "Would you be willing to play games again, or is that nonnegotiable with you?"

"If you want to pay me to play games, I won't say no."

"Glad to hear it," said the Fox. "Do you have any questions for me?"

I hate asking questions during an interview. My ADHD-raddled brain can listen to someone for only about three minutes before it starts looping Muzak and my brain goes into energy-save mode. Luckily, this trait is balanced out by my narcissism, which allows me to remain focused for a good hour and a half, so long as we're mostly talking about me. It's a great combination for staying focused during a job interview, but it's terrible when it comes time to ask questions, because I probably haven't picked up enough information to form any reasonable inquiries. At best, when someone asks, "Do you have any questions for us?" the most honest response I could give is "No?" or "Can we keep talking about me?" Neither of which is appropriate.

Something was different on this particular day. Maybe I was feeling especially full of myself, or I was feeding off the Fox's natural French elitism. Who knows? Whatever it was, something possessed me, and for the first time ever, I asked a question during a job interview.

"When you say you're looking for feedback on your games, do you mean honest feedback, or do you just want a yes-man who will tell you everything is great?"

My brain didn't catch on to what I was saying until it was halfway out of my mouth. I had just enough time to regret everything before speaking the final word. Before the Fox had a chance to respond, I heard my dad's voice in my head. "When will you learn to shut the hell up?" It was something he'd been saying to me for two decades. For once, I agreed with him.

The Fox and I have never spoken about this moment. If I had to guess, he was likely thinking, "What the hell sort of question is that? Who does this kid think he is?" He should have laughed me out of the room, shouted me down and put me in my place. Instead, he offered me a job.

Wayne and the Fox gave me a couple of days to think it over.

Was this really what I wanted to do? I moved to New York to become a writer. So far, that had been a nonstarter. That didn't mean I should give up, right? No doubt working in video games would be fun. But it wasn't writing.

I sent a text to the director of my Jamaican crime script. "Hey. Any word on the movie?"

His response: "Let's talk tomorrow. Have a new idea to run by you. What if Scarface drove a bulletproof Rolls-Royce? Bring weed."

On second thought, I could definitely work in video games until my writing career took off. Even better, the salary and health insurance would keep me alive until it happened.

I emailed Wayne: "I'm in."

4

EAT SHIT OR DIE TRYING

When I joined 2K Games in August of 2005, the company was just beginning to stretch its legs. We were small, no more than forty people. 2K's sister company, Rockstar Games, was an unstoppable juggernaut. Even in the aftermath of the Hot Coffee scandal, there was little concern people would stop buying their games. For Rockstar, controversy was—and still is—little more than a bump in the road. You need only look at their sales figures to see the truth of that. It's difficult to get accurate sales figures for video games, but *Grand Theft Auto: San Andreas*, the bearer of Hot Coffee, has sold almost 21 million units since its release in 2004. The franchise's most recent installment, *Grand Theft Auto V*, released in 2013, sold 32.5 million units within its first six months.

As newcomers, we weren't looking to attack the throne. 2K was building something new that could stand proudly beside Rockstar and leave its own mark on the industry. However, we didn't have a franchise like GTA. Our schedule of upcoming games was, to put it lightly, schizophrenic. The most immediate projects were licensed games based on movies and TV shows, such as *Charlie and the Chocolate Factory* and *The Da Vinci Code*. Further down the line were releases from acclaimed developers Firaxis and Irrational Games. Peppered throughout were various sports titles—tennis and boxing were already in development, with racing and *lucha libre* possibly to come. For a catalog, it was scattershot, unfocused. But that was the point. We'd cast our net wide, looking for the game upon which our house would be built.

Our offices were located on the third floor of a small building in SoHo. The elevator opened onto a waiting area, where Miriam, the receptionist, would greet you from behind a desk. From there, you passed through a locked door into the main office. A dim, wood-paneled hall led you past the glass-walled conference room, where a statue of a knight wearing a red clown wig stood guard over the meeting table. From there, you emerged into a long, bright room whose windows overlooked the corner of Broadway and Houston.

It was an open floor plan: no cubicles, only long, thin desks placed back to back. Each workstation was decorated as you might expect—action figures, swag from old projects, Japanese brochures about the apparent evils of pubic hair—you know, the usual stuff. The office walls were classier, bearing framed art that managed to look both uninspired and expensive. If you're familiar with the work of Damien Hirst, you know what I'm talking about. The art wasn't ours, by which I mean 2K's, but rather from the personal collection of Ryan Brant, founder of our parent company, Take-Two. I don't know the effect it had on anyone else, but for me it was a daily reminder that I wasn't in Louisiana anymore. This was the big time. New York City. Corporate America at its best.

Seated at the desk next to mine was D. T.—real name unimportant. To get the measure of this man, all you need are the initials D. T., for a tattoo he planned to have inked on his taint as a symbiotogram. Viewed from one angle, the tattoo would read "Dickhead." Flip it upside down, and it would read "Twatface."

D. T. had removed his belt and wrapped it around his forehead as a means of holding a telephone receiver to his ear. He was listening to the weekly marketing call while playing one of our upcoming games. For the last half hour, he'd been firing a gun at two enemy corpses, trying to nudge their hands onto each other's crotches. He had almost achieved this goal and wasn't about to stop just for a phone call.

"Walter," he called to me, without turning his head. "Hey, Walter." I didn't respond. "Guh! C'mon, Walter." I tried to shut out D. T.'s voice, but he wouldn't stop. "Walter! I'm dying over here, and you're ignoring me? You're an animal, Walter! An animal!"

D. T. was getting himself worked up. He wouldn't stop until I acknowledged him. Best to get it over with.

"What do you want, D. T.?"

"Do you ever worry that someday you'll be walking down the street near Central Park and you'll pass one of those horse-drawn carriages and the horse will accidently step on your foot, and you'll scream so loud it'll spook the horse, causing it to rear back and take a massive dump in your screaming mouth, and then you'll literally eat shit and die?"

This was my neophyte brother, the yang to my yin, the PR assistant to my game analyst. We were the new guys, employees #40 and #41. The entry-level grunts straddling the aisle between Production and Promotion.

Product development, or PD, was my domain. Our job was to interface with the studios developing our games to ensure they were on time, under budget, and up to quality. D. T. was on the promotion side—marketing and PR, two similar but very different things. Marketing is consumer focused. It's their job to sell you something, whether you want it or not, so they handle commercials, ad campaigns, and the like. PR is focused on the press. It's a job built on relationships. They organize events, manage press tours, set up interviews—everything journalists want to provide their readers and publishers need to promote their games.

D. T. and I interacted with each other's departments. As the rookies, we were the catchall. We reviewed builds, provided milestone feedback, made beer runs, took screenshots, captured videos, carried heavy boxes, and filled out submissions for the Entertainment Software Rating Board (ESRB), the organization responsible for assigning games an age-appropriate rating based on content. That's what it's like when you're starting out in a creative field. You do everything so that one day, if you rise to the top, you understand how it all works. Sure, you shovel a lot of shit, but that's because there's a lot of shit that needs shoveling, and the people above you are too busy to do it themselves. It's called paying your dues. Come out the other end and you'll be hardened enough to handle the pressures of the real job. Crumble under the weight of menial tasks and you'll be gone in no time, your expulsion a mercy killing. If you can't handle the shit at the bottom, you're not cut out for the job at any level.

D. T. AND I were playing *Serious Sam 2*, the fifth—not second—game in the Serious Sam franchise. The game was nearing completion, soon to be shipped around the world, and we were looking for game-breaking crashes.

Crashes are bad. A crash means your game has broken in such a way that it needs to be restarted. Every game is full of crashes before it ships. In fact, most games ship with some crashes still in the code. These crashes are usually triggered by an almost impossible set of circumstances. A game might crash if you start the second stage with the rocket launcher equipped and then throw a grenade at the exact moment you open the first door. We weren't looking for these. Our goal was to find any game-breaking crashes—the kind that make it impossible to complete the game. For example, if the game reboots every time you enter the first door in the second stage, that's a game-breaking crash. If we could make it to the end without a crash, the game would be one step closer to reaching gold. (When a game "goes gold," it's ready to be released.) Once that was achieved, *Serious Sam 2* would be sent to manufacturing. Discs would be pressed, boxed, and shipped across the globe.

We'd been playing for two days and having a hell of a time. I'd never heard of Serious Sam, but from what I could tell, the series was about "Serious" Sam Stone, a muscle-bound man from the twenty-second century sent back in time to ancient Egypt to defeat Mental, an alien overlord who wanted to rule the universe. In *Serious Sam 2*, Sam visits the planet Sirius, home of the technologically advanced Sirians, where he must locate the five pieces of an ancient medallion needed to defeat Mental. The story was ludicrous; not even worth our attention. The gameplay, however, was fun and frantic; every stage was a madhouse that only escalated until we reached the game's final stage—a vast, grassy field underneath a clear blue sky.

A pyramid stood in the distance. This was the Mental Institute, where we would finally face off against our mortal enemy. All that stood between us and victory were a series of impassable walls and an enemy force bigger than anything we'd faced before. Waves of enemies broke against us: albino cyclopes, green-skinned footballers, cyborg dinosaurs, giant robot spiders, demons with tank treads for legs and cannons for hands, bodybuilders with bombs instead of heads, even clowns riding unicycles. Yes, we fought them all.

At the entrance to Mental's pyramid, we faced one last foe—a lifesize, wind-up rhinoceros. It charged from across the field. We stood our ground and opened fire. Mere seconds after the mechanical monstrosity had fallen to our bullets, the screen faded to black. We gripped tight our controllers. Together, D. T. and I had survived the gauntlet. It was time for the final battle, the ultimate boss fight. We were ready to face Mental in deadly combat.

We waited a very long time.

The publishing producer on *Serious Sam 2* was a man we called Geekjock. He was Jersey to the bone—sleeveless tee, store-bought tan, and finely sculpted facial hair. But the muscles and bravado only served to hide his inner nerd. Comic books, fantasy games, *Dungeons & Dragons*—this guy was the Vin Diesel of video-game publishing. At a party, I once saw him stop talking midsentence, look around the room, and ask, "Are all the ladies gone?" A guilty smile spread across his face. "Who wants to play some *Magic: The Gathering*?"

As publishing producer, Geekjock had one job—ship the game. This is a gross oversimplification, like saying a plate spinner's only job is to not chip the fine china. With *Serious Sam 2* waiting to go gold,

Geekjock was well into the weeds. If he could ship the game on time, that would be great. Within budget, even better. If he could pull off both while also ensuring the game wasn't a steaming pile, he'd be a goddamn miracle worker.

To maintain focus, he'd recently enacted a "no questions" policy. Whatever you needed to ask, you had to first ask yourself, "Could this wait until later?" Sitting on Geekjock's desk was a medicine ball. If he didn't think your question was urgent, he wouldn't answer. Not until you sat down, spread your legs, and let him roll that ball at your junk.

"Are you sure this is the gold candidate?"

Geekjock looked up from his desk. He saw me eyeing the medicine ball, my hands lingering over my crotch. I didn't relax until he'd placed the ball under his desk. The question was approved; my testicles were safe.

"What's wrong?" he asked. "Did the game crash?"

"It's not that. It's just there's no final boss. You play through the final level, reach the bad guy's pyramid, and that's it. Cut to the final cut scene, roll credits, the end."

"That can't be right. There has to be a final boss. The developer said it was going to have the biggest boss fight in video-game history."

"There's a wind-up rhino."

"Please tell me it's a giant wind-up rhino."

I shook my head.

You don't expect to watch a man's heart break when you tell him the wind-up rhinoceros you just killed was only normal size, but that's the sort of thing that happens in this industry.

"This is bullshit." Geekjock yanked his phone receiver from its cradle and dialed a number, pausing long enough to say thanks. "I appreciate you catching this."

"What are you going to do?" I asked.

"I'm going to find out what went wrong. Then, I'm going to figure out how we can fix it without changing anything." Ah—the publishing motto. Fix everything, change nothing. Improve a game without causing new problems. It sounded like nonsense, the kind of bullshit platitude one aspired to but could never actually achieve. It only took Geekjock thirty minutes to prove me wrong.

Turns out the issue with the final boss was timing. The development team had planned to create the biggest boss ever, but they unfortunately ran out of time and decided it was better to have no boss at all. They'd meant to tell 2K, really they had, but somehow it fell through the cracks. As a sign of good faith, they offered to resolve the issue by implementing a final boss, posthaste. Sure enough, *Serious Sam 2* would ship with the biggest boss ever—Mental's pyramid. They turned the giant pyramid at the end of the game into a boss by having it rise up on tank treads and roll toward you while launching fighter jets and pummeling you with assorted weaponry. Problem solved, nothing changed.

"That should solve everything," said Geekjock. "Now, you have a passport, right?"

Once the final boss was implemented and the game was deemed bug-free enough to ship, *Serious Sam 2* would be sent to the manufacturer so it could be pressed onto discs and sold across the world. The problem is, there is a whole community of pirates who would love to get their hands on a gold master so they can crack it, rip it, and upload it to torrent sites. At the time, we were terrified of handing off our games to a random courier service, not knowing what might happen to them during transit. That meant someone from 2K would have to hand deliver the gold master to the manufacturer, all the way in London.

To make it fair, D. T. and I would both show up to work with our passports and a carry-on bag. There, we'd draw straws. The short straw would climb into a town car waiting downstairs and head straight to JFK airport. Seven hours later, he'd disembark and place the gold master directly into the hands of Klaus, a man you'd swear was the bastard German son of Lemmy Kilmister, who would then get the courier nice and drunk before putting him on a flight back to New York.

"My girlfriend's gonna be pissed," said D. T. "I have to go home tonight and tell her I might be flying to London. We were supposed to get dinner with a friend, or a coworker, or someone. I don't even know where my passport is. I'll be up half the night trying to find it."

"It's okay if you don't have one," said Geekjock. "Walt can go to London. But you'll have to run demos with Bruce at a convention this weekend."

Bruce was a product manager in the PR department and D. T.'s direct superior. His real name was Roose, but whenever he gave his name, people usually thought he said Bruce. After years of correcting people, he finally decided to just roll with it. He made the mistake of telling this to the office, after which we refused to call him anything else. The only person who didn't use it was D. T. He had a different name for Bruce.

"On second thought, London sounds great," said D. T. "Anything's better than spending an entire weekend with that Persian goat snake."

It was a surprisingly pointed insult from D. T. It almost would have struck me as racist if Bruce hadn't silently appeared from behind a cubicle wall and said, "I have had many names: the Carpathian. En Sabah Roose. Daddy. Now, Persian goat snake. I certainly wouldn't classify myself as underhanded and devious, but I understand why lesser beings would see it that way."

As Bruce walked away, he kept his eyes on us, making sure never to blink.

IT WAS AGREED THAT D. T. would ferry the gold master to London, and I would accompany Bruce to a comic convention in Chicago, where we would demo a forthcoming game. The plan was to meet him at the office on Friday morning and leave from there to the airport.

I found him waiting in the lobby with one large suitcase and two bulging duffle bags.

"I'll let you carry these," he said, motioning to the bags.

"You're not going to help?"

He shook his head. "One of the perks of being a product manager. I don't have to carry things anymore."

I grunted as I slung the bags over my shoulders. "What's in here?"

"Just swag. T-shirts. Maybe some posters."

Swag is promotional junk masquerading as sought-after collectibles: hats, stickers, patches, posters—anything someone might wear or display. Swag is great. You reward fans with something they can't buy in stores, and in return, they agree to be your walking billboard. You might wonder who'd want this shit.

"Am I allowed to take a shirt?" I asked.

It doesn't matter what industry you're in—never pass up a free T-shirt, especially if it's one you can wear to work. Clothes cost money. Swag is priceless.

DEMOS, LIKE MANY ASPECTS of promotion, are a lie. A demo may look like a game, and it may play like a game, but it is not a game. The game is still being built and is in no position to be shown to the public. The demo is a separate entity, designed to represent what the final game will be. It's highly scripted digital theater, meant to be seen and not played.

Developers hate demos, mainly because production must come to a grinding halt to create these promotional experiences. We don't build one level to final quality before moving on to the next; most levels are built simultaneously. For a demo to look its best, a team has to shift their attention away from the main game to focus on a fake one. And no, once a demo is finished you can't just put it into the final game. Demos are so specialized and scripted that in order for them to work in the final game, they would have to mostly be rebuilt from scratch.

Presenting a demo usually requires two people: a driver who plays and a presenter who talks. Every moment has been scripted, even those built around uncertain outcomes. This helps maintain the illusion that the demo is representative of the final product. When you see someone playing a game, you assume that game is playable, and that whatever happens on screen will be present when you finally get your hands on it. It's a simple manipulation that works almost every time. Follow the script, and the demo will show viewers exactly what you want them to see. Attempt to deviate, and it all falls apart.

Demos suck.

"I was thinking you could do all the demos this weekend," said Bruce. We were at the convention, setting up our booth before the first wave of attendees came through the door. "You'd drive and present, and I'd just stand here, talking to people. How's that sound?"

I could tell he was joking, so I ran with it. "Fine with me."

Maybe my delivery was too deadpan, because Bruce took me seriously. "You'd do that?"

"I will if you buy me something from the convention."

"Well, I mean, I dunno . . ." Bruce began to waffle. I expected him to back down. Instead, he said, "We'll need to set some ground rules. It can't cost more than fifteen hundred dollars."

It took every ounce of self-control to keep my mouth from falling on the floor.

Fifteen hundred dollars? Are you kidding me? I was hoping for twenty-five. And all I have to do is play a video game all weekend? If I were home, I would have done it for free.

I rolled my eyes and tried to look annoyed. If Bruce found out he'd overshot the mark by a few miles, he might renege on the deal. "I guess that's fine. But I'm going to need at least a five-minute bathroom break every few hours. And thirty minutes on Sunday to look around the convention and decide what I want."

Bruce held out his hand. "You got a deal."

I spent the majority of the next two and half days hidden behind the thick black curtains of our promo booth, where the demos took place. From start to finish, the demo took around ten minutes. Whenever I finished, my audience of fifteen to twenty people would file out, and then a new audience would be sent in. With five minutes between each presentation, I usually ran through the demo four times an hour.

Outside my dark room, our booth workers drummed up excitement to ensure I always had a packed house. In the past, it was common for the booth workers to be young, attractive women in scanty outfits, colloquially known as booth babes—the idea being that the only thing a bunch of geeks wanted more than comic books and video games was sex. All you had to do was stick a few booth babes outside your stall, and the boys would come running. Some companies still use them, but the practice has become less common. As our industry has grown more mainstream, it has slowly moved away from objectifying women as a marketing strategy. Some conventions actually ban the use of booth babes. I'm glad, because it was always a cynical move. If your game is good, you don't need flesh to convince people they should check it out. More importantly, the gaming demographic has grown beyond the stereotype of nerdy, white males. Our consumers, developers, and gaming press are more diverse than ever before. Events and conventions should be inclusive; no one should feel out of place or uncomfortable.

2K didn't employ booth babes. Instead, our promo team had gathered a mix of young men and women dressed in branded T-shirts and black pants. They were attractive, for sure. Definitely above average. But that had more to do with hiring them through casting agencies rather than off the street. None of them understood fully what they were doing. A few of the guys played video games, but I don't think any of them had ever read a comic book. This place was alien to them. Still, they gave it their all. They memorized all the talking points, delivered them with believable excitement, and never once looked down their noses at the people spending their weekend buying toys and dressing up in spandex.

During one of my negotiated bathroom breaks, I noticed one of our young ladies crying behind the booth. I asked Bruce what was wrong. Apparently she had flubbed some of the talking points. Someone from the developer had overheard it and yelled at her for the mistake.

I felt bad, so I invited her to watch my demo a few times. Watching someone else pitch the game might help her retain the information. A few hours later, I heard her enthusiastically recounting what I'd said, word for word. Good for her. I stuck my head out so I could proudly survey my work. To my horror, I saw she had grabbed Joe Quesada, editor in chief of Marvel, by the shoulders and was politely yelling into his face.

"HAVE YOU HEARD ABOUT—"

"No no no no no!" I rushed over and gently removed her hands from Mr. Quesada. "It's okay, you can stop. He knows all about the game, and he doesn't care." Joe laughed it off and went on his way. For a split second, I considered stopping him to find out if that guy from the mail room ever gave him my résumé, if only to bring the story full circle. But he'd been accosted enough for one day.

"Did I say something wrong?" the girl asked.

"You did perfect. He's just a very important person."

"Oh, like an actor?"

It occurred to me that "very important person" might be a relative term in this situation. "Yup." I smiled and nodded. "He's an actor."

WHEN I'M PLAYING AND presenting a demo at the same time, my eyes stay focused on the screen. Like trying to walk and chew gum simultaneously, there's just too much going on for me to pay attention to anyone else in the room. I welcome everyone as they enter and wish them a great afternoon when they leave, but that is the extent of our interaction.

If the kid hadn't attended two demos in a row, I never would have noticed him. I didn't say anything to him when he came in the second time with a different crowd. Either my eyes lingered too long or he saw the recognition in my face, because he burrowed down into his seat, as if trying to hide. Not very helpful, seeing as he was in the front row. I barely made a note of it before launching into my usual spiel. Ten minutes later, everyone filed out, kid included. Two minutes after that, the kid strolled back in, this time with a new group. He stuck to the back row and held a stack of comic books tight against his chest so as to hide his lanyard. It must have been holding a three-day pass, the kind you bought in advance that came printed with your name on it.

Even though I only gave my audience a cursory glance, there was no way I could have missed the kid. Show up to three demos in a row, and you're going to stand out.

"You must really dig the show, huh?"

The kid blushed and ducked his head. "Yes, sir." He didn't look my way again until I'd started the demo. As I went through my script, playing and speaking, I made sure to look away from the screen a few times, just to see what he was doing. His eyes were wide and locked on the game playing out before him.

Wow, I thought. He actually was digging the show.

Afterward, the kid hung back while the group shuffled away. Now that I was paying attention, I guessed that he was somewhere around ten or twelve years old.

"I'm sorry." He looked ashamed, like he'd been caught stealing. "I shouldn't have snuck back in here."

"You didn't do anything wrong. If you want to watch the demo, come watch it. That's why we're here."

"Even if I already saw it?"

"Hey, if you like it so much you want to keep watching it, that's awesome. You can check out the demo as many times as you like."

I've only seen pure, unadulterated joy twice in my life. The first time was when I brought a big, empty duffel bag to where the Girl Scouts were selling cookies and told them to fill it up with Tagalongs until it couldn't hold anymore. The second time was in that demo booth.

The kid stuck around for three more demos. In between, he'd ask questions about the game, and I'd give him little bits of "confidential" information. They weren't actually secrets, but they weren't part of my presentation, either. He didn't know any better, and it made him feel like he was getting to see something really special. After six presentations, he finally decided to head back to the convention floor. Before he went, I gave him as much swag as he could carry—shirts, posters, everything we had.

"Do you know if there are any more games here?" he asked.

"That's a good question. I honestly have no idea. They keep me locked in here, playing demos all day."

"Oh. Okay. Well, thanks again!" He passed through the curtains and, so I believed, out of my life forever.

Presenting demos can be a thankless job. You'll occasionally have someone ask a question, like "When's it coming out?" "What platforms will it be on?" "Will there be multiplayer?" All of which require the PR-approved response of, "We're not talking about that yet." The best you can hope for is that you might tell an off-the-cuff joke during the demo and the room will laugh. That always makes you feel good, but it's just showmanship. Showing demos for the press can be even worse. You'll get game journalists who try not to show any emotional response so as not to betray their opinions. It's like talking to a wall, until you reach the end and they ask, "When's it coming out? What platforms will it be on? Will there be multiplayer?"

Side note: Please stop asking if there will be multiplayer. There won't be.

I'd only been at the job for a few months, but a lot of the magic had already worn off. When you work hard on something, it's exciting to show it off. But there are only so many times you can look into the practiced, unimpressed stares of game journos or read the angry comments of unfulfilled grown-ups before that excitement begins to fade. Eventually, you learn to manage your expectations. Hell, you're trained to do it, like a dog that gets hit with a rolled-up newspaper every time he jumps on the couch. "This is just how it goes," you tell yourself. "At least people are seeing it." Inside, a tiny piece of your dream dies, and you move one step closer to viewing your career as just another job.

But then some random kid wanders into your demo booth and you get to make his day by letting him know your game is waiting for him in the future, and for a little while you both get to be excited because holy shit, video games are awesome.

The kid showed up again toward the end of the day.

"Back for another round?"

"No," he said. "I just wanted to bring you something, since you don't get to leave the booth." He handed me a promotional comic book—a team-up between *The Darkness* and *Witchblade*. The symbol in the corner indicated that it was a convention exclusive. A fresh autograph was scribbled across the cover in silver ink. "The artist was signing copies at one of the booths."

"Wow. That's really nice of you to do, but I can't take your comic from you."

He held up a second copy. "It's okay. I got two of them."

I don't like when strangers do nice things for me. Whichever part of my brain controls external responses can't seem to figure out an appropriate reaction. On one hand, a random act of kindness deserves a heartfelt response. On the other, some of us get weirded out by it. When someone is kind to me, my emotional cortex trips all over itself. Whatever I say, I end up coming across like a lizard-person who killed a guy, put on his skin, and then tried to mimic human emotion.

Maybe the kid could tell, because he spared me having to respond. Instead, he thanked me again for letting him watch the demo and for giving him all that free swag. Then out through the curtains he went, forever this time.

As THE CONVENTION DREW to a close on Sunday, Bruce stuck his head into the demo booth and gave me a nod. "You got thirty minutes. Make 'em count."

I already knew what I wanted. The convention was too big. I knew thirty minutes wouldn't be enough, so I'd been using my periodic bathroom breaks as a way to scout ahead, each time taking a different route to and from the booth. Turns out I didn't have to go far. What I wanted was one row over from ours.

Alex Ross, the award-winning painter, had a booth at the convention where his dealer was selling some of his original sketches and paintings. I'd been a fan of his work for years, but never imagined I might one day own a piece of it. Among the items for sale were some of Ross's preliminary art he'd done for the opening credits of the film *Spider-Man 2*. There were four pictures on two pages. Combined, they cost a total of $1,750. That was $250 more than what Bruce had agreed to pay. I would have paid the difference myself, but I didn't have that kind of money. I thought about getting just one, but couldn't bring myself to choose. The only other option was to give up and find something else.

While I agonized over my decision, Bruce casually slid up beside me in that quiet, creepy way of his. "Alex Ross, huh?"

He listened while I explained the situation, occasionally nodding without saying a word. When I was done, Bruce flagged down the art dealer.

"I think I want to get these two Spider-Man pieces. How's $1,500 sound?"

The dealer didn't even hesitate. "Yeah, I can do that. I'll bag them up for you."

What the hell had I just seen? Was that haggling? I had no idea. I'd only tried to haggle once in my life, with a guy selling used books on a sidewalk in New York. My attempt was so feeble, not only did I end up paying full price, I also apologized. Like so many things, everything I knew of haggling I had seen on TV. I knew you started low, countered high, and then went back and forth until both parties settled on a reasonable price. Bruce had done none of that. He'd basically thrown money on the floor and said, "Pick that shit up and bring me my art."

"Are you a wizard?" I asked.

"Yes." Bruce arched his eyebrows and made his best approximation of an arcane gesture. "Don't tell anyone." He dropped the pose and pulled out his wallet. "I'm also friends with the dealer. I get first dibs anytime there's a new Wonder Woman piece for sale. Alex Ross has a lot of my money."

The dealer returned and handed the art to Bruce, who in turn handed it to me. "You earned it."

In the years since then, I've acquired a small but respectable collection of original art. It's on the small side because I'm picky; I only buy art that has a direct connection to an important moment in my life. The various pieces decorate my entire house, but I always hang the Alex Ross pieces near my desk. It's easy to get bogged down in the daily work and forget what you love about the job. Looking at that art helps me remember important things. Like it's okay to spend the entire weekend playing a video game, and that there once was a time when promoting a game at a comic convention was a grand adventure.

THE FOLLOWING MONDAY, D. T. and I returned to a quiet office. Our inboxes were empty. We went to every producer, associate producer, project manager—they had nothing for us. No tasks, nothing to review or play. We decided to take a long lunch.

D. T. shouted at me through a mouthful of cheesesteak. "We're unnecessary, Walter! Redundant!"

At the time, it seemed plausible. During my original interview, the Fox said 2K was hiring a game analyst to handle the extra work producers couldn't find time for. Now that the work had dried up, it made sense they would no longer need us.

"This is our fault," I said. "We finished our work too fast. How long do you think it'll take before they realize they don't need us anymore?"

"A week; maybe two. This is a major corporation, Walter. There will be no shit-or-get-off-the-pot moment. They will squeeze us out and move on. I'm telling you, our days are numbered."

We finished our twenty-four collective inches of Cheez Whiz–slathered beefsteak in silence. The dream was over. It was time to think about getting a real job.

Back in the office, Geekjock waved us over. "The Fox's been looking for you."

We had underestimated 2K's efficiency. D. T. and I shared a sad, knowing look, then went to meet our fate.

The Fox didn't sit in the open with the rest of us. He had a small, glass-walled office set off to the side. The only chair was his, tucked behind his desk. D. T. and I had to share a low, leather-clad bench, which gave the Fox a significant height advantage. It was a classic power play, albeit with a twist—hanging above the Fox was a stuffed moose head. The head was massive. Alive, the animal must have weighed a literal ton. We were trapped in its glassy, dead-eyed stare.

"So . . . what are you working on?"

"Nothing at the moment," I said.

"Really?" The Fox cocked his head, a bit like a confused puppy. "I heard you were both very busy." Was this some kind of put-on? Maybe he was trying to let us down easy.

"We were, but we finished everything. We're just waiting for the next thing."

"Hmmm . . ." Without warning, the Fox clapped his hands together. "Well, good news! I've got a task for the both of you. One each, because I am a very generous man."

I voiced a silent prayer to God, thanking him for ignoring my many heresies and giving me a second chance. This time, I'd play it smart; make the job last as long as possible.

"Walt, I want you to take a look at *Top Spin 2*."

Wait—a tennis game? Not a chance.

"Yeeeah, I'm not really sure I can do that. I hate tennis." Emboldened by the realization I wasn't getting fired, I apparently decided to shoot myself in the foot. "It is a boring, stupid sport, and I don't understand it."

I tried to appear apologetic. The look on the Fox's face said it wasn't working.

"You think you should be excused from doing your job because you don't like tennis?"

"That's not what I said at all." Actually, that's exactly what I said, but copping to it wouldn't do me any favors. "What I'm saying is, I won't be able to provide helpful feedback. If the game is bad, I won't like it. If it's good, I still won't like it. It could be the best tennis game ever made, and I'd have no idea. Does that make sense?"

The Fox studied me for a moment, measuring whatever response he was about to give. Finally, he said, "That's a fair point. But I don't like it. D. T. will take over *Top Spin*. You can check out *Oblivion*."

Then my heart exploded and I died.

LET ME TELL YOU about a little video-game franchise called The Elder Scrolls. Developed by Bethesda Softworks, The Elder Scrolls are a series of fantasy games known for their expansive worlds and nonlinear gameplay. I never played the first two games in the franchise, *Arena* and *Daggerfall*, but I had a long history with *Morrowind*, having purchased it three times in my life.

The first was during my freshman year of college. I'd noticed the PC version on sale in the campus bookstore and was intrigued. I'd already decided which classes I wouldn't bother attending, so I sold back those books and used the cash to buy the game, all in the same transaction.

My computer ran *Morrowind* as well as I might run a marathon. Even with graphical settings tuned to the lowest levels, it would work only in fifteen-to-thirty-minute stretches before hard-crashing. Growing up, I didn't play PC games; everything was console. I had no concept of system requirements. Still, I was not deterred. My first experience with *Morrowind* was unpolished, low-res, and laggy, but I was enthralled nonetheless. With every reboot, I couldn't wait to get back into that world and see what I'd discover next. The only reason I eventually quit was because *Morrowind* was too good. After a few weeks, I finally gave it to a friend. Seeing it on my desktop, knowing I couldn't immerse myself in the game for hours at a time, just hurt too much.

Four years later, while working at the mall in Austin, I saw the Xbox version on sale and quickly scooped it up. I didn't own an Xbox, but my friend did; and that friend owed me a favor, so it was like I owned an Xbox. I called in my chit, and he brought it over that afternoon.

"You didn't buy the Game of the Year edition?" he asked.

An hour later, I bought *Morrowind* for the third and final time. My wallet was pissed, but my body was ready.

On the surface, The Elder Scrolls is similar to what you'd find in *Dungeon & Dragons*. It takes place in a medieval, vaguely European world populated by humans, elves, orcs, cat-people, and lizard-people. The player's available skill sets fall into the usual categories of stealth, swords, and sorcery. These similarities don't make the series derivative. A world and its people are just a starting point. What makes a story unique is how those elements are used. *Morrowind* used those familiar elements and remixed them to create a world both alien and familiar.

Vvardenfell, home of the gray-skinned Dunmer elves, was a land of stone and ash, where giant mushrooms grew alongside centuries-old pines. I was its hero, Indoril Nerevar, reincarnated as Walt, the Dunmer thief. I could have tried a new class, like fighter or mage, but I just didn't see the point. Why waste time working my ass off for money and power when so much of it was sitting around in people's houses, waiting for me to take it? I'd need both if I was going to challenge the immortal Dagoth Ur, whose defeat I was prophesied to bring about. Luckily, Dagoth Ur and his followers were trapped inside the Red Mountain, which meant I was free to bum around until such time as I could be bothered to deal with his slaggy ass.

The first thing I did was head straight to Vivec City, the largest city in Vvanderfell, where I broke into the treasure vaults of House Hlaalu and became the richest adventurer to not reach level five. I murdered my way to the top of an assassins' guild, led an imperial cult while serving as the patriarch of my native Dunmer religion, became grand spymaster to the Dragon Emperor of Tamriel, and worked as a double agent in the Thieves and Fighters Guilds. By the time I reached Solstheim, a frozen island to the north, I was so immersed in the game that I hung blackout curtains over my windows and turned the AC down to sixty-seven degrees. Outside, it was summer, but I wanted to feel the cold, biting wind. My body sat on the floor in nothing but my boxers while my mind roamed icy Solstheim as a Dunmer-turned-werewolf, wreaking havoc just for the hell of it. Somewhere in all that, I made a quick stop to Red Mountain so I could teach Dagoth Ur that immortality didn't mean shit with someone like me running around. Then it was right back to living large.

I miss the days when I could immerse myself in a game so completely. It's easy to think life has gotten in the way, but really it's the games. There is no lack of open-world games out there, but almost none have come close to matching the quality and richness of *Morrowind*. It's still one of the best games I've ever played. It was four years from when I got my first taste of *Morrowind* on PC to when I could finally sink my teeth into it on Xbox. And believe me, it was absolutely worth the wait. I almost want to buy it three more times, just because I think Bethesda deserves the money.

The Fox knew of my love for *Morrowind*; I'd mentioned it in my interview. Being sent to meet its creators and play the sequel, *Oblivion*, was nothing short of a gift. I took no care to hide my fanboy excitement. That's why the Fox pulled me aside the day before I was scheduled to take a train from New York to Bethesda, Maryland. He wanted me to know that it was okay to be excited, but I also needed to be careful. This trip would not be without danger.

The relationship between a publisher and developer can be tricky to navigate. A development studio makes the video game; they are artists working hard to bring their vision to life. Unfortunately, making a video game costs a lot of money, especially if it's categorized as AAA. I'm not going to hit you with a lot of math right now, but imagine a developer with sixty employees who make on average a salary of fifty thousand dollars, and that it takes three full years to make a game. Then you're looking at a nine-million-dollar price tag, not counting marketing, PR, bonuses, and a whole load of other stuff. Most developers don't have that kind of money lying around, so they turn to a publisher. Every deal is different, but for the most part, a publisher will front the cost of development and promotion in exchange for the financial returns. If the game sells enough copies, then the developer will begin to earn royalties. However, most games don't earn royalties. This is basic business stuff; nothing too contentious. The real trouble is around the question of creative control.

It would be easy, if not incorrect, to say a developer is to its publisher as an artist is to its patron. The comparison draws a semisolid line of demarcation between the two parties; the former creates art, the latter commissions it. While a patron is certainly entitled to request art on a certain topic or theme, the artist-patron relationship generally assumes an artist is free to interpret that request through his or her own creative vision. This is a harmful simplification of the developer-publisher relationship because it reinforces the false belief that publishers are creatively bereft, and developers are perfect stewards of their own talent.

To get at the truth, we have to dispel the myths we've built around developers. AAA development studios are not artists; they are companies founded on the premise that you can make money by making art. There's nothing wrong with that—greed and artistic intent are not mutually exclusive, and we all have bills to pay. Creating marketable games with broad appeal does not make you a greedy, corporate whore. The reverse is also true; creating pure, vision-driven games does not exclude you from being a money-grubbing, credit-hogging asshat.

If developers aren't necessarily pure of heart, then we can't assume publishers are devoid of it. Holding the purse strings doesn't make you Ebenezer Scrooge. Most publishers are collaborative curators using their resources to empower studios to create on a scale they never would have reached on their own. If a publisher sometimes overshadows their developers, it's because the publisher's reputation carries more weight. That's the risk you run when dealing with a curated system—an audience will flock to the name they most associate with quality, even if it doesn't belong to the creator.

Developers operate on a smaller scale, allowing us to humanize them by giving a face and name to their corporate identity. We fetishize them because their beauty enriches our lives, and we are hardwired to equate beauty with value, regardless of how either is defined. It's a lot easier to villainize a publisher for being a cold, distant corporation. A publisher doesn't create; it simply capitalizes on the hard work of others. Whatever happens, there's always someone you can trust and someone for you to blame. It's a convenient arrangement for everyone involved.

So, who gets the final say—the developer who makes a game or the publisher who funds it? Almost everyone would say the developer, but that's not always the case. Both parties want the game to succeed and make a ton of money. That doesn't mean they're on the same page. A developer might want to make a single-player game, whereas the publisher thinks the game will sell more if it includes a multiplayer mode. The developer doesn't agree, the publisher threatens to cancel the project, and suddenly there's a multiplayer mode. This is an extreme example, but you get the idea. Honestly, most publisher meddling comes in the form of suggestions and notes like, "Tone down the difficulty to make the game more accessible"—innocuous stuff that makes a developer cringe all the same.

The Fox warned me that while visiting Bethesda, I would be 2K's official representative; the publisher made flesh. Many at the studio would view my appearance as an ill omen. They would be cagey, hesitant to answer questions for fear I might trick them into revealing vital secrets. I'd do well to watch my back. A dev team nearing the end of a multi-year project is not unlike a ship's crew too long at sea. The monotony has warped their minds and dulled their senses. For them, there is no escape; only the work, and the hope of land on the horizon. Under such circumstances, even the most stalwart developers can be driven to paranoid superstition. You hear rumors of visiting publishers going missing, their bodies later found in a ditch with throats slit by the jagged edge of a broken CD-R. Who can say if these rumors are true? Not me. You can ask about the scar on my neck, but I'll swear it's from spinal surgery.

In contrast to the warning I received, the staff at Bethesda was very welcoming. Everyone I met was friendly and excited to share what they'd been working on. It probably didn't hurt that I was wide-eyed, like a kid in a candy store. It must have really put them at ease, because during a tour of the studio, they made sure to lead me down a row of cubicles tucked away in the back.

The guy leading the tour gave me a sly smile. "Uh-oh. Don't look to your right or you might see some concept art for *Fallout 3*." It was clear from his tone that I absolutely wanted to look to my right.

"Cool! What's *Fallout*?" Only one of the most beloved and celebrated PC franchises of all time. Which meant I'd never heard of it.

His eyes flashed shock, disappointment, and finally disdain. ". . . Follow me, and I'll show you where you'll be playing the game."

That was it. End of tour.

I played as long as I could—eight to ten hours at least; barely a drop in the bucket. Playing an Elder Scrolls game is a commitment. As open-world games, they have a lot of content for the player to discover. Not all of it is mandatory. If you only play the mandatory missions, it might take between twenty and thirty hours to complete. To finish every optional mission, master every skill, and track down every piece of equipment would take almost two hundred hours. I'd have to play all day and night if I wanted to see a sizable chunk.

Oblivion was very different from *Morrowind*. This time around, I was no reincarnated hero. I wasn't even a first-time hero. I was nobody, just some schmuck in a jail cell. The only reason my character was even caught up in the story is because someone was trying to kill the emperor, and his secret escape route happened to go right through my cell. It was sheer luck that brought Emperor Uriel Septim VII and I together. When the assassins finally caught up with him, I was the only one still alive to hear his last request—I was to locate the emperor's illegitimate son and place him on the throne. Failure to do so would break an ancient covenant and open the gates of Oblivion, allowing the demonic Daedra spirits to invade and destroy our world. It was a lot of responsibility to put on someone who wasn't the foretold reincarnation of a legendary, god-killing hero. I wasn't sure how I felt about it.

As the hours wore on, I became aware that I wasn't alone. Bethesda couldn't leave me, the publisher, free to roam their halls without supervision. I was at the office, and so were my handlers. They had lives waiting for them at home, but instead they were babysitting me. Around 10:00 p.m., I thanked everyone for their hospitality, then excused myself to the hotel across the street. I didn't return the next morning. Instead, I caught a train back to New York and went straight to work.

"So?" asked the Fox. "Will they be ready to ship by end of the year?"

It dawned on me how ridiculous the question really was. I could have made an uneducated guess, based on additional questions such as: Was it very buggy? Did it crash a lot? Were all the systems in place? Was it missing large chunks of content? These were valid technical questions. And maybe that's all the Fox was asking. But I got the sense he was digging deeper: Does Bethesda consider the game technically complete? Does "technically complete" equal good? At what point should a creator be satisfied releasing their work to the public? When is good considered good enough?

The Fox had to know I couldn't answer his question with any certainty. Even if you ignore that it's an impossible question, I was clearly not experienced enough to provide a real answer. He had to know. But if he did, then what was it all for? What was the takeaway? What was the Fox trying to teach me?

"I don't know" was the only acceptable answer I could give, but it wasn't the answer I gave. "I think they'll be done by the end of the year." *Oblivion* didn't ship until the next year, around the end of March.

5

THE CRUEL TUTELAGE OF PETER GRIFFIN

I must have done something right at Bethesda, because the next thing I knew, I was headed back to Chicago, this time to meet with another developer—High Voltage Software.

The project was a licensed game based on the popular cartoon *Family Guy*. Take-Two had picked up the license during the show's original cancellation. However, when *Family Guy*'s DVD sales began raking in the dough, the show was given a second life. This reversal of fortune extended beyond the show to our game. What was once intended as a small project aimed at a cult following was suddenly the official licensed game of the most popular cartoon on television. For that reason, the Fox wanted someone working closely with the developer to ensure the game reached its newfound potential. After spending a weekend watching *Family Guy* DVDs, the Fox decided that person should be me.

This wouldn't be an overnight trip, like the one I'd made to Bethesda. The Fox wanted me to embed with HVS for an extended stay. Forget that this was only my third month on the job—I was to be the publisher's on-site representative to ensure the game lived up to its potential, in the hopes it would make 2K and HVS a lot of money.

"It's a test," said D. T. "It has to be."

"Not to sell myself short, but it seems insane that he'd send an entry-level guy into such a high-risk situation."

"Could be he's setting you up to fail. Ever think of that? He knows the game won't be any good, so he's making you the patsy."

"I don't think the possibility of failure has ever crossed the Fox's mind. Where others see the impossible, he sees opportunity."

"It's trial by fire. The Fox wants to know how brightly you'll burn if he douses you in gasoline and then hands you a match."

There was only one problem: I was twenty-four. This meant I couldn't rent a car (a necessity, since the developer was located forty-five minutes from the airport). I'd also never owned a credit card, which meant I had zero credit. Traveling for business is expensive. You have to pay for transportation, hotels, food. It's not bad for one or two days, but it adds up when you're gone for weeks at a time. It's all reimbursable, but that means nothing if you don't have a large enough credit limit to afford it in the first place.

I was able to solve the car situation by having my parents cosign the rental from Louisiana. Regarding the issue of the credit card, I had a better idea.

"I need a corporate card," I said. In my head, I envisioned steak dinners, rented convertibles, and top-shelf cocktails garnished with tiny umbrellas. TV had taught me a corporate credit card was a blank check, a needle jammed straight into the company's rich, money-filled veins.

The Fox laughed. "Not a chance."

"Guess I'm staying here, then."

"Like hell you are. It's bad enough having you around being a smart-ass all the time. Half the reason I'm sending you to Chicago is to get you out of my hair."

"How am I supposed to pay for it?" At his insistence, I applied for a credit card, but my limit would cover only three days—not nearly enough.

"Don't worry about it. Just get on the plane, and I'll work it out."

Fair enough. I arrived to find the city blanketed in snow, with more falling every minute. This was a serious problem. As a native of Louisiana I was familiar with the concept of snow, but had never driven in it. In the back of my head, I remember something about snow tires. I didn't know what they were, but they sure sounded like something you'd need for driving in the snow.

I sat in the parking lot for thirty minutes before finally calling the Fox.

"Are you at the hotel?" he asked.

"No. I'm at the rental-car place."

"What's wrong? Do the rental people not have a car for you? I thought you got a confirmation."

"No. I have a car. It's just . . . it's snowing."

"So, what? You stopped to make a snowman?"

"I've never driven in snow. Am I supposed to put chains on my tires or something?"

To his credit, the Fox did not mock me. He explained everything I needed to know about driving in the snow; the first thing being that tire chains were not necessary. Comforted, and cautioned to take it slow, I headed north.

When I checked into the hotel, the desk clerk asked for my credit card, as they always do.

"I was told the room would be paid for."

"It is," said the clerk. "I'm to charge the room to your card until it's reached its limit, then put the rest onto a card for . . ." She searched for a name on her screen. She found it, read it back to me. The Fox.

In my room, I sent him an email. "Why not put the whole thing on your card?"

"So you can build up credit," he wrote back. "Trust me. You can thank me later."

He was right. Every month, I maxed out my card, and every month I paid it off. Always on time, never a penalty, all thanks to the magic of expense reports. Pretty soon, I had enough credit to manage the trips without his help. Of all the lessons the Fox could have taught me, this wasn't exciting or even game related, but it was one of the most important. He saw a backwoods kid who didn't understand how the world worked and set him on a path to become a functional, modern adult.

It was a very human, paternal thing for him to do. I'm not sure I ever thanked him for it, but I also never forgot.

LIVING IN A HOTEL can mess you up.

Living out of a suitcase is like doing time in prison, a statement I feel qualified to make as I have seen every episode of the HBO original prison drama Oz. Whether you're gone for days, weeks, or months, it all comes down to compartmentalization. You have to shrink your life into a series of bite-size chunks in order to cope with the fact you won't be going anywhere for a while. Acceptance is the key. Resign yourself to where you are and what you are there to do. Find ways to fill your life for one hour, then another, and another, until each day melts into the next, and time itself has lost all meaning.

My trips to HVS would last anywhere from one to three weeks, including weekends. When planning for these extended stays, I always made sure I would have access to three essential things. The first was alcohol. Nothing takes the edge off hotel habitation like a bottle of top-shelf hooch.

The great thing about working on-site is being able to expense your meals. There was a limit to how much I could spend each day, but no regulation on what I spent it on. If my body could digest it, my report could expense it. Every bar was a gateway to experimentation, an opportunity to develop a sophisticated palate on someone else's dime. To ensure I always drank well, I developed a system built around the hotel's free continental breakfast. Every morning, I'd eat until I was full, and then stock up on the three Bs—bananas, bagels, and bacon. I could keep these staples in my bag until lunch, so long as I wrapped the bacon in a napkin. That covered two meals per day without having to spend a single cent. Dinner was usually a cheap and greasy five-dollar burger, followed by a liquid dessert of Lagavulin 16, as many glasses as my limit would allow.

That brings us to the second item on my must-haves list: a gym.

If I was going to be stuck in one place for a while, it seemed a good idea to spend time on self-improvement. Clearly, my dietary habits were not the best: a lot of carbs, fat, and cholesterol with the occasional vending-machine dim sum sprinkled throughout. Hitting the treadmill three or four times a week not only helped to keep off the weight, it also helped battle depression. Hotels are lonely places, devoid of the personal baubles and trappings that triggered my sense of comfort. The longer I stayed in one, the more disconnected I felt from myself. This was only exacerbated by the alcohol I guzzled on a nightly basis. Remember, alcohol is a depressant. The sadness it brings will sneak up on you. For me, regular exercise fought it off, but only for so long. Eventually, I would have to resort to the third item on my list.

If you're going to live in a hotel, you have to bring your own entertainment. This is easy to accomplish these days, but iPhones and iPads weren't a thing back in 2006. My only options were analog—books, comics, DVDs. If the TV in my hotel room had the proper hookups, I'd even bring along my PlayStation 2. I always packed too much. Better to have too many options than none at all. Working my way through a book or show gave me some sense of accomplishment, enough to convince me the hotel wasn't syphoning off what limited time I had left on this earth. Eventually, I streamlined my entertainment to focus only on complete runs of classic TV shows. I didn't care what the show was about, so long as every season was available on DVD. Reading and games were fun, but I needed something that required a minimal amount of focus. I often got insomnia when I traveled, and it absolutely wrecked my cognitive abilities. If I hadn't slept in forty-eight hours, the written word took on an incomprehensible, alien swirl. All I could do was lie in bed like a coma patient, absorbing stimuli by osmosis, never fully awake or asleep— whatever it took to ensure I wasn't alone through those long nights. Being alone only led to questions, the kinds you never want to ask.

Terrible, right? Wrong. Working on-site was fantastic, and I'll tell you why.

Money.

You may not have heard, but New York City is expensive. While my job came with all the perks and benefits, it was still an entry-level position. I was paid a reasonable salary for my role and experience. Reasonable won't always cut it, though.

When working on-site at the studio, my daily cost of living was covered by the company. Food, shelter, and transportation could all be expensed—basically free money. If I'd been working in the New York office, I would have paid for food and transportation out of pocket. When you're young and just starting out, extra cash is very enticing. It's great for paying off loans or building up a savings account. You just have to be able to resist its siren call.

"I'm thinking of giving up my apartment," said D. T. We were catching up over lunch. Both of us had been on the road for a while, and this was a rare opportunity to sit down and talk. "I'm never in town. When I am, I usually just crash at my girlfriend's place. Might as well save some money."

"Is she going to be cool with you moving in?"

"Cohabitation? Walter, what are you thinking?! This is freedom we're talking about: no apartment, no rent, nothing. Imagine how much money you'd have if you weren't paying rent every month. Just living in hotels, expensing all your meals like a professional hobo."

We hadn't been around long enough to realize money could only get you so far. There's actually an emotional arc that occurs when your earnings suddenly increase. You start by convincing yourself to work harder, as if you need to prove you're worth it. As the stress rises, your mentality shifts, and you accept that you are being adequately compensated for what you're doing. The more you prove yourself, the more people begin to rely on you alone. You've always been able to handle things in the past, no matter what it took; there's no reason for that to change. It's then that the truth finally hits you—you're not paid nearly enough to deal with this shit.

Money is necessary to our physical survival. That's just capitalism.

To keep our spirit alive, we also need a sense of purpose. How you find that depends on the type of person you are. Maybe you're working on your dream project, or you want to show the world what you're capable of, or perhaps you're just the kind of broken, malformed mutant for whom the work itself is enough. Whatever does it for you, heed my advice—find it fast, then suck every last drop of marrow from its bones. Without its nourishment, you will not be long for this world.

For me, that purpose was writing. Eventually, HVS would get around to writing the script for the *Family Guy* game. I knew if I hung on long enough, I'd get to be part of it. Then, I'd show 2K, the Fox, and everyone else just what I was capable of.

When the time came, it was decided to bring in the *Family Guy* staff writers; that way the game would match the quality and humor of the show, plus it would be a great selling point. I was instantly opposed to the idea. I wanted to write the game, or at least part of it. If the show writers got involved, they wouldn't need my talents. Luckily, the *Family Guy* staff didn't have time to write the script; they were too busy making a TV show. We floated the idea of HVS writing the first draft and then sending it to the show writers for a final polish. They agreed. This was my chance. All I had to do was find a way to insert myself into High Voltage's writing process.

If you've ever wondered why so many games have bad writing, it's because developers don't usually have a dedicated writer. It's more common now, but a few years ago, it wasn't out of the ordinary for a script to be cobbled together by anyone who cared enough to force their way into the discussion. It was a train wreck of designers, coders, and artists pushing for their ideas. This sort of thing doesn't happen in other disciplines. Art and design occasionally, but take programming, for instance. Try telling programmers you want to do a studio-wide review of their code and see which breaks first—the game or your legs. I don't know why, but when it comes to story, suddenly everyone's a writer. The script you end up with won't necessarily be bad; oftentimes it's perfectly passable. But there's a wide margin between good enough and great, and the quality jump is always noticeable.

The script HVS sent us was, in my opinion, rough. I freely admit I was biased; after all, I didn't write it. On top of that, it just didn't read like *Family Guy* to me. I told the Fox we couldn't send it to the show writers; they'd have to start over from scratch. As far as I could see, the only way forward was for me to rewrite the entire script. All I needed was five days.

In college, I had a process for writing a lot in a short amount of time. I'd isolate myself, usually by dragging a desk into a storage closet. Then I'd write by hand, using different-colored pens to help me keep track of sections and corrections. Once I'd written fifty pages, I'd type them up, print them out, and sleep for six hours. When I got up, I'd slash and burn the printed pages until I was left with ten to fifteen pages of usable material. Then I'd pick up where those pages left off and do it all over again. I did this Monday through Friday, every week. It was an effective process, and even though I'd have to modify it for working in the office, I knew I could use it to finish this script within five days.

The Fox didn't buy it. "I've never worked with a writer who could write a script in just five days."

"To be fair, none of those other writers were me." Cocky, I know. I had to be, because I had nothing to back it up.

Being an artist isn't like being an accountant or a doctor. People need medical care. If you can provide it, you will never want for patients. People also need art. It speaks to who we are as individuals, as well as a species. That doesn't mean they need *your* art.

Anyone with a proven track record can be confident. When you're just starting out, you have to convince yourself that you are talented and worthy of recognition; otherwise, you'll be held back by self-doubt. In other words, fake it until you make it.

My arrogance and narcissism must have resonated with his French blood, because he gave me the go-ahead. Hidden away beneath a stairwell, I spent the next week rewriting the game's script. In my opinion, the resulting product was pretty good. Even the Fox agreed. We fired it off to the developer and went home for the weekend.

Come Monday morning, there was an email from HVS's producer waiting in our inboxes. To my surprise, he wasn't angry; he was disappointed. His team had worked hard on the script, and he couldn't understand why it had been rewritten. "This isn't a rewrite. It's an entirely new script. The whole thing is just an excuse for Walt to replace our stuff with his." All valid points, but it didn't matter. This was the plan the Fox and I had agreed upon. HVS's script never would have passed muster had we sent it to the show writers. We were on a tight schedule, and there was no time to make sure everyone's delicate egos remained unscuffed.

A week or so later, we flew from New York City to Los Angeles to meet with the show writers and discuss the script. I was over the moon. I'd written a full game script—based on the hit TV show *Family Guy*. That script had been read by the show's actual writers. Just a few months ago, I was unemployed with no career prospects. Now, I was flying to Los Angeles to visit the FG offices and meet with the people who made the show. This was my moment. Anything was possible.

"The script is bad. Like, really bad. One of the worst things I ever read."

It turns out anything *was* possible, including having my script ripped to shreds. So much for my dreams of collaboration. I tried to hide my disappointment, but my poker face is weak. I think the show writers could see they were tearing my heart out, because they toned down the criticism. No concessions were given, not even a "Nice try" or "It wasn't all bad." But they stopped calling it the worst thing ever, instead choosing to focus on how much work it would take for them to fix it.

The Fox and I left the studio completely dejected. We thought we'd brought our A game, but Hollywood shut us down real fast. We were just a video-game publisher. The "real" writers would take it from here. I'd been shut down in the exact same way I'd shut down HVS. Had I been wiser at the time, I might even have learned a lesson from it all: It doesn't matter how good you think you are. It doesn't even matter if you're right. All that matters is the opinion of the next person down the line.

MONTHS PASSED, AND WE finally got the final script from the show writers. The story was basically the same, but the words and jokes were different. That is, every joke except for one.

It was at the end of a scene in which Carter Pewterschmidt and the police show up at the Griffin house, looking to arrest Brian for once again knocking up Carter's prized dog, Seabreeze. Brian denies the allegations, but Carter won't hear it.

> Carter pulls a stack of cash out of his pocket and hands it to the Cop.

> **CARTER**
> He's lying.

> Carter hands the Cop a second stack of cash.

> **CARTER**
> And he's not Caucasian.

> The Cop runs into the room and beats Brian with his nightstick.

"Good for you," said the Fox. "I'll make sure you get an additional credit on the game." And he did. When the game shipped, I was credited under *Additional* Writing and Design, which is a nice way of saying I put words and ideas in the game, though not in any official, titled capacity.

The Fox dropped what looked like a tube of toothpaste onto my desk. "Here. I got you something." He'd been traveling overseas the previous week. He must have bought souvenirs.

The tube had a picture of a reindeer on it. "What is it?"

"Consider it a bonus for all your hard work."

I uncapped it and squeezed some onto my finger. It looked disconcerting: a grayish-white paste with bits of darker gray things scattered throughout. Was it some weird, foreign Christmas treat? No. It was pureed reindeer. And it had already gone bad.

As I stood gagging in the office kitchen, trying not to vomit in the sink, I couldn't help but feel like I'd won somehow. One joke wasn't much, but my foot was now in the door. From there, I could move on to writing generic lines, a whole character, maybe even a script for an entire mission—more and more, until every word was mine.

6

ENRAPTURED

ENRAPTURED

In 2006, Take-Two Interactive announced it had acquired acclaimed developer Irrational Games. Founded by Ken Levine, Jon Chey, and Robert Fermier, the company had made its name developing the PC games *System Shock 2*, *Freedom Force*, and *SWAT 4*. All three were former employees of the legendary Looking Glass Studios, which gave the world the beloved System Shock, Ultima Underworld, and Thief franchises.

You might be curious why a developer of such caliber would choose to sell itself to a publisher. I wish I could tell you; unfortunately, I don't have any special insight. Every acquisition is different. That said, if I owned my own development studio, I can tell you why I would want to be acquired.

Developing games is hard. As an independent developer, even a successful one, you're reliant on contracts and other companies for publishing, marketing, distribution, and more. It's exhausting, and can feel like you're always on the verge of collapse. There's stability in being acquired. You'll always have projects to work on and enough cash flow to cover payroll. It removes some of the pressures of being a salesperson for your company and its games, as the publisher now becomes your advocate. More importantly, you gain access to their marketing, distribution, and sales force, which in theory should lead to more success for everyone involved. There are trade-offs, of course. You might give up some creative control, along with any intellectual property and franchises you might own, but that's not necessarily a given. Like I said, every acquisition is different. It all comes down to the contract.

Once acquired, Irrational's latest project, *BioShock*, became part of 2K's lineup. The game was a story-driven first-person shooter (FPS) set in Rapture, a city of scientific wonder founded on Objectivist ideals by industrialist character Andrew Ryan. For a video game, that wasn't nearly enough of a hook. Rapture wasn't just a fantastical city; it was also an impossible one, having been built at the bottom of the Atlantic Ocean in the late 1940s. And while it would have been fun to shoot your way through a city of cultural elites who ran away to live in a private ocean paradise, it wouldn't have been much of a challenge. Luckily, those upper-class hoity-toities had been transformed into superpowered drug addicts who killed little girls to feed their need for ADAM, an addictive, gene-altering wonder goo.

BioShock merged the intellectual elitism of Ayn Rand with the low-class entertainment of beating things to death with a wrench. It walked the line between serious and absurd, and in doing so embodied exactly what I love about video games. I couldn't wait to work on it.

BioShock was planned as a spiritual successor to Irrational's first and most celebrated game, *System Shock 2*. Set aboard a spaceship in the year 2114, *System Shock 2* is a first-person shooter/survival game about a soldier who teams up with an evil computer named SHODAN to destroy the Many, an alien hive mind that threatens to consume every living thing it encounters. *System Shock 2* is a celebrated game for many reasons, first and foremost being the game's terrifying villain. It's also beloved for its unforgiving level of difficulty. Your in-game character is physically weak, while the enemies you encounter can often kill you in just a few hits. Your weapons degrade every time you use them, until they become worthless. Even if you manage to kill all the enemies in a given area, you're not safe; they can respawn anywhere, anytime.

To play *System Shock 2* is to understand that you are a fragile, mortal being whose life could end at any moment. I've never played *System Shock 2*—and probably never will—and this is the reason why. As I see it, life is hard enough. I don't need to be tortured in my free time. I'm sure *System Shock 2* is a fantastic game, it's just for a different type of gamer. I want the games I play to be fun; other people want games that hate them on a primal level.

With *BioShock*, Irrational promised to bring the dark narrative and immersive gameplay of *System Shock 2* into the modern console era. This terrified the Fox. Games had changed a lot since 1999. Console games were far less difficult than the PC games of old. The Fox knew *BioShock* would be phenomenal, but he was afraid it would be too punishing for a mainstream audience. He wanted to keep an eye on the game, just to make sure it didn't become insanely difficult.

"We're going to Boston next week to meet with the team," said the Fox. "You're invited to come, but on one condition." Anything. "I need you to not do that thing you do during meetings." Thing? What thing? "You know, the look you give to whoever is speaking. The one that says, 'You are the dumbest person I've ever met.' "

"Do I give you this look?" I asked.

"All the time."

Oh, shit. ". . . Am I giving it to you right now?"

"No. Right now, you look scared."

Of course I was scared. I'd just learned my face was constantly telling my boss to fuck off. "So, here's the thing about my face—"

The Fox waved off my explanation. "It's fine; I'm used to it. Just don't do it to Ken."

I wasn't going to be part of the difficulty discussion. The only reason I tagged along was so I could meet the team and discuss the creation of promotional assets, aka screenshots.

When you think about screenshots, you probably think of fakery: pictures of a game, purported to accurately convey its look and feel, taken from impossibly dramatic angles, touched up using Photoshop— all to make you think a game looks better than it actually does. They call this a bullshot. It's an appropriate term, but if we're being honest, even an accurate screenshot is a lie.

Video games are kinetic. They are expressed through motion and sound, interaction and reaction. A screenshot is cold, dead, frozen. You're taking a moment—one frame out of sixty; not even a full second—and presenting it as an accurate representation of a living, breathing interactive experience. It exists only to be seen; nothing more. And yet, when produced properly, a screenshot can embody the full spirit of the game.

A bad screenshot is a blatant lie. It shows you a game that doesn't exist, and sells you on a promise it will never fulfill. A good screenshot is art. It lies truthfully by capturing the emotional essence of *playing* the game. The image won't be something you'll see in-game because it will utilize common techniques such as dramatic lighting and framing. But when you look at it, you will know how it feels to be locked in deadly combat with an ironclad behemoth who has a drill instead of a hand. And yes, you read that correctly. Screenshots may be promotional assets, but they are still art. It's called photography, and it's a medium that happens to be older and more sophisticated than ours. It doesn't matter if the photograph is being used to sell sixty dollars' worth of first-person shooting; there is an art to capturing a single moment capable of conveying all that is unseen, unheard, and unknown.

Ahead of our visit, I put together a screenshot portfolio for Irrational to review. My work had already been used for advertisements, retail boxes, and featured magazine articles. I wasn't worried; my screenshots were solid.

It wasn't long after we arrived at Irrational that I was approached by someone I'd never met. "You're Walt, right? The screenshot guy?"

I nodded, unsure of where the conversation was going.

"Your screenshots are . . ." he searched for the words. "Well, they're not good."

"Oh. That's . . . okay. Is there something specific you don't like?"

"Everything, really. Sorry, I know that's not helpful." He kept turning to look down the hallway. I got the impression he was supposed to have been somewhere five minutes ago.

"No, that's fine. Just let me know what you're looking for, and I can do that."

He shook his head. "I don't want to give feedback that might constrain your creativity."

"Ken!" shouted someone from down the hall.

It dawned on me who this was.

Ken Levine poked his head down the hall and shouted back, "Yeah, on my way." I took the opportunity to vigorously rub my face. Had I been giving him the look? I had no idea. If I had been, maybe I could massage it away and he'd forget all about it.

"Sorry." Ken turned back to face me. "I have to go to a meeting. Just give it another shot. And whatever you did last time, don't do that." Then he was gone.

Left alone to ponder our brief interaction, I started thinking about Ken's feedback. Like he said, it wasn't very helpful. Still, his blunt, honest response clicked with me. He hadn't found the words to articulate his criticism, but he'd left me with a clear direction—do something different.

My first round of screenshots had tried to capture *BioShock*'s first-person combat. That must have been my mistake. Combat was too frenetic; the particle effects caused by weapons looked unnatural in freeze-frame. For the second round, I chose to ignore gameplay entirely. I would pretend I was photographing a place instead of a game. My focus would be on framing, composition, lighting, and most of all, telling a story using a single image.

A video game is more than a challenge; it's an experience. The presence of gameplay is not the only appeal. Our digital worlds can feel as real as the one we inhabit. If we treat them as such, players will come. If all we do is present a game, then we're just telling players what they already know.

The next day, Ken hurried past my desk as he was being led to another meeting by Alyssa Finley, the project lead. He saw me and stopped.

"The screenshots. They're amazing; beautiful. I don't understand. What did you do?"

"You wanted me to do something different. I just did what you told me to."

"No, no. I've never given feedback that made someone go from terrible to genius. This . . . this is something else."

Alyssa put a hand on his shoulder. "Ken, we're already late."

"I know, I know." He turned back to me. "You're my screenshot guy. Keep doing what you're doing. It's great. Amazing stuff." And then he was gone.

In a minute and a half, Ken had given me more positive reinforcement than I'd received from the Fox in two years. The Fox thrives on creating conflict. He sees it as a catalyst for creation, like the heat of a kiln, melting iron so it can be crafted into something purposeful and strong. The Fox is no fool, though. He knows fire is hot, and prefers to keep his distance. If you asked, he'd say he's more of a lover than a fighter. Really, he just wants you to do the fighting for him. That's why he avoids positive reinforcement. He wants you uncertain, striving.

As a management strategy, I almost buy it. Almost. As it were, all it took was a sincere "attaboy" from Ken, and I was ready to follow him to hell, snapping screenshots all the way down.

I WOKE UP EVERY morning around 7:00 a.m., when my floor began to vibrate. There was a laundromat directly beneath my apartment. The vibration caused by the washing machines would make my apartment tremble and hum well into the night. It was a small price to pay for living in a two-bedroom apartment on the Upper West Side, a block away from Central Park and the D train. My room was large enough to hold a twin bed, a folding chair that doubled as a nightstand, and the plastic bin I used for a dresser. My lone window faced a brick wall five feet away. If my room ever saw sunlight, I was never around enough to know.

The Fox had told me I should be at work by 9:00 a.m. Even though my bed was only a fifteen-minute subway ride from my desk, I wouldn't arrive until sometime after eleven. I promised to try harder. It wasn't a lie; I meant it. I just never did it. Those extra hours in the morning were my time. Eventually, the Fox stopped bringing it up. I think it helped that, on a slow day, I wouldn't leave work until 8:00 p.m. Normally, I would be there well after midnight, taking screenshots and editing videos. Whatever it took to get the job done.

I might enjoy taking screenshots more than I do writing. It gives me the chance to experience a game without having to hunt, survive, or kill. When I play a game at home, I'm interacting with it according to its design. Enemies fight me, and I fight back. I use the tools at my disposal to vanquish them, which in turn makes me feel clever and powerful. The problem is, not everyone shares the same power fantasy. Some of us find strength in going unnoticed, watching from the sidelines. That's the fantasy I experienced as I searched the game for screenshots. Walking the halls of Rapture, *BioShock*'s underwater city, I was unseen and untouched. It allowed me to see a world most players never would.

The residents—Splicers, as they're called—were insane. They had been normal, once—as normal as you can be, living in a city at the bottom of the ocean. When you live a fantastical life, it's hard not to view the world through a lens of your own hubris. Egged on by their mastery of the world around them, Rapture's citizens turned their focus to personal perfection. Genetic splicing granted them extraordinary abilities, at the cost of their minds and bodies. The Splicers looked and acted like monsters, but in truth they were sick. ADAM, the miraculous substance used to alter their genetic makeup, was highly addictive. Once these people began splicing, they couldn't stop. The need was so strong, they would literally rip people apart on the chance their organs might contain just a drop of ADAM. Left alone, the Splicers would stroll through their crumbling metropolis, whistling to themselves, twirling a pipe or pistol as if it were anything other than a murder weapon. They roamed where they pleased, choosing to dwell where they felt most comfortable—like the sprawling gardens of Arcadia, or Fort Frolic, the city's entertainment district—locations tied to who they once were. These poor souls, robbed of humanity, were desperately trying to recapture what they could.

I was the ghost in their midst. Using debug commands, I passed through walls and floors, flew through the air, and even became invisible. It was freedom, but it was also necessary. One glimpse of me, and the Splicers would explode into a murderous rage. Once that switch was flipped in their brains, there was no going back. No longer would I be a silent observer; instead I would become just another target.

During my daily trips to Rapture, I would snap nearly one thousand photographs. Almost all of them were worthless. Relying on the godlike power of debug commands, I would slow down time to a snail's pace. The game would creep into frame, exactly where I needed it to be. A defensive turret in the background, a Splicer in the foreground, a burning corpse just offscreen, its flame giving the room some proper mood lighting. When everything was in place, I'd spam the screen capture button on my desktop. I grabbed every frame available to me; freezing them, so I could pore over them later, in search of that one perfect shot.

At the end of the day, I'd send fifteen to twenty screenshots to the PR department. Maybe a fourth of them would be approved.

This was my life from morning until night, five days a week, for more months than I can remember. I never ran out of things to photograph.

By the time I would finally head home, my train would have switched from local to express, meaning I had to get off at Seventy-Second and Broadway and walk seventeen more blocks to my apartment. Just outside the station was Gray's Papaya, a twenty-four-hour restaurant known for cheap hot dogs, which are three words I find irresistible. I rolled into Gray's every weeknight around 2:00 a.m. and bought as many dogs as I could carry. Munching happily, I'd head north, walking straight down the middle of Amsterdam Avenue. At that time of night, there was no one to bother me, no cars to run me down. Those seventeen blocks were mine. I passed through them like a ghost, unseen and untouched.

But with hot dogs.

TAKING SCREENSHOTS FORCED ME to play *BioShock* using every possible weapon, tactic, and Plasmid. Plasmids were like super powers. The Electro Bolt Plasmid gave players the ability to fire electricity from their hands. Sonic Boom would create a powerful gust of wind to knock back enemies. Cyclone Trap spawned a miniature tornado that would fling Splicers into the air. There were eleven Plasmids in all. Irrational thought that might be too many. Designers were reporting that they didn't use all the Plasmids, because they just weren't useful.

I had to agree. During my daily excursions to Rapture, I'd perfected the one-two punch—stunning a Splicer with Electro Bolt, then killing them with a quick shot to the head with my revolver. I only used other Plasmids if I needed them for a screenshot. My familiarity with the gameplay made me a valuable resource, so when Irrational called a design meeting to review the Plasmids, the Fox wanted me involved.

"I think we should cut Cyclone Trap," said one designer. "It's just Sonic Boom, but it throws Splicers in the air instead of shoving them backwards."

"No way," said another. "I use Cyclone Trap all the time. I'll lure Splicers down a hallway, use Inferno to set a fire on the ceiling, then launch them into it with Cyclone Trap."

A third designer leaned forward. "Really? I just use Inferno to light Splicers on fire, and then when they jump into water to put themselves out, I fry them with Electro Bolt."

If one designer thought a Plasmid was useless, at least two others thought it was indispensable. There wasn't a problem with the Plasmids; they had been perfectly designed to give players a choice in how they played the game. This was brilliant design.

After that meeting, the Fox had D. T. and me review *BioShock* for opportunities to "say yes to the player." Saying yes to the player is a design mantra, built on the idea that every action the player takes is a question—"Do my actions affect this world?"

A lot of our feedback was focused on the question "What can I do with a dead cat?"

In the fiction of *BioShock*, cats were smuggled into Rapture as a means of pest control. When the game starts, the cats are all dead. Their corpses can be found lying throughout the city.

"Can I pick up a dead cat using Telekinesis and use it to kill a Splicer by throwing the dead cat at its head?"

A bit obvious, but yes. You can do that.

"Could I set a dead cat on fire and use it to light a bunch of other things on fire?"

Hah! That's more like it. The only better torch than a dead cat is an actual torch, and we don't have those in the game.

"Would it be possible for me to cover every inch of a dead cat with highly explosive adhesive grenades, thereby turning said kitty's corpse into a pressure-detonated weapon of mass destruction?"

Yes, you beautiful bastard! A thousand times yes!

"If I freeze the dead cat using the Winter Blast Plasmid, will it shatter into a cloud of blinding ice dust when I throw it?"

No.

"Well, why the hell not?"

Ice doesn't work that way in the game.

"Splicers shatter if I freeze them and then smack 'em with my wrench."

Right, but that's because the enemy AI has a frozen state which is triggered by the use of the Winter Blast Plasmid, allowing for the AI model to be replaced with the shattering ice particle effect when you hit it. Since the dead cat isn't an AI, it doesn't have a frozen state. You can hit it with Winter Blast, and it will appear to be frozen due to a temporary texture layover, but it won't actually be frozen in the way you want it to be. Does that make sense?

"..."

You still want exploding catcicles, don't you?

"You're goddamn right I do."

D. T. was adamant. Every list we presented to the Fox had those cats right at the top—FROZEN CATS SHOULD SHATTER WHEN HIT.

After one week, the Fox had had enough. He demanded frozen cats be removed from any future lists. When D. T. refused, it sparked a shouting match.

"Why do you care so much about these damn cats?"

"I don't!" said D. T. "But you told us to make a list of ways we can say yes to the player, and some players will want to shatter a dead, frozen cat!"

"Why, huh? Why should they be able to do that? What is the point?"

"The point is that we're selling this game on the premise that players can do whatever they want!"

The Fox scoffed. "We have never said such a thing! Not once!"

"Really? Because I'm pretty damn sure we just released a bunch of T-shirts that say '*BioShock*: What Would You Do?' across the back in big, bold letters!" He was right. We were gearing up for E3, the Electronic Entertainment Expo, one of our industry's largest, most visible trade shows. We'd produced a lot of new swag for the event. That shirt was a fan favorite.

"Oh shit. We did, didn't we?" The Fox sat down, the fight having completely left him. "We need to look into what it would take to freeze those cats."

D. T. and I continued thinking of ways we could ask the game, "Can I do this?" We strove to answer that question in the affirmative as often as possible. We'd finish a list and send it to the Fox, and he'd forward it to Irrational. It was a thrill to see our ideas manifest in later versions of the game, but some never appeared. Sadly, shattering catcicles was an idea too pure for this world.

Where saying yes to the player got tricky was in *BioShock*'s moral choices. If you say players should be able to shoot out a light bulb, people might think that's kind of cool. If you say players should be able to murder kids in order to gain superpowers, those same people will probably stare at you in horrified silence while slowly backing out of the room.

Stick with me, okay? This part's going to get weird.

In the world of *BioShock*, ADAM is the chief currency of power. According to the game's fiction, it is excreted by rare sea slugs found on the ocean floor. However, the sea slugs are incapable of producing enough ADAM to meet the demand of Rapture's citizens. The only way to increase the slugs' output is for them to be surgically implanted into the digestive tract of a young girl between the ages of five and eight. Unsurprisingly, not many families were willing to fork over their daughters for the purpose of slug bonding. So, the necessary girls were either kidnapped or bought from orphanages, so they could undergo unspeakable medical procedures, transforming them into brainwashed slaves known as Little Sisters.

When *BioShock* opens, Rapture lies in ruin. ADAM addiction has turned its population of cultural elites into murderous junkies. Little Sisters roam the halls in search of corpses. The dead still carry ADAM-rich fluids capable of being harvested; they simply need to be extracted. To this end, the Little Sisters carry an oversize syringe which they use to draw fluid from a corpse—fluid they then drink, passing it through the sea slug in their stomach. The process is effective, but it turns the Little Sisters into walking treasure chests filled with liquid gold. That's why everyone in Rapture, including the player, is dying to get their hands on a Little Sister. With her ADAM, the player can buy Plasmids—special genetic enhancements granting fantastical power. The question is, how far is the player willing to go in the name of power and survival?

If that was too confusing, let me break it down for you. In *BioShock*, there are special weapons that can only be purchased with special money, which can only be found inside the bodies of special brainwashed girls (ages five to eight).

The player acquires ADAM by way of a moral choice. They can "Rescue" a Little Sister, which sets her free but awards an insignificant amount of ADAM. However, for every three Little Sisters rescued, the player receives a gift containing a very substantial amount of ADAM. The player's other option is to "Harvest" a Little Sister and rip the ADAM-rich sea slug from her body, earning a large amount of ADAM in the process. So, you know, it's a trade-off.

D. T. and I were presenting *BioShock* to the PR team. They wanted to watch experienced players play the game, to get a better idea of what it was like.

The demo proceeded as you'd expect. D. T. fought his way through hordes of Splicers, showing off the game's variety of weapons, both traditional and fantastic. The PR team was impressed, but wanted more.

"Can you show us a Big Daddy fight?" asked someone seated behind us.

D. T. wandered the level until the screen began to shake with the sound of heavy, metallic footsteps. We heard a sad moan, like a cross between a whale and Frankenstein's monster. A Big Daddy was near. Turning the corner, we saw it—a hulking brute sealed into an old diving suit. It lumbered behind a Little Sister as she skipped down the hallway toward a tasty-looking corpse.

"Is that a Little Sister?"

"Oh yeah," said D. T. "Check this out." He equipped a machine gun and opened fire on the girl. The Big Daddy roared to life. The ironclad beast was no longer slow and docile; it was gripped with a berserker rage. It charged D. T., unrelenting in its brutality. The Big Daddy would not let up until one of them was dead.

When the battle was over, the Big Daddy's body lay steaming on the ground. Its Little Sister stood over it, head in hands, crying tears for the protector she called "Mr. Bubbles."

"Whoa," said faceless PR person number two.

D. T. giggled to himself. He knew what was coming, and so did I. "If you think that was intense, wait until you get a load of this."

He switched weapons, this time choosing a large adjustable wrench. The Little Sister didn't even look up as he approached. With the touch of a single button, D. T. struck the girl on the head, killing her. Instantly limp, her body fell to the floor.

D. T. pressed another button. In the game, he lifted the girl's body, cradling it close to the camera. Then, he took her ADAM-gathering syringe and plunged the needle into her chest. He sucked the ADAM from the corpse, then discarded her on the floor like an empty bottle.

"Ka-ching!"

Flush with cash, D. T. headed to the Gatherer's Garden—a vending machine where he could buy new Plasmids. He selected Telekinesis, the ability to lift and throw objects using the power of your mind.

With his new Plasmid, D. T. lifted the Little Sister's corpse into the air. "Watch this."

He entered the next room, where a Splicer was waiting. D. T. flung the dead girl at the ADAM junkie's head, killing him. D. T. giggled as both bodies collapsed on the floor in a heap.

"If you think that's cool, check this out."

For the next five minutes, D. T. made full use of that dead girl's body. He juggled her, froze her, turned her into a bomb by covering her with sticky grenades, and lit her on fire to use as a torch for lighting other people on fire.

D. T. was having a great time, and I'll admit, so was I. One of the things I always admired about him was his ability to find his own fun within a game. What he was doing on-screen was terrible, but it was also just a game. None of it was real. On top of that, it was ridiculous. When you say, "I used the body of dead girl to bludgeon a man to death," yeah, it's a little messed up. But when you say, "I used the body of a dead girl to kill a teleporting fisherman while in an art deco city at the bottom of the Atlantic," it's hard to take seriously.

We couldn't hear the PR team over the sound of our laughter. But even if we'd been silent, we would not have heard a peep. They were mortified. Looking back, I can't blame them.

A few weeks later, the Fox gathered us together to see the new Little Sister design. Players would still acquire ADAM by way of a moral choice revolving around the Sisters. What changed was how the choice played out.

The Fox approached a Little Sister and was presented with a choice. "Harvest" or "Rescue." Selecting "Rescue" caused him to pick her up. The Little Sister struggled against his touch, but only until he laid a glowing hand on her head. A white light momentarily filled the screen. When it faded, the Little Sister had been healed, her deathly pallor replaced with the rosy cheeks of a living girl. The slug in her stomach had been dissolved, her mental conditioning undone. Finally free of her servitude, she scurried off into a dirty vent, as little girls are wont to do.

Next, the Fox chose "Harvest," and a similar scene played out. The Little Sister struggled against his grasp, this time with good reason. Instead of raising a safe, soothing hand, he raised one that appeared evil and clawlike. The Little Sister recoiled in horror as the hand lunged at her. The screen went black. The sound of a dying heartbeat played over the darkness. When it finally receded, the Little Sister was gone. In her place, the Fox now held a writhing sea slug, the implication being that he had ripped it from the girl's body with his bare hands.

"So, you killed her," said D. T.

The Fox shook his head. "I harvested her."

"You're holding a slug that was inside her body. It stands to reason you killed her."

"You don't know that. If she's dead, where's the body? I don't see a body. Do you?"

"You think the problem is we're making a game that lets players kill little girls. The problem is we made a game where killing girls is so much fun, no one will want to save them."

"Except we don't kill girls; we harvest them. It's completely different."

"People aren't that stupid."

"You're right. They're smart enough to understand the difference you refuse to grasp."

D. T. DIDN'T GET out of the office much after that. The Fox kept him in New York, working on *BioShock* and any other game that needed an extra hand. Meanwhile, I was flying around the country with Ken, demoing the game for the press. *BioShock* never failed to excite, even outside of our scheduled meetings.

One afternoon, I arrived in San Francisco, on the third leg of a multicity promotional tour. For whatever reason, Ken and I had ended up on different flights, so I arrived at the hotel before him. After settling into my room, I returned to the lobby to leave him a message at the check-in desk. "I'm in room blah-blah-blah, my number is one two three, etc . . ." That sort of thing.

As I turned to walk away, a voice called out to me.

"Excuse me?" It was the concierge. "Sorry, I didn't mean to eavesdrop, but did you just leave a message for Ken Levine?" Strange, but not, like, creepy strange. Just unexpected. Maybe I was confused about the travel arrangements and Ken had already arrived.

"Uh, yeah."

"As in Ken Levine, creator of *System Shock 2*?"

"Yessss?" Everything in my body clenched. My lips pulled back unnaturally and my eyes bulged outward as I tried to mimic the appearance of a happy, comfortable person. I've never been able to smile on cue; any attempt makes me look like a dehydrated corpse. No doubt it's a defense mechanism left over from a more primal time, when my taut, terror-filled face might have discouraged predators from going to town on my scrumptious muscles and organs. Sadly, in our modern, civilized age, its effect is minimal.

"Oh my God, what is he working on? Does he have a new game coming out? What's it called? Can you even tell me? Oh my God!"

"Itiscalled*BioShock*andiscomingoutinOctoberitisgreatyoushould buyitsorrygottagobye!" I scuttled away to the elevator, for some reason turning back to wave nervously at the man. It had finally happened—I'd run into a fan. It was off-putting, but also kind of invigorating. It was like being recognized, only one step removed. I got to experience the excitement of a fan and then go about my business, without any fear of being hounded or followed. Better than that, it showed me just how important *BioShock* would be. Knowing that made the endless hours and constant travel worth it. Even when I'd get worn down, I could fall back on that.

I wish I could say the same for D. T. Whenever I was in New York, I could see the stress wearing on him. Normally loud and off-putting, he had begun suffering in silence. After weeks of bottling up every ounce of stress, he was finally beginning to boil over.

One day, as I was taking more screenshots in the 2K office, I heard D. T. sigh in pain. I turned to see him hunched over his keyboard. "Are you okay?"

He pushed back his hair and looked at me with glazed, blinking eyes. "Yeah, why?"

"You just sighed, and it sounded like a sad balloon committing suicide."

"Huh. Didn't even notice." It was the third time that day. He hadn't noticed the other two, either.

That evening, we left work early to grab a drink. It was a Monday. I know because that was the only night we ever went out. Friday-night drinking was for suckers. After a hard week, the last thing we wanted was to fight a crowd for the privilege of gulping down overpriced cocktails. If we drank on a Friday, we did it at home. In the dark. Alone. Just as God intended.

Recently, whenever we did go drinking, D. T. would get sloshed within an hour and spend the rest of the night flicking peanuts into the faces of passing strangers. This led to us being banned from our usual haunt in favor of a bar that didn't serve peanuts.

"Are you doing okay?" I asked.

"Honestly? I don't think so." He was picking through a bowl of standard bar mix in search of ammunition. The ratio of peanuts to other bits was low enough that I figured we could get a few rounds in before he caused any problems. "You know how I woke up this morning? I was on the couch—shirt and jacket on, pants off. Like a filthy animal. I don't even remember how I got home. It was humiliating, Walter!"

D. T. found a large wasabi pea buried in the bar mix and flicked it at some guy's face. He was too drunk to make contact, but it got close.

"What the hell, dude?"

D. T. shrugged. "Do something."

Looking to me, the guy said, "Your friend needs to calm down."

"Thank you. Have a good night." I waved. I don't know why; I just did. It must have been another one of those primal survival instincts—a way to let a predator know I was not a threat to his virile manhood and should be allowed to live, if only out of pity.

I punched D. T. in the shoulder. "What the hell is wrong with you?"

D. T. didn't react; he just put his head down on the bar. "I'm tired."

"Then take a vacation. Call in sick and take a mental health day."

"No can do, Walter. There's too much to do. A man chooses; a slave obeys."

He was quoting Andrew Ryan in *BioShock*. Those six words—"A man chooses; a slave obeys"—were *the* line from the game's big twist, and D. T. had taken to saying it whenever he felt completely helpless.

The twist occurs two-thirds of the way through *BioShock*. The player has fought through the underwater city of Rapture with the help of Atlas, a citizen seeking a way out. The player has been trying to reach Andrew Ryan, the city's founder, in order to kill him and end the city's lockdown. Ryan is no innocent man. He is a despot gone mad; a true antagonist. His death is warranted.

When the player finally confronts Ryan, he's behind a glass window, unreachable. "The assassin has overcome my final defense. And now, he's come to murder me."

As Ryan speaks, the player watches him casually putt golf balls on a strip of green Astroturf. "In the end, what separates a man from a slave? Money? Power? No. A man chooses; a slave obeys.

"You think you have memories: a farm, a family, an airplane, a crash, and then this place. Was there really a family? Did that airplane crash, or was it hijacked? Forced down by something less than a man, something bred to sleepwalk through life until activated by a simple phrase from their kindly master? Was a man sent to kill, or a slave?

"A man chooses; a slave obeys."

Ryan opens the door to his sanctum. The player enters.

"Stop, would you kindly?"

The player stops; the controller ceases to respond. All power has been stripped away. The player now moves only at the whim of Andrew Ryan, who proceeds to reveal the game's untold truth.

The player is not the person they were led to believe they were. Instead of a being an unfortunate stranger from the outside world, they are actually a bioengineered slave created and artificially aged in Rapture, and then sent to live above the waves. It's no accident the player has returned to the city of their birth; they were summoned back to complete their purpose—killing Andrew Ryan. To ensure the player complies, they have been programmed with the trigger phrase "Would you kindly." It's a phrase they've heard almost every time they've been given a goal to complete.

As a final act of control, Andrew Ryan hands his golf putter to the player. "Kill."

The player can only watch as their hands beat Ryan to death. You can probably guess his final words: "A man chooses; a slave obeys."

This was D. T.'s point in quoting Andrew Ryan—he could no more control his own life than the player could control theirs.

Everything Ryan says is true. Nothing you do in *BioShock* is of your own volition. Your goals, tools, and actions are all predetermined by the developer. Any sense of power and control you might have is just an illusion. Even the character you inhabit is a lie. What little you know of your character's past only exists to support the illusion. As with every video-game character, the person you control in *BioShock* did not exist until you started playing.

Nothing you believe about video games is true.

A traditional game is a challenge in which a player's skill comes up against a rigid set of rules. Turn-based strategy, multiplayer death match, platformers—these are traditional. The modern, high-end, blockbuster AAA game is not a skill challenge. If it were, the player might fail and be disappointed, and then we wouldn't sell as many copies. The rules are fluid. We change them to create tension, surprise, or excitement. Saying yes to the player only goes so far, and that distance is the exact length required to make you feel in control.

Feel. That's the key word. We can't make you powerful, clever, or important, but we can design an experience that will make you feel that way. It's a fantasy, though not a frivolous one. Our desires lead us to dream; our dreams lead us to create. If we can make you feel like the person you want to be, even just for a moment, then you might be inspired to go out and become that person. That's the real strength behind what we do.

Fantasy is good.

BIOSHOCK WAS RELEASED AUGUST 21, 2007, for Xbox 360 and PC. The reviews were phenomenal. On the review website Metacritic, the console and PC versions both received an average score of ninety-six out of one hundred. The response was so positive that the value of Take-Two's stock jumped nearly 20 percent the following week. The Xbox 360 version sold almost five hundred thousand copies its first week, making it the third-best-selling game of August 2007.

It was a great moment for everyone at Irrational. Their hard work had paid off. Those of us in publishing were just as excited. *BioShock* was the game we'd been looking for, something we could point to and say, "This is who we are. This is what we can give you."

In the following months, *BioShock* was nominated for awards all over the world, including an astounding twelve nominations by the Academy of Interactive Arts & Sciences, arguably the gaming equivalent of the Oscars. The award show was held at their annual summit, D.I.C.E., which stands for four pillars of game development—design, innovate, communicate, and entertain. As a thank-you for our hard work, 2K flew the publishing team to Las Vegas for the awards. Of its twelve nominations, *BioShock* won four—Outstanding Achievement in Art Direction, Story Development, Original Music Composition, and Sound Design. I can't speak for everyone else, but I was a little disappointed we only won four out of twelve. The big award, Action Game of the Year, we lost to *Call of Duty 4: Modern Warfare*. But it's hard to be too upset when you lose to one of the most intense and visceral games of the last ten years. The open bar also didn't hurt.

After the awards, I tried to slink away to a roulette table, but Geekjock grabbed me by the arm. "Come on. I want to introduce you to a friend of mine." Damn that manly grip and artificially tanned bicep! There would be no escape.

He dragged me over to a circle of couches where a group of people was just ordering drinks. One man in particular looked up and smiled. Geekjock introduced us. "This is Walt, my game analyst. Walt, this is Mark Cerny."

Mark Cerny is a bit of legend in game development. He's done it all—design, programming, production, even business. He was the lead architect for Sony's PlayStation 4 and the PlayStation Vita. If that's not enough, his body of work includes more successful, beloved franchises than that of anyone else I can think of: God of War, Resistance, Ratchet & Clank, Jak and Daxter, Uncharted, Spyro the Dragon, Crash Bandicoot. But all these accomplishments paled in comparison to one.

"So, you're the guy who made *Marble Madness*?"

"Oh God . . ." Mark cringed. "Are you seriously going to bring that up?"

Booze always loosens the tongue, but it has nothing on the freedom that comes in the aftermath of battle. And make no mistake, game development is a battle. Our universe is one of law and logic. To create is to shatter those laws, to reach inside yourself and produce a thing where once there was none. The universe doesn't like that. It will set everything it has against you—time, space, and everything in between. When the fight is over, it's easy to forget how hard it was. No one will fault you for speaking the truth. You've achieved the improbable, and they know how that feels.

I gave Mark a drunken, shit-eating grin. "You misunderstand. I'm not geeking out. *Marble Madness* was the first game I ever rented as a kid. I never got past the second level. I just wanted to take this opportunity to say 'Fuck you.'"

Laughter. Clinked glasses. Cheers all around.

These are the moments that make it all worthwhile.

I'VE NEVER WORKED ON a game I didn't hate.

As the saying goes, familiarity breeds contempt, and there is no greater intimacy than that obtained through creation. By the time *Bio-Shock* was released, I'd played the game more than two hundred times. My cursor had caressed every hair, blemish, and wart on its digital frame. I'd seen everything, except the final game 2K had shipped to stores across the world. *BioShock* had gone gold without me. I had no idea what changes had been made in the final stages of development. I didn't want to know. When the Fox gave me my retail copy of the game, I tucked it away in a drawer. There was no way I could play it. The memory of working on *BioShock* was still too fresh.

A person is just an animal with a very high opinion of itself. We don't like to think about it too much, but we're as trainable as dogs. If an action is continuously repeated, our mind will build connections between the action and associated stimuli. Video games demand everything of their creators. With *BioShock*, I wasn't even involved with its creation; I was just the guy taking pictures, and it still wrecked me. Three months passed before I found the energy to play it.

On a Saturday morning, I placed the game in the disc tray of my Xbox 360. The game spun up; the 2K and Irrational Games logos appeared and then faded from my TV screen. When the start menu appeared, I did nothing. It was night. Moonlight streaked the cloud-covered sky. The game's logo—an iron-cast plate bearing its name and an abstraction of a city skyline—floated above the Atlantic Ocean, at the base of a lighthouse. The water rippled gently; the rays of moonlight moved in time with the clouds. It was the first time I'd seen the final menu, and it was beautiful. When I saw that, I knew I was finally ready.

I selected "New Game" and descended back into Rapture. Minutes later, as my bathysphere surfaced inside Rapture's welcome terminal, the game froze. At first, I thought the game had simply crashed. Even with high-profile releases like *BioShock*, it wasn't out of the question for a game to ship with bugs still inside. Then I noticed the power button of my Xbox 360. Normally green, it was now surrounded by three flashing red lights. My console had suffered a general hardware failure that the gaming community had dubbed the Red Ring of Death. I was ready to play *BioShock*, but my 360 clearly wasn't. It had fatally shat itself and was now an expensive brick, broken beyond repair.

For the first time in a long while, I went outside and enjoyed the day.

7

MADE MEN

A few years into the job, life took a turn.

I was in a long-term relationship. It ended. The details aren't relevant to what we're talking about, except for one—I was more willing to commit to my job than to my personal life. Coming out of college, I had no career prospects. Now, I was working for a major video-game publisher, traveling the world, and standing near brilliant people creating spectacular things. It was easy to be seduced.

She wanted to move back south. I said no. This job was for me; New York City was for me. It hurt, but I needed to stay.

The day after she left for good, I was on a plane to Berlin. Work didn't stop for doubt, regret, or heartbreak. That night, the Fox grinned at me from across a table in the bar of our hotel.

"So . . . What do you think of San Francisco?"

The mischievous twinkle in his eye said everything his question had not.

"I think you're an asshole."

2K was growing and needed more room. The plan was to trade our single-floor office in SoHo for a converted airplane hangar in Novato, California, a small town thirty miles north of San Francisco. Publishing wouldn't be alone; we'd be sharing it with 2K Sports; their main developer, Visual Concepts; and our newest internal dev studio, 2K Marin.

The Fox didn't expect me to blindly follow him to the other side of the country. An offer was made—a generous one, which included a promotion from game analyst to associate producer. It was tempting, but

I was in no rush to accept. I was one day removed from my last major life change, and was suddenly facing another. If I went to California, I'd be leaving the first city that had ever felt like home to me. On the other hand, if I didn't accept the Fox's offer, I'd be out of work. Staying in New York meant finding a new job, and there weren't many video-game options in New York. It was possible I could have transferred to Rockstar, but I had no desire to. There was nothing wrong with them; their games just weren't my style. The open-world design of Grand Theft Auto was interesting, but the series's core crime fantasy didn't appeal to me. Most likely, I'd have to abandon video games entirely and find employment in a new field. The third option was to leave New York and 2K, move back south, and attempt reconciliation.

A month before, I had had a fiancée, a career, and a great life in New York. I should have known it was too good to be true. Something had slipped by in the paperwork, and the cosmos had finally noticed the error. The choice ahead of me was the universe's way of saying sorry. I was only supposed to get one of the three.

IT HAD BEEN AWHILE since I tried the comic-book thing, so I updated my résumé and sent it off to Marvel and DC Comics. Would you believe it? For the first time ever, I got a response.

With Marvel, I got a few rounds into the hiring process for an assistant editor position. Through an accidental slip in conversation, I learned I wasn't the only person at 2K vying for the job. A few of us had secretly applied, all for the same reason—we didn't want to move. Marvel was our Hail Mary, but none of us managed to pull it off. I don't know how it went down for everyone else, but I can pinpoint exactly where I went wrong.

As a test, Marvel had me edit a few comic scripts. The first one was fine; I corrected typos, called out inconsistencies, kept it simple. Making it to the next round must have gone to my head, because the second script was less an edit than a full rewrite. It was a bad habit, one the Fox encouraged but no other company would tolerate. Rewriting the Marvel script was a bad decision, made even worse by the fact it had been written by Chris Claremont, the most prolific X-Men writer in comic history. Two of the six X-Men movies are based on his classic stories "The Dark Phoenix Saga" and "Days of Future Past." Claremont is the guy who transformed Wolverine from a vertically challenged Canadian nobody into one of the most popular comic-book characters ever created, arguably making him the godfather of Hugh Jackman's entire acting career.

I never heard back from Marvel after that. I'm still holding out hope for the mail-room job, but only because I've now mentioned it three times. Like Beetlejuice or Candyman, an email from Marvel's hiring department should appear in my inbox any day now, just to say, "We have received your application and regret to inform you . . ."

DC Comics was a different story. I was browsing through a comic-book store one afternoon when I got a call. Someone at DC had seen my résumé and was so excited that they wanted to cut straight to the chase. My credentials were perfect for the position, but they were afraid I would want too much money. I'd been working an entry-level position while living in New York; too much money was not a concept I was familiar with. All I knew was what I needed to get by, month to month. DC came in five grand lower and couldn't budge, so that was the end of it. I had missed my window of opportunity: after years spent applying with no response, I was now overqualified.

There were no other jobs in New York that excited me at the time, so my options were down to two: go west or go home.

In the end, it all came down to Berlin. Up to that point in my career, every game I worked on had been someone else's project, a work I had joined in progress. The game being made in Berlin was different. I'd been involved with it since the beginning, and in that way, it was mine. Even though it was still in the early stages, I knew it had the potential to be unique. If I stuck with 2K, I could help guide it. I'd finally have an original AAA game on my résumé, one that showed what I was capable of. Once I had that, I could go anywhere—maybe even find work down south. When I looked at it from that angle, it really was the only option.

We were still in the final days of shipping *BioShock*, so there wasn't time for me to visit the Bay Area and find an apartment. The best I could manage was a place near the new office that would allow me to sign a lease from New York. Once that was done and *BioShock* had shipped, I loaded my stuff onto a moving truck and then flew to Prague to meet with a developer. Work wasn't going to stop for something as trivial as moving across the country. One week later, I flew from the Czech Republic straight to San Francisco, where my new life was waiting.

CALIFORNIA WAS BRIGHT.

Where I lived, in San Rafael, there were trees and mountains and one road. The 101 was the Mississippi River of highways. All roads were tributaries, leading me back to that black stretch of asphalt.

They said the weather was perfect, though based on what scale I can't even imagine. It would rain for a few months and then burn for a few months. The rest of the time, it was simultaneously hot enough to make you sweat and cold enough to require a jacket.

The closest food was always fast food, but I won't count that as a negative.

More than anything, though, it was bright. I don't know if it was the lack of clouds or ozone, but it always felt like there was too much sun. My body is made of marshmallow; pale and lumpy but delicious. The prospect of a sun-kissed life did not appeal to me the way it did to my friends. By the time I arrived, they had all taken up hobbies, like hiking, softball, or windsurfing. California had shown them our industry's version of the Holy Grail—the elusive work-life balance. They had been transformed into healthier, happier, tanner versions of themselves.

Not much had changed for me. I'd roll into the office around 10:00 a.m. and roll out after sundown. My Red Bull habit, once one can a day, had grown to four before lunch. Every so often, someone would stop at my desk and look down at me with a white-toothed smile and say, "We're going to get something to eat. Wanna come?"

"Fools!" I'd shout. "Blind fools! You're all living a lie!"

Our job required regular human sacrifice; blood was needed for the gears to run smoothly inside the gaming mill. My coworkers believed their lives had improved, but I knew there would be weeping and gnashing of teeth when our dark digital gods grew hungry once again. Only I would be deemed worthy, for I had stayed the course and never abandoned my righteous misery for the false promises of surf and sun.

I didn't get invited out a lot in those days.

Said a coworker, "It's nice to know if anyone ever asks what type of person Walt Williams is, I can say, 'He's the type of person who gets angry when you invite him to lunch.'" I know I shouldn't be proud of that, but goddammit, I honestly am.

WITH MY PROMOTION TO associate producer, 2K was left without a game analyst. *BioShock* had shipped, but *BioShock 2* was already gearing up, plus *Mafia II* and *Borderlands* were just around the corner. "We need Walt 2.0," said the Fox. "Who do you know?"

There was a guy—Young Philippe, a friend from my college days. He loved video games more than anyone else I'd ever met, and there was a period of time when we had the same haircut and people thought we were brothers. These are not the best criteria for hiring someone, but when the Fox said he needed Walt 2.0, this is what popped into my head.

I called Young Philippe to see if he'd be interested. "So, how are things?" I asked.

Things were good for Young Philippe. He was about to graduate from college, his final exams were done, and he was free as tap water for the next two weeks.

"I'm loving life, and it is loving me right back," he said.

This type of unfettered positivity usually made me nauseous. Coming from Young Philippe, it was contagious. His excitement and hope were rooted in childlike wonder. At some point in life, he simply decided to not grow old and bitter. This was enough to recommend him for the game analyst position. New blood is important in the game industry; there's nothing more uplifting to a team of bitter developers than bright-eyed enthusiasm.

I explained the situation—we were looking to hire a new game analyst, and he was perfect for the job. If he was interested, I'd see about getting him an interview.

"For real? Oh, man. I really appreciate that, but honestly, I already have plans. After graduation, I'm moving to Austin to become a rock star and an astronaut, so I'm pretty well set. But thanks for thinking of me!"

There was such conviction in his voice; I didn't have the heart to tell him it was ridiculous. The conversation was over. I had offered Young Philippe his dream job, and he passed so he could become Ziggy Stardust. Nothing beats Ziggy Stardust.

Two weeks later, I woke up to a text message at 5:00 a.m. on a Sunday morning. It was Young Philippe. "Hey, man. Were you serious about that video-game job? Because I graduated yesterday and it just hit me I don't have any job skills."

Of course I was serious. "Send me your résumé. I'll see what I can do."

I've always been aware of how lucky I was to find a job at 2K when I was just starting out. I owed a lot to Wayne, the hiring manager who'd been willing to give me a chance. I'd always planned to pay that kindness forward. Young Philippe just so happened to be the guy to pay it to.

The Fox took some convincing. He didn't see the point in interviewing someone in Waco, Texas, when there were plenty of great candidates in the Bay Area. Even if Young Philippe got the job, 2K would never pay to relocate him for an entry-level position. I told him reloca-tion wouldn't be an issue. To sweeten the pot, I even promised that if 2K flew Philippe out for an interview and chose not to hire him, I would personally pay back all travel costs. That did it. We set a date and pre-pared for Young Philippe's arrival.

"Should I wear a suit?" he asked.

"Absolutely not," I said. "Don't even pack one."

"Everyone says you're supposed to wear a suit to a job interview."

"Everyone is a liar. You are to wear jeans, tennis shoes, an untucked dress shirt, and your GWAR belt buckle."

Silence on the other end of the line. Then, "I don't think that acces-sory is appropriate." Were this any other job, Young Philippe would be correct. GWAR is a hard-core heavy-metal band known for their grotesque costumes and concerts filled with over-the-top violence and gore.

"Trust me. Wear the damn belt buckle."

WHEN YOUNG PHILIPPE SHOWED up for his interview, he wowed every-one in product development. He was smart, inquisitive, and driven. The kid knew this was his only shot at working in video games, and it pumped him full of adrenaline, keeping him at the top of his game.

The Fox was Young Philippe's last interview of the day. Before going in to meet Philippe, he stopped by my desk.

"So, is there anything I should know before I speak to your friend?"

An idea popped into my head, sudden and mischievous. "He ma-jored in French."

The Fox's eyes lit up. French, after all, was his native language. "Oh! This will be fun."

I watched the Fox enter the glass-walled conference room where Young Philippe was seated. The door closed. The Fox sat down, put his feet up on the conference table. His lips began to move. Young Philippe's body instantly tensed; he sat up straighter in his chair. I knew the Fox would have launched right into speaking French, and I smiled to myself.

It couldn't have been more than ten minutes later when the Fox exited the conference room.

"How'd it go?" I asked.

He tossed Young Philippe's résumé on my desk like it was garbage. "His French is terrible."

Oh, no. Had my joke just cost Philippe the job? "I'm sure he's just rusty. Aside from that, what did you think?"

Never one to give an easy compliment, the Fox shrugged. "Eh. He's a good kid. I think he'd fit in well, but . . ." His voice trailed off, and his brow scrunched down in thought. "Was he wearing a GWAR belt buckle?"

"Yeah."

"Then why the fuck haven't we hired him yet?"

YOUNG PHILIPPE MOVED TO California a few weeks later, with nothing but a suitcase full of clothes. He wouldn't last long in San Francisco on his own, so he moved into my apartment in San Rafael, where he lived on my couch. I knew it was a mistake almost instantly.

At work, Philippe was amazing. Our desks sat next to each other. Against the wall, behind us, we began building what we called the Death Shrine, a pile of empty cigarette packs and Red Bull cans. Every day, we added one pack and four cans. To us, it was a sign of how hard we were working. To everyone else, it was a trash heap. Like me, Young Philippe was aware of how lucky he was to work at 2K. It felt like at any moment the shoe would drop and someone would realize he didn't belong. Philippe's fear of being fired and returning home a failure kept him at the top of his game. At home, however, he was just so damn happy.

My day-to-day life in California was simple. I woke up around 8:00 a.m., watched some TV, took an hour-long bath, and eventually went to work around ten. The office was an easy, breezy five-minute drive from my apartment. Sometime around seven or eight in the evening, I'd drive back home, play some games, eat some dinner, and fall asleep. That was my life, and I loved it. When Young Philippe arrived, that all changed. He was excitable and energetic, like a puppy, always looking for new things to do. I was not a doer. My number-one hobby in California was making plans on which I never intended to follow through. There was the time Young Philippe and I decided to join the San Francisco curling league and qualify for the 2010 Winter Olympics. And that other time when we planned to take all the cigarette packs and Red Bull cans from our Death Shrine and use them to build the body of a robot we had already named the Offense-o-Tron Deathousand. My personal favorite was when we were going to rent a pirate ship to sail us into international waters so we could set off illegal fireworks. These were some of our best adventures, and I never had to do any of them.

Young Philippe wasn't content living a life of dreams. He wanted to experience California. Since he didn't have a car, I was his only transportation. If he went to work early, I did, too. If he wanted to check out a brewery in Lagunitas, I had to take him. Visiting the beach at Point Reyes, hiking on Angel Island, touring pubs all across San Francisco—I was there for all of it. On the nights I convinced Young Philippe to stay home, it was just as bad. Inevitably, we'd play video games, which brought out his competitive side. It didn't matter what game we played. If it had multiplayer, Young Philippe had mastered it. He couldn't stand the thought of losing and had spent many boring Waco days perfecting his skills. I couldn't care less about playing the "correct way." I was a button-masher, meaning I just pressed buttons on the controller and hoped something good would happen. I never stood a chance. It was all too much for my grumpy, lazy bones.

After a month, Young Philippe got a car. That saved me from a life of "doing things." He was free to have adventures, while I huddled in my dim apartment like a subterranean creature whose eyes have grown blind from lack of light. A month after that, I made him get his own place so I could regain control of my living room. He still didn't have any furniture, so I gave him one of my chairs. It was a small price to pay for peace, quiet, and the freedom to walk around my apartment without pants.

THE ONLY OTHER PERSON who shared my attitude about moving to California was Carlito, our production director. He was Italian, angry, and perpetually clad in black. It was like someone broke off a piece of Long Island and chiseled it into the shape of a man. His title was production director, but his job was jack-of-all-trades. He handled contracts, licensing, outsourcing, casting, motion capture, voice direction, video editing, creative direction, level design, and script writing. He was the rock of product development.

You didn't see much of Carlito; his numerous responsibilities kept him on the road most of the year. He kept a private office in the Novato hangar, but it was more symbolic than functional—something to acknowledge that he was still an employee. The majority of his work took place off-site, usually in a developer's office, hotel room, or recording studio. For a while, he worked out of a secret editing suite hidden above a deli. Whether his offices were temporary pop-ups or permanent installations, they were always fully stocked with everything Carlito needed to survive: blackout curtains, pallets of energy drinks, crates of protein bars, a minifridge filled with cold cuts, and a couch for those rare moments when sleep could no longer be ignored. Inside those darkened hovels, he was more beast than man. Nothing existed for him other than the work and his most basic human needs.

Every so often, Carlito would select a kid from PD, someone to serve as both assistant and apprentice. Working with Carlito was like going through basic training. The physical and mental demands were high; the comforts and freedoms were next to none. Those who could learn and adapt would eventually move on to key creative roles on future projects, because if you could survive Carlito, you could weather anything a developer threw at you. Those who weren't up to the task would stick around for a month or two and then quietly show themselves the door. One kid was so affected by his time with Carlito, he began to dress like him, even gel his hair the same way. None of us realized he was counting the days until the project ended and he was free. Last we heard, the kid had left the industry to become a man of the cloth. True story.

When I got an email from Carlito one Friday afternoon, I knew my time had come.

"You got plans this weekend?"

I replied, "Do I ever?"

"Good. I need you in the office. We got work to do."

The 2K office was in Hamilton Landing, a former military base that had been converted into a subdivision of Novato. Carlito was 450 miles south of there in Santa Monica, writing and recording dialogue for *Mafia II*.

Originally developed by Illusion Softworks in the Czech Republic, Mafia is an open-world crime franchise, in which players take on the role of a mafioso during the mob's golden age. A normal game will keep the player confined to a level: you start at Point A, move to Point B, then teleport to the next level and repeat. An open-world game is different in that its levels are contained within a vast world that players are free to explore. These games have a critical path you can follow, if you wish, but their appeal comes from what can be done when you're ignoring that path. You can drive a car, ride a horse, fly a jet pack, watch TV, hunt Bigfoot, skin bobcats, find a serial killer's dumping ground, play poker, work out, get fat, buy houses, invest in the stock market, own a bar, grow a beard, move to a shitty trailer in the desert, pretend you're a different person. It takes a big team to populate an open-world game with enough options to make it worth playing. The possibilities are not endless, but they can feel that way.

To make an open world seem real, it has to be filled with NPCs, or nonplayer characters. These are the computer-controlled characters you meet when playing the game. NPCs can be enemies or noncombatants. They act and react based on how their AI, or artificial intelligence, has been programmed. Imagine you're playing *Mafia II*. Your character is walking down the sidewalk and passes a man in a suit. If you punched that man in the face, he might run in fear, fight back, or sprint to the nearest police officer to report your crime. You, the player, don't know how that man will react. That variety and surprise created by NPCs is part of what makes an open world feel alive. But it doesn't stop there. To make the illusion seem real, those NPCs need to talk, which is where writing comes into play.

In the hierarchy of game writing, you have many levels. At the top is your core script. This is the main story a player will experience in a game. It's like a screenplay, mostly linear and noninteractive. Next are barks, or generic lines as they're sometimes called. These are nonscripted, nonnarrative lines that are triggered when a certain event occurs. For example, the player shoots a guy in the knee. The guy falls down and screams, "Ow!" or "Why'd you do that?" or "Oh no, my adventuring knee!" The line that plays is chosen randomly from a pool of relevant choices. Barks make a game feel more alive by having its artificial inhabitants react to the things happening around them.

Below barks are tertiary lines. They're background chatter, unimportant noise used to simulate an active, living world: two people chatting on a street corner, a soldier talking to himself on guard duty, a shopkeeper explaining her wares. These lines give color to your world and make it feel alive, which is funny because writing them makes me want to kill myself.

Carlito needed two thousand tertiary lines by Sunday night—a drop in the bucket for the entire game, but a lot for an impromptu weekend marathon. The amount of lines didn't worry me; numbers can always be overcome with the right approach. It was the nature of what I'd be writing that made me want to vomit. Writing a core script can be fun. It has rhythm, progression, flow. If I can tap into that, it's easy to get carried away. My eyes glaze over, muscle memory kicks in. The next thing I know, eight hours have passed and my script is thirty pages longer. Barks and tertiary lines are devoid of such pleasures.

Writing the tertiary lines wasn't like writing a script. Instead, I was filling in a spreadsheet. I worked my way down, filling in one cell at a time, my words matching the character and action listed in the cell beside it. For example, "Gun Store Clerk—Hello," meaning the guy who runs the gun store would say the line whenever the player entered. I wrote something like:

GUN STORE CLERK

If you're looking for a gun, you came to the right place.

But I couldn't stop there. It would get repetitive if the clerk always said the same thing, so I wrote four more lines.

GUN STORE CLERK

Good afternoon, sir. Care to see what we got?

GUN STORE CLERK

Hello. If I can help, just let me know.

GUN STORE CLERK

Come on in.

GUN STORE CLERK

Hi.

With each line, I felt my life draining away. That was five hellos for the gun store clerk, but I still wasn't finished. I needed to write five "hello" lines each for the other seven gun store clerks, who all looked, sounded, and acted differently. Then, I had to do the same for the clothing store clerks, the barbers, the waiters, the car salesmen, the gas-station attendants, the shoe shiners . . . You get the picture.

After three sets of hellos, I began to wonder how many of my fingers I could bite off before passing out from pain and blood loss. But I persevered and wrote a hundred variations of "Hey, guy! Lookin' to buy?" Then I moved on to the next set of lines: Gun Store Clerk—Good-bye.

GUN STORE CLERK
See you next time!

If I bit down hard enough, could I sever a finger in one chomp, or would I have to gnaw through the bone like it was a stubborn piece of gristle?

THAT WEEKEND, I WROTE lines for every store in the game. Hellos, good-byes, idle chatter, and helpful descriptions of everything the player could buy, from hot dogs to hand grenades. After a while, it felt like my skull was filling up with smoke.

Spend enough years writing and you find your breaking point, your body's way of letting you know it's time to stop. Skull smoke was my red flag. I knew a migraine was on its way, soon to be followed by fever naps and vomiting. To get past it, I had to trick my brain into not thinking; I had to write with my gut, not my mind. I turned to a method I developed in college to survive speed-writing papers at the last minute.

The next set of lines on my spreadsheet was Gun Store Clerk—Tommy Gun. Easy enough.

GUN STORE CLERK

I heard you're in the market for a Chicago piano. Well, I'm your guy.

GUN STORE CLERK

This here's a classic. Same one Al Capone uses, hand to heart.

GUN STORE CLERK

Now, this is a top-notch tommy gun. Never hear any complaints,

if you get my meaning.

GUN STORE CLERK

It shoots bullets really fucking fast. What more do you need to know?

The last line was for me. It wasn't clever or terribly funny, but it's how I felt as I tried to come up with something else to say about tommy guns. Giving voice to my frustration was enjoyable. I didn't care if one out of every four lines wasn't usable. It took some of the pressure off, and relieved the pain building inside my head. It was the Tom Sawyer effect. It wasn't work if I could convince myself I was having fun.

When I got to work on Tuesday, there was an email from Carlito waiting for me. The subject read "THIS IS GOOD WRITING." Attached to the email was an audio file. The voice on the file was unmistakable: Curtis Armstrong, best known for playing Booger in *Revenge of the Nerds*. I was so surprised, it took me a second before I recognized what he was saying—it was one of my throwaway lines.

SHOE SHINER

You know, it's a shame more women don't get their shoes shined.

You ever stopped and looked at a woman's shoe? I mean, really looked

at it? They're so slim, so beautiful. They just make you wanna . . .

I dunno . . . smell 'em.

The email itself was one sentence long. "When can you come to Santa Monica?"

I FLEW FROM SAN Francisco to Santa Monica and drove straight to Pacific Ocean Post, where Carlito had rented an audio-recording studio for the month. I arrived around 10:00 a.m. and found Carlito in the studio with our four actors: Ricky, Nicky, Bobby, and Tony. They were flipping through a binder full of menus, trying to decide what to order for lunch.

Bobby was going back and forth between two different pizzerias. "Is it sissy if I order the veggie pizza?"

"Depends," said Ricky. "What's the veggie pizza?"

"It ain't got no meat on it."

Nicky, who'd been talking to Carlito, turned to Bobby. "You ordering a plain cheese?"

"Who the fuck said anything about plain cheese? I'm talking about pizza with vegetables and shit on it."

Tony grabbed the binder out of Bobby's hand. "What? You a fucking vegetarian now?"

"No . . ." Embarrassed, Bobby almost blushed. "Just trying to lose some weight."

These guys were full of Italian machismo, but they were also professional actors. Keeping it tight was something they could relate to.

"Nah," said Ricky. "That ain't sissy."

Tony looked up from the menu. "It's only sissy if you order the side of cock."

"Well, shit." Bobby looked devastated. "The cock's the best part."

I had somehow ended up in the dinner scene of a mob movie.

Ricky slapped Bobby on the shoulder to get his attention. "Hey, Tony. Did I hear you on the radio last week?"

Tony shut the binder and placed it on his lap. "I knew this was gonna happen." He sat back, squared his shoulders, and crossed his arms. "Go on. Let's have it."

"What'd he do?" asked Bobby.

"Five words," said Ricky. "All-you-can-eat breadsticks."

Bobby's eyes went wide. "You did an Olive Garden commercial? You fucking sellout."

"You act like I'm the only one. Nicky did one for . . . whatcha call it?"

"It was Macaroni Grill," said Nicky. "And it was classy as shit."

Ricky, Bobby, and Tony looked like Nicky had just spit on their sisters, mothers, and grandmothers.

"I'm talking about the commercial! I classed it up. The food was . . ." He waved it off. "Eh, you know how it is."

WE DIDN'T GET STARTED until lunch had been delivered, served, and digested.

A recording booth usually has room for only one actor at a time. This forces the actor to perform alone. It's not ideal. Carlito liked to record all his actors at once, so they could react to one another. He booked the larger studio used for automated dialogue replacement, or ADR. In film, ADR is the process of rerecording dialogue after filming is complete. It requires an actor to perform his or her lines while watching the film. Since the ADR studio had to house a projection screen, that meant it was big enough for all of us to be in there at once. Ricky, Nicky, Bobby, and Tony sat in long-legged director's chairs, separated from one another by sound-dampening partitions. I handed each of them a script and a pencil, then joined Carlito at a long table.

We were recording scratch for *Mafia II*, which means none of it was final. The script was still a work in progress, or WIP. That's not to say it was bad or unfinished; it's just that the game design was still in flux. If your game is WIP, then so is your script, because as sure as the sun will rise, the game will change. And when the game changes, the script changes. These are the rules.

Just because scratch isn't final doesn't mean it's not important. Scratch dialogue lets us get a feel for the story and plot cinematics, and just get lines in the game so we can see what the final experience may feel like.

The recording with Ricky, Nicky, Bobby, and Tony was a blast. Since our cast was only four guys, each of them did multiple voices. Al Pacino, Christopher Walken, Marlon Brando—we recorded every impression they could pull off.

I asked Carlito, "Do we need to get people's permission for this?"

"Nah. This shit won't make it into the final game, not in a million years."

"Then why do it?"

"Because it's fun. These guys are recording a huge script and playing too many characters. It's important to keep things light. Besides, the more fun they have, the more they'll want to work with us. Trust me. There's a reason for everything."

The group session was only four hours long. When the time was up, Ricky, Bobby, and Tony said their good-byes and headed home. Nicky stayed behind to record his barks and grunts.

A grunt is like a bark, except there are no words to it. It's an exertion noise. We call them grunts because that's what they are—sighing, panting, grunting, all the noises you unconsciously make over the course of your day. Video-game characters make the same noises, whether they're lifting a box, jumping down from a ledge, or taking a shotgun blast to the face. It's a dangerous world out there for a video-game character; a new, wholly improbable death awaits them at every turn. As writers of the barks and keepers of the spreadsheets, it was up to us to make sure we recorded every grunt we could imagine.

I like to separate grunts into four categories: normal, bad, hellish, and sexy. Normal grunts are exactly what you'd think—jogging, sprinting, catching your breath, lifting something heavy, small jump, big jump—stuff like that. Bad grunts are sounds you might make on a really bad day—sounds of pain and struggle, like having the wind knocked out of you, being kicked in the face, or taking an arrow to the knee. Hellish grunts are sounds you've probably never heard, or made, in real life. If you have, then it's possible you're currently dead or severely traumatized. Curb-stomped, burnt alive, face sawed in half—these are hellish grunts. How dark and disturbing they get is entirely up to the director. The last category, sexy grunts, are different than all of the above. We'll get to them a bit later.

Before we got started, Nicky had some questions about the script. "I'm not sure what you guys want for this stuff. The first line just says 'grunt-comma-punch.'"

Some writers will give their actors scripts filled with *hrghs*, *umphs*, and *gahs*. That's a rookie mistake. Your actors are professionals, not comic-book characters. They don't need their grunts literally spelled out for them; they just need direction.

"Lemme see," said Carlito. He grabbed a copy of the script and found the line. "Right, okay. So, this is the sound you'd make if someone punched you hard in the chest."

"Okay, cool. Ready when you are."

Carlito signaled the audio engineers in the booth behind us. One of their voices came over the intercom. "Recording."

Carlito nodded to Nicky. Nicky gave us three grunts as if he were being punched in the chest, and then we moved to the next line.

MOBSTER
[Grunt, small scream]

"This is like a bullet grazed your arm. It stings, but not enough to slow you down."

MOBSTER

[Grunt, big scream]

"This time, the bullet hits you but goes clean through your shoulder. It hurts, but you're still on your feet."

MOBSTER

[Death gurgle]

"The bullet has torn through your jugular. You're lying in the street, cold and alone, bleeding out. You know you're dying; you're trying to sob, but it's hard to cry when you're choking to death on your own blood."

"Gotcha."

In any other medium, a character choking to death on his own blood would be "A Moment." For us, these were generic lines. Nicky's dying tears would play a hundred times over the course of the game. This was one more sound thrown into a pool of death gurgles from which it could be randomly selected whenever an enemy died. This was the ambient sound of combat, death and despair as white noise.

"Great," said Carlito. "Let's move on to the next page. These are taunts you're shouting at the player while trying to kill him."

Nicky nodded. He took a swig of water and cleared this throat.

He snarled into the recording mic, murder in his voice. "Your head'll look good stuffed and mounted on my wall!" He did three takes, as usual. They were good. It was a perfectly menacing line, but I felt like it could be better.

Carlito looked sideways at me. "Call it—A, B, or C?"

For every read of a line, he had me mark down A, B, C, and so on. That way, we remembered which take we wanted to use when it came time to implement them in the game.

"Maybe C?" I wasn't sure if there was a wrong answer, but it felt like there was. "Yeah, I think C."

"Good. Mark it down."

I did as I was told, then leaned over to whisper to Carlito. "I think I have an idea for an alternate take on that line."

"Yeah? Let me hear it."

"Your head'll look good stuffed and mounted on the end of my dick."

Carlito gave a snort. I couldn't be sure if it was laughter or derision. "That might be too much. These guys are bad, but not that bad. I like that you're throwing out ideas, though."

As WE LEFT THAT evening, we passed the studio's head manager. Carlito had basically been living at the studio for the past month, so the two of them had grown familiar.

"We're going for dinner," said Carlito. "Wanna come?"

"Wish I could, but I've got a director going long. I can't say who, or what he's working on, but it's a game. The poor guy's freaking out. Apparently he's on take one hundred ninety-seven of the same line."

Carlito shrugged like it was no big deal. "Maybe tomorrow."

As we got in the car, I asked, "How do you end up doing one hundred ninety-seven takes of one line?"

"I bet whoever's directing that session is a fucking writer. These guys write a line and think they know exactly how it should be delivered, then they come in here and fuck up the entire session trying to get it exactly the way they hear it in their head. They all think they're Stanley Kubrick.

"Listen, forget one hundred ninety-seven takes. If your actor can't get a line in ten, it's not because they can't get it right. It means you wrote a shitty line. You have to trust your actors. This is what they do. It's why we pay them to show up and talk into a microphone. When you hand off your script to someone else, it has to stand on its own. You can't control it every step of the way. I don't give a fuck if you wrote a great script; it's not all you. It will never be all you. This is why you never let writers into a recording session."

"... I'm a writer."

"Yeah, but you don't know shit. I can teach you to do the job right. At least then you won't make extra work for me."

"Good to know."

"One hundred ninety-seven takes . . ." Carlito sneered as he pulled out of the parking lot. He wasn't angry; it was more like he was disgusted. "Just walk away," he said, quoting the Humungus in *Mad Max 2: The Road Warrior.* "Just walk away and there will be an end to the horror."

MY SANTA MONICA EXCURSION was scheduled to last two weeks. That was fourteen days of living like Carlito. By design, my world was reduced to a hotel room and a recording studio, both in Santa Monica. The distance was short enough to walk, but I never did. My schedule did not allow for leisurely walks. Every day had to be fast, focused, and familiar. Too much downtime and I started asking questions—dark, terrible questions with answers I didn't want to know. Questions like, "Why?" If I asked myself that question, I would have passed the point of no return. To avoid it, I lost myself in the routine:

0800—Wake up.

0803—Wash down Adderall (20 mg) #1 with Sugar-Free Red Bull (12 oz) #1.

0810—Shit.

0830—Shower.

0840—Shuffle downstairs.

0850—Drive 1 mile to studio. Drink Sugar-Free Red Bull (12 oz) #2.

0900—Eat donut. Drink Sugar-Free Red Bull (12 oz) #3.

0930 to 1200—Record VO.

1200—Eat lunch. Something brown, preferably fried.

1230—Adderall (20 mg) #2, Sugar-Free Red Bull (12 oz) #4.

1300 to 1800—Record VO.

1810—Drive to hotel.

1820—Drop bags in hotel room.

1830—Start drinking.

1900—Eat dinner. Steak or hamburger, alternating nightly.

1930—Review scripts for tomorrow.

2100—Take melatonin (5 mg) and Advil PM (ibuprofen,
200 mg/diphenhydramine citrate, 38 mg).

2105 to ????—Listen to an audiobook until I pass out.

The audiobook was a source of escape that I could enjoy. The uppers and downers weren't fun; they were necessary to keep my brain in the game. The first half of my day was ramping up; the second half was ramping down. I was chemically controlled, around the clock.

One morning, Carlito found me downstairs in the hotel lobby, sitting on a bench with a half-full can of Red Bull in my hand. The ever-present dark circles under my eyes had reached undead levels. I was staring at the pattern of tiles on the lobby floor.

"I'm tired," I said. "My brain won't turn over."

He put a hand on my shoulder. "What you're experiencing right now? This is the job. It doesn't get better. We all float down here."

THAT AFTERNOON, RICKY WAS preparing to record his grunts when Carlito said to me, "Why don't you direct this one?"

"Are you sure?" Off the top of my head, I could think of many reasons why I shouldn't.

"Yeah, why not? If you fuck it up, it's just scratch." Fair enough.

I directed Ricky through the first page of grunts. It was the easy stuff, like running and panting. He was doing great, burning through them at a rapid pace. I was starting to think I was born to direct, until the session literally screeched to a halt.

The line was:

MOBSTER
[Shot, scream]

Ricky let out three short, high-pitched cries. I won't say they sounded girlish, but his voice had definitely undergone a sudden and drastic rise in pitch.

I raised my hand and said, "Cut," because that's what I'd seen people do in movies.

"Something wrong?" asked Ricky.

"No, that was good. But do you think we could try it again with a little more intensity? Remember, you're getting shot."

"You got it."

Ricky took a deep breath and then unleashed a string of sounds that could only be described as squealing gasps.

Ugh, God, this was hard. I had no idea how to properly word my feedback. How could I get him to make a sound that didn't sound like a ten-year-old girl stubbing her toe? I tried to be diplomatic. "Your pitch went a little high on those. Let's try it again, and keep it low this time."

Eager to please, Ricky gave me another three. "How was that?"

To his credit, he went from sounding like a ten-year-old girl to a fifteen-year-old girl who'd been sneaking cigarettes behind the gym. Unsure of what to do, I just came out with it.

"Is there any way you could sound manlier?"

Ricky slowly leaned forward in his chair. "You want me to sound manlier? While I'm getting shot?"

"Yes, please." When someone repeats your question back to you, it is a clear sign that you have fucked up.

"Have you ever been shot?" he asked.

"No."

"I have." He was still leaning forward, closing the distance between us. "Do you know what happens when you get shot?"

"No, sir."

"You scream like a *bitch*." On the last word, he jumped forward, causing me to flinch away. I nearly fell backward in my chair. It was not my finest moment.

Properly chastened, I blushed and lowered my eyes to the floor. "The grunts you did earlier were a lower pitch, with more gravel in them. Think we could get some like that? We'll need them all to match."

Ricky smiled and leaned back in his seat. "Sure thing."

"How do I get from where I am to where you are?"

The question had been on my mind for a while. We were nearing the end of my second week, and I'd seen enough of Carlito to know he had everything I wanted—autonomy, control, respect, and, of course, money. In other words, freedom. Not freedom to do anything he wanted, but freedom to do things his way.

He said, "Don't wait for an opportunity to arise. Find the thing you can do that no one else can, then keep doing it until they realize you're indispensable. Or until it kills you."

"I'm surprised you didn't say, 'Build it and they will come.'"

"Too easy," said Carlito. "Look, we're all gonna die. The only question is how you check out. Do you want it on your feet, or on your fucking knees, begging? I ain't much for begging. Nobody ever gave me nothing. So I say fuck that thing. Let's fight it."

"You lost me. What are we fighting?"

"The xenomorph. I was quoting Charles Dutton in *Alien 3*."

"Would you believe I've never seen the Alien movies? Actually, no, that's not true. I saw *Alien: Resurrection*. I liked it."

"How the fuck are you working in video games?"

"I met a guy in a bar—"

He held up his hand. "I don't want to know how that story ends."

MY LAST DAY IN Santa Monica, Tony brought his wife, Janice, to the studio to record some lines. We had a few female characters to record, but only enough lines for a half day's recording.

The days leading up had been a nonstop tirade of ball busting and shit talking. Nothing was off limits except getting offended. I don't know if it was the presence of a woman or the fact that her husband was also in the room, but when Janice arrived, we suddenly became more polite. There was a little less cussing and a lot less talking about ex-girlfriends, ex-wives, and women in general. Honestly, it was kind of refreshing.

If we didn't need Janice to record sexy grunts, it would have been a lovely afternoon.

Sexy grunts are the fourth and final category of exertion noises. You can probably guess what type of exertion I'm talking about. I hate recording sexy grunts. Call me old-fashioned, but there is nothing I find more uncomfortable than paying a woman to fake an orgasm so I can record it. I won't say sex has no place in games; there's a time and place for everything. The problem is, video games are terrible at sex.

Our sex is passable when it's implied, like in a PG-13 film or on CBS before 10:00 p.m. Nothing shown, nothing lost. One of my favorite games of all time, *Fable II*, is full of sex. After I was crowned king of Albion at the end of the game, I celebrated by inviting every sex worker in the kingdom back to my castle for an orgy, because it's good to be the king. And it all happened offscreen. The game faded to black, then played a short moan of pleasure for everyone who was involved. That was forty-three consecutive moans. Fade back in, and voila! Congratulations, player. You have sexed. Enjoy your new STDs. Where sex goes wrong is when we put it on camera. There are many reasons, but off the top of my head I'd say it boils down to the fact we're watching poorly designed crotchless dolls pretend to have the most vanilla sex you can imagine. It's both creepy and boring.

When playing a game, you can avoid any content you don't want to experience. You don't have that luxury as a director. If your game calls for sexy grunts, you just have to buck up and power through.

"Give me about fifteen seconds of sensual moaning." One Mississippi, two Mississippi, three Mississipi . . . "Thank you. For this next one, start with moaning, build to an orgasm, and then climax for another fifteen seconds." Oh goddammit, is this seriously turning me on right now? Don't look her in the eyes, don't look her in the eyes, don't look her in the . . . Oh, thank God, it's over. "Great! Quickly moving on, let's get one that is obviously fake. So unconvincing it hurts. You're bored and tired, and you want this guy to know it." Huh. That's not quite right. "Can you make it sound meaner? Maybe with a Russian accent?" Yeah, there it is. I feel emasculated just listening to it. "Perfect. Let's grab one more. Same thing—you're faking an orgasm—but this time, you're weeping with uncontrollable sadness."

Yeah.

Luckily, my first experience with sexy grunts was vanilla as they come.

There's a scene near the beginning of *Mafia II* in which Vito, the main character, has returned to the city of Empire Bay after fighting overseas in the Second World War. Vito is invited to the apartment of his old friend, Joe. When he arrives, he can hear music inside—the normal kind you find on a record and the sweet kind you make with someone else. Apparently Joe decided to throw an impromptu party with a pair of prostitutes.

Prostitutes played by Janice.

Carlito put on his serious face. "All we need is about thirty seconds of gasping, moaning, that sort of stuff."

Janice smiled. "Not a problem."

"We're rolling," said the sound engineer.

Carlito nodded at Janice. "Whenever you're ready."

There was a soft, sudden intake of breath. Janice made a slight sound, not quite a moan. It trembled, almost involuntarily, her lungs reacting to an imaginary sensation we could all visualize far too easily. Every eye dropped to the floor except for Tony's. With crossed arms and flared nostrils, he scanned the room to see which of us assholes would be dumb enough to look at his wife while she pretended to cum into a microphone.

Thirty seconds later, Janice's ecstasy reached its peak, then fell off into quick, desperate gasps, each growing softer and slower as the oxygen saturated her blood, until they finally faded into relaxed silence.

"How was that?"

Carlito cleared his throat, signaling the recording was over. The rest of us responded by shifting in our seats and looking anywhere except at Janice. Tony was still staring us down, searching for any sign we might have enjoyed his wife's orgasmic moans.

"Yeah, I think we got it," said Carlito. "Let's move on."

Out of everything we recorded, it was the only line that didn't get a second take.

8
LOST AT SEA

The AAA game industry is a franchise operation. If you're not working on an established franchise, you're trying to start a new one. A new franchise is the dream. It's a clean slate, a chance to create something new, free from the expectations of fans and publishers. No one can get in the way of your vision, except for the publishers (who will expect your game to reach a certain scope and marketability) and the players (who will expect it to measure up to a subjective level of quality and value established by companies with near-endless resources). But aside from that, it's all yours! If you're lucky, it'll be so successful you have to churn out new installments until you quit, get fired, or die.

This is the franchise trap. The only way to escape it is to make a game that doesn't sell well enough to warrant a sequel. I know because I have made many of them. I am free in the way most AAA developers are not, both from franchise exhaustion and any sort of profit sharing.

A franchise is marketing shorthand. We create a character and concept for a player to inhabit. Stepping into that role allows a player to inject a bit of him- or herself into the character. If it's relatable enough and provides a certain level of joy, then we've done our job. Once players are hooked, we don't have to sell them a game—we can sell them a feeling.

"Remember how it felt to be twelve, playing *Super Mario World* in your bedroom during Christmas vacation, when your mother brought you a red paper plate filled with sausage balls and butterscotch crunch, and every molecule in your body felt electric as you ate your favorite treats and uncovered the secret Star Road for the first time?

"Good news! You can feel that way again by picking up any of the games in the Super Mario, Mario Party, Mario Kart, Mario Golf, Mario Baseball, Mario Tennis, Mario Strikers, Mario Sports, Mario and Sonic at the Olympics, Paper Mario, or Mario & Luigi series." Nintendo's Mario franchise is the best-selling video-game franchise of all time because Mario is a beloved character whose name is synonymous with childhood, quality, and entertainment. It also doesn't hurt that he's appeared in nearly three hundred games across thirty-nine platforms since 1981.

There's nothing wrong with franchises or building an industry around them. I'm a die-hard *Doctor Who* fan, so I understand the appeal. There are only three photographs in existence that show me smiling—me at my wedding, me holding my daughter, and me standing inside the Ninth Doctor's TARDIS. I've devoured the show's entire fifty-year run, even going so far as to track down the audio tapes of lost episodes. Even when the show is bad, I can't get enough. A beloved franchise is a warm blanket in the middle of a very long, cold life.

The problem with franchises is that they can never rest. The longer a franchise runs, the more people it'll try to reach. Each installment becomes a balancing act between innovation and familiarity. *Assassin's Creed 15: The Seattle Grunge Assasscene* might be your fifteenth Assassin's Creed game, but it's the first for someone else. It has to please both newcomers and the faithful, while also trying to win back fans who have left the franchise behind. It's enough to drive developers mad.

"We love what you did," scream the fans. "Now, do it again, but better."

PART OF MOVING THE company to California was the formation of our newest developer—2K Marin. Founded by former staffers from Irrational, the studio was tasked with creating *BioShock 2*, a sequel to a game many considered to be sequel proof. The game had been self-contained, with a clear ending. A sequel flew in the face of that and seemed to scream, "Cash in!" The fact that Ken Levine, the visionary behind the original *BioShock*, would not be involved only seemed to prove that *BioShock 2* was unnecessary.

None of this was factored into the decision to make a sequel. We were making *BioShock 2* because the original *BioShock* had been a financial and critical success. That's just how franchises work. It doesn't mean we're cashing in; we're just trying to keep our business running while giving you what you want.

COMING OFF OF *MAFIA II*, my ego was at an all-time high. I survived Carlito and in the process saw what a writer could do when given a little freedom. Carlito's story for *Mafia II* was a tragic tale of two friends driven to ruin by their ambition as well as their loyalty to each other. You don't see many games like that in this industry; we like to pretend the player is a hero no matter what type of character he or she is controlling. You can be a mobster or a bloodthirsty Spartan or a mute physicist—we'll jump through hoops to ensure whoever you're killing is way worse than you; that way you're never not having a great time.

Carlito didn't do that. He played to the expectations of a mob story, while also being true to the risks inherent in that lifestyle. It was a monkey's-paw fantasy, in which a wish comes true and reveals itself to be a curse. I loved it, and was proud to have worked on it. If I could get my hands on the kind of power Carlito had, I knew I could tell a story just as good, if not better.

There was a problem, though. Carlito had been in a special situation. The dev team was writing *Mafia II* in Czech and then having it poorly translated into English. Carlito, being the cultural custodian, was then rewriting the script so it actually reflected the voice and tone of an Italian mafioso in the forties and fifties. This gave him the opportunity to tweak the narrative beats as well. If something was too outlandish or unbelievable or simply off point, he'd rework it and take it back to the team. Normally, that sort of power was reserved for a creative director.

In the game industry, there are three types of writer: creative director, narrative designer, and script writer. A creative director is the person in charge of a game's creative vision. A narrative designer writes a game's quests, or missions, and implements them in the game engine. A script writer writes the script.

Script writers and creative directors are two sides of the same coin. The key difference is authority; creative directors have it, script writers don't. Both jobs are unique, as they require you to see the big picture. To do either job well, you must incorporate every aspect of the game; art, sound, design—nothing can be left out. Neither position is required to implement ideas in the game. I won't say it never happens, but normally implementation falls to the designers. That's why the narrative designers sit in the middle. Implementation affords them a measure of creative freedom, but it doesn't grant them authority over other disciplines.

I wanted to be a creative director. I just didn't know how to become one. So far, every creative director I worked with had been a founder of their company. The job appeared to be synonymous with, "I own this place, so you do what I say." That changed with 2K Marin. The studio's creative director, Jordan Thomas, had been a designer on the original *BioShock* and *Thief: Deadly Shadows*. He was a fiercely talented designer who aimed to create something new within the AAA space. Seeing him rise to creative director showed me there was more to the position than simply being the boss; talent and ambition could be rewarded.

I liked Jordan. We'd hung out a few times during the making of *BioShock*. He was funny, dry, and intelligent to the point of almost being intimidating. Since moving to California, we had passed each other in the hall a handful of times. Names had been remembered, greetings were exchanged. I took it as a good sign. Normally, a publisher and developer wouldn't cross paths so regularly, but we both shared the same office hangar. A dev team needs freedom to brainstorm and experiment without the purse holders peering over their shoulders. On the other side, a publisher's presence should be limited so it will carry the proper gravitas when necessary. The publisher-dev relationship is one of checks and balances; too much familiarity can wear down those carefully constructed walls.

It was that familiarity that convinced me to reach out to Jordan via email.

"Hey. Congrats on the creative director thing! We should get drinks some time. I'd love to pick your brain about how to get from where I am to where you are." It seemed okay to me—just a simple, straightforward request to exchange booze for knowledge.

Jordan never responded. I don't know why, but I can hazard a guess. He was the creative director of a brand-new studio. Giving career advice to some kid in publishing would not have been high on his to-do list. Odds are my email briefly crossed his eyes before being shoved deep into his inbox by a flood of other emails, all more important than mine. Looking back on it now with more wisdom and empathy, I completely understand. At the time, however, I was a petty little bitch. Jordan and I weren't exactly friends, but I thought we had hung out enough to at least warrant a reply. In my mind, there was only one logical reason why he wouldn't—that bastard thought he was better than me. Well, I'd show him. I was a vengeful idiot, desperate to prove I was a better writer than a guy who did nothing worse than ignore me.

I pestered the Fox until he gave me the green light to review the scripts for *BioShock 2*. Jordan would be too busy for me to bother, so instead I turned to Gage, 2K Marin's narrative producer. It was Gage's job to monitor story development and track script content. Everything in a script is an asset someone will need to create. When a new character is introduced, the team has to create and review concept art, model the character, rig it for animation, hire an actor, record the lines—there's a lot involved. The same goes for locations, items, story beats, etc. Everything you write in a script creates work for many other people. A narrative producer tracks these dependencies to ensure a game's story doesn't sink the entire production.

Gage and I had worked together briefly when I helped write text for the *BioShock 2* multiplayer mode. I suggested naming a pistol upgrade "Extended Clip" because it allowed the player's pistol to hold more bullets. Gage responded, "The pistol is a revolver, and revolvers don't have clips. Everything in *BioShock* needs to be realistic."

Revolvers do use clips. They're called moon clips, and they can hold either a full or half cylinder's worth of cartridges. I sent Gage a link to a website where he could purchase these very real items, along with my personal evaluation of *BioShock*'s realism—"Your game takes place in a city at the bottom of the ocean and lets me shoot bees out of my hands."

We didn't get along.

None of the scripts were ready to review. That didn't stop me from hounding Gage until he relented and sent me an early draft of the game's first chapter. I scoured the pages looking for mistakes, bad grammar, plot holes—anything I could show the Fox to prove *BioShock 2* needed me as its editor. What I found was text for an audio log about diving bells.

"This is sloppy work," I said to Gage in an email. "The audio log mentions two different types of gas, but a diving bell would only use one of them. Is no one reviewing this stuff?"

In the Fox's office, I leaned forward and spoke in a low, controlled voice. "*BioShock 2* needs me." You couldn't come at the Fox with anger. If he thought you were being emotional, he'd write off anything you had to say. The key to making him listen was to remain calm, maintain eye contact, and press your point.

"If we don't stay on top of this project, the whole thing is gonna crash and burn."

GAGE STARED AT THE Fox and me from across the conference table, his arms crossed in a petulant manner. This was the last place he wanted to be.

"I don't see the point in these meetings," he said. "I understand that as the publisher you can arrange meetings where I sit here and explain the story to you. What you need to understand is that I have complete faith in this story, and these meetings will only slow down my ability to work on it. But again, this is your prerogative, and I am obliged to be here. Just recognize your actions are delaying my work."

The Fox grinned back at him. Gage was emotional, which put him at a disadvantage. To the Fox, a meeting was like a fight in an old-school kung fu film. Every word was a blow whizzing through the air. People would come in swinging, thinking to make quick work of this Frenchman, only to grow frustrated as each attack failed to connect. Then, when his opponents were ready to explode with righteous fury, the Fox would deliver a swift blow to the chest and knock them on their asses. He was a drunken master of not-so-passively aggressive confrontation.

"We appreciate you taking the time," said the Fox. "There are just a few things we would like to discuss, so we have a better understanding of what you're trying to accomplish."

"Such as?"

"The dialogue, for instance."

Gage stiffened. "What's wrong with the dialogue?"

"Eh . . ." The Fox wiggled in his seat, like he was hesitant to speak until he found the right word. "Everything."

Before the Fox could say another word, Gage threw his hands in the air and shouted, "How is that at all helpful?"

"Maybe you'd find out, if you gave him a chance to explain," I shouted back.

I'm not like the Fox. In meetings, I'm a mirror. Come at me with politeness, that's what you'll get. Try to start some shit, and I will burn your goddamn bones.

The Fox laid a hand on my arm. It wasn't time for that yet.

"The dialogue isn't bad," said the Fox. "The problem is it uses a lot of ten-dollar words. English is not my first language, and I'm having a very hard time understanding what the dialogue is trying to say." That wasn't the only thing that stumped him. Some of the dialogue had also been written phonetically to emphasize different dialects. Even Gage had to admit it was a fair point.

Any admission of fault was a weakness, a chance for me to strike fast and bring the entire narrative crumbling down. "The dialogue is just indicative of a larger problem. Story is a big part of what makes BioShock such a unique franchise. Right now, we can't tell what that story is going to be."

"We recorded a story video," said Gage, reverting to his stubborn posture. "Watch that."

To avoid spending time explaining the story whenever he was asked, Gage had sat Jordan down in front of a camera and had him recount it from start to finish.

"Gage—the video is ninety minutes long. The Fox and I aren't going to spend the time watching it when you could just tell us what we need to know, right now. We don't need a full summary or a beat-by-beat breakdown. All we need is for you to tell us what the story is about."

He took a deep breath and sighed. His eyes glazed over as he stroked his chin in thought. Whatever he was searching for, he was digging deep. A moment later, Gage lowered his hand and looked me straight in the eye.

"Solipsism."

I DON'T THINK GAGE was trying to be a dick.

Actually, I take that back. I do believe he was trying to answer my question as succinctly as possible. He just did it in a way I found to be kind of dickish. He might have done it on purpose, but I can't tell you for sure. Even if he had, being kind of a dick is very different from being a total dick, especially since he did answer my question. He just answered it with a word I'd never heard before.

If you're like me, let me save you a Google search.

solipsism: *noun*; 1) the theory that only the self exists, or can be proved to exist.

    2) extreme preoccupation with and indulgence of one's feelings, desires, etc.; egoistic self-absorption.

Anyone else would have said egoism or narcissism. Neither word fully encapsulates solipsism, but it would have gotten me close enough to understand what Gage was talking about. Instead, all it did was piss me off.

LET'S GO BACK IN time, to a little over a year prior to my conversation with Gage. I was still living in New York, working on the original *BioShock*. I was putting together a video trailer for the game; it was a big deal. In a week, the first playable demo would become available on Xbox Live, Microsoft's online gaming service. This demo would be the first time consumers had been able to play the game, and when they were finished, they'd be presented with a video. It needed to be impactful and hint at everything the game had to offer, while also enticing people to preorder from their local game store.

"Think you could put something together?" asked Geekjock.

I'd done some video editing in college but had never captured and edited a professional-quality video. "Yeah, I can do that." If you want to learn how to fight, you have to throw yourself to the wolves.

I started on Monday. The video had to be delivered to Irrational on Thursday night, or before they arrived at work on Friday morning. I was there from 9:00 a.m. to 2:00 a.m. every day, putting everything I had into that trailer. I wanted to prove I could do it, that they could trust me.

Thursday night, I didn't even go home. I stayed at the office, putting the final touches on the trailer. When I finally sent it off Friday morning, it was too late for me to leave. I had a conference call scheduled with Irrational at 9:00 a.m.

I was alone in the conference room. In Boston, Geekjock and the team sat around a speakerphone, listening to me explain what was still needed for the trailer. It had been edited without music; they would need to either find a track that matched the edit or record an original piece of score that afternoon. I talked nonstop for a good seven or eight minutes. When I was done walking them through the trailer, I sat there waiting for someone to respond. There was nothing but silence on the other end of the line.

Goddammit, I thought. Did the call drop? How long had I been talking to no one?

I was about to call them back when muffled laughter came through the speaker, followed by someone affecting a fake southern accent.

"So, what part of the South are you from?"

When I brought it up with Geekjock later, he told me I apparently said the word "y'all" quite a bit, and they just couldn't help themselves. I'd worked really hard to give them a fantastic trailer, and they couldn't see past my use of a fairly common contraction.

When Gage said "Solipsism," for some reason it brought that moment rushing back into my mind.

In the trunk of my car was a pink softball bat I had purchased when I was on the 2K softball team. My involvement lasted two practices before my travel schedule made it impossible to continue. It was pink because I felt stupid buying a softball bat. I didn't know what type or length I should get, so I went with the most audacious. There may have been some serendipity in that purchase, because let me tell you, people notice when you carry a pink softball bat around the office.

That pink bat went everywhere. When I spoke to people at their desks, I rested it on my shoulder, like I could take a swing at any second. During meetings, I laid it on the table in front of me, for everyone to see. I was angry and wanted people to know it. As terrible as this was, I have to admit, people did not argue with me so long as I carried that bat.

After a few hours, the Fox showed up at my desk. "You can't walk around with the bat anymore."

"Why not?" I wanted to hear him say it.

"People are starting to complain. They think you're going to break something."

"That is ridiculous!" Not really. "I would never do something like that." True, but I was hoping no one knew that. "What the hell is wrong with these people?" Because how dare people get upset when I actively try to intimidate them?

The Fox didn't buy it. "I don't care. Just stop it before someone reports you to HR."

THE NEXT STORY MEETING didn't go much better. For an hour, the Fox and Gage's assistant sat back and watched us yell at each other. There was no discussion or concession, just venom. The only time we found common ground was when I called the game's main villain impotent, causing Gage to instantly begin nodding. "That's true. She doesn't really do anything right now."

As we left the conference room, the Fox leaned in and whispered in my ear. "I think Gage was about to jump across the table and punch you in the face." I didn't know it at the time, but Gage's assistant was making the same observation about me. I'm not entirely sure they were wrong.

"We're getting nowhere," said the Fox. "You need to fix this."

Fair enough. I took a long walk around the hangar and circled back to Gage's desk.

"Look, I know you're busy, but could you please just write a one-paragraph summary of the story and email it to me? Nothing longer than what we'd put on the back of the box." I was haughty and full of myself. If I'd been capable of ditching my bullshit pride, I'd have added something like, "I hate bugging you for this stuff, but I've backed myself into a corner here. I know we fight about literally everything, but I have to be honest—I'm out of my depth. No one's ever given me this much responsibility before. There's a lot of pressure on you and the team to make a great game; I get that. But now that I'm on this project, I have to prove I can work with a developer to get them to deliver whatever publishing needs. Right now, I need a summary. So, please, can you just help me out?"

We're always so afraid to be vulnerable, as if admitting our fear and uncertainty will somehow prove us to be unworthy. Instead, we puff out our chests and put on a show, because God forbid we admit to one another that we're all making this up as we go along.

Thirty minutes later, Gage emailed me a short story summary. It was heady, with a lot of big words, but I wasn't angry about it. He delivered what I asked. That was a big deal. In the moment, it felt like we had crossed a bridge.

I shot back an email: "Thanks. Can we get a version anyone can understand?"

You'd think a writer would be better at wording his emails. In my head, what I wrote read as, "Thank you very much. Can we get a version that uses more plainspoken language?" Everyone else read, "Thanks for nothing. Now, can you do one that's legible?"

Multiple people came to my desk, demanding to know why I sent that email. Once I realized how it had been received, I was beyond apologetic. It was too late, though. I had become disruptive to the process. After a discussion with the Fox, it was decided I would no longer be included in the *BioShock 2* story meetings.

"YOU'RE LIKE CANCER," SAID Lily.

"Explain." I lifted my head off the desk where her dog, Crepe Suzette, had been licking my hair in moral support. Crepe Suzette was a long-haired dachshund, small enough to lie on Lily's desk without getting in the way.

"You find something you don't like and you let it eat at you until there's nothing left. Then you find anyone who's happy and you whisper your problems in their ear until they end up as miserable as you."

I smiled. "That's true. I do enjoy watching happy people fall apart."

Lily Rose Flowers was our community manager, which made her the liaison between our developers and gamers. It was her job to facilitate dialogue between company and customer, usually involving special events, promotions, and ARGs—alternate reality games—that helped players feel meaningfully involved with the franchises they loved.

For some reason they had never been able to articulate, Lily's parents had saddled her with a full bouquet of a name. She never forgave them for it. To their credit, her parents understood completely. Going through life as Lily Rose had whittled her attitude down to a finely-pointed shiv. She was my sister in hate. If ever I needed to rant or rave, she had always been ready to dive into whichever sea of shit I was currently swimming in.

This time, however, she'd had enough. "You're being extra cancer right now. I hope you realize that."

I shrugged. "Gage is a narrative tyrant who can't handle how valid my feedback is. Now, I'm just worried the game will ship and be a huge success."

"That is the dream."

"Is it, though? I mean, of course we all want the game to be a success, but if that happens, what does that say about me? Am I so far off the mark I can't even recognize a good game? It's like, I don't want the game to fail, but at the same time, I kind of do."

Lily gave me the side-eye and shook her head. "You need to let it go. Stop being cancer."

THAT FRIDAY, I WALKED into the Fox's office and dropped a script on his desk.

"I rewrote the entire script for *BioShock 2*. That's all the feedback I've got; use it if you want. I'm done."

I let it go like a fucking hand grenade.

A WEEK LATER, THE Fox called me into his office.

"I think it's important for people to be validated, under the right circumstances." He pulled my script out of his desk and flipped through the pages. "Your script was very good. There was never a chance we would have used it, but I still thought you should know."

"What's the fucking point, man?" I was full of myself, still riding the wave of my own righteous indignation.

He threw the script back into his desk and slammed the drawer. "Why are you like this? I give you a compliment, and you instantly become combative."

"That's not a compliment. 'Hey, your story is so good we threw it in the garbage.'"

"You get this way with every game," he said. "You think you should be the writer, but it's not your job to tell developers what to do. A studio needs ownership over its game."

"What about my ownership? If you tell me to edit a script and that script turns out badly, it's my fault. If I have to shoulder the responsibility, I should have a say in how it turns out."

"These aren't your games."

"Maybe they should be. Did you ever think of that?"

"Yes!"

"I'm sorry, what?"

"I called you in here so I could tell you your script was good and that I think we should find a project for you to write, but you didn't give me a chance."

"You're going to let me write a game?"

"I was thinking about it. Is that okay, or would you like to yell at me some more?"

"No, I think I'm done."

"Great. I'm glad we had this talk. Now, get the hell out of my office."

HAVING THE FOX RECOGNIZE my talent was apparently all the validation I needed. There was nothing left for me to prove. The development of *BioShock 2* went on without me. My bitterness softened, guilt crept into my bones, and slowly I began to understand I'd been a real shitheel.

Let me be clear: I'm ashamed of how I acted toward Gage, Jordan, and everyone else at 2K Marin. Rewriting the script was wrong and way outside the bounds of my job. Sure, it worked out in my favor; the Fox decided to let me write a game. But I can't count this as a personal victory. I mean, holy shit; an associate producer has no business rewriting a developer's script without their knowledge or permission. If my script had ended up being used, it would have set a precedent so stupid and irresponsible, it would have transformed our entire development process into something like *Game of Thrones*. What a tire fire of a legacy that would have been.

The week *BioShock 2* shipped, I sent Gage an email. "Hey. I know we never saw eye to eye during production, but I wanted to say congratulations on shipping a great game. You should be proud."

Like with the email that started it all, I received no response. This time, I wasn't upset. Gage had good reason to ignore me. I had stood in direct opposition to everything he tried to accomplish, for no better reason than my own pettiness and egoism. No response was better than I deserved.

When I played the final game, I was blown away. *BioShock 2* was a master class on how to write and design a compelling sequel. The original *BioShock*'s story was about great men and women whose hubris destroyed the lives of everyone around them. By the end of the game, those great minds had died, along with their city. Many felt that Rapture had no more stories to tell, but they were wrong. Jordan, Gage, and the rest of 2K Marin cut deep into BioShock's world to tell a heartbreaking story of what happens to the lowly and the ruined once the great men and women are finally gone.

You play as Subject Delta, an outsider who accidently found his way to Rapture in the city's early days. Sent to prison, you eventually become a Big Daddy, horribly mutated and trapped inside an iron diving suit. You awaken in Rapture after the events of the first *BioShock*, separated from your Little Sister, the genetically manipulated girl you are programmed to protect. Her name is Eleanor Lamb, and she has been taken by her mother, Dr. Sofia Lamb, who now controls Rapture. Dr. Lamb wants to use Eleanor as a vessel that will contain the collected minds of everyone in Rapture. Subject Delta wants to rescue her and, in so doing, save himself. Delta's biological programming requires he find his Little Sister, or else he will fall into a coma and die. It's an exploration of how far some will go to leave their mark, regardless of whether they have any right to do so. Needless to say, it put me in my place.

The next time I saw Gage was at the launch party.

When playing the final game, I noticed certain story elements had been cut. It wouldn't be right for me to go into details; that's not my story to tell. But I will say they were things Gage had championed during development and that I agreed were fantastic. I don't know why they were cut, and was disappointed they weren't in the final game. I can only guess how Gage felt. Watching him from across the room, I imagined this celebration probably felt different for him. Maybe I was projecting, but something about the way he was standing—alone in a crowd—made me think he wasn't very happy.

"Hey," I said, as I sidled up beside him.

Gage spared me a glance. "Oh. Hey." He turned away and kept his eyes locked on the crowd. I could tell he didn't want to talk to me, but fuck it. I had something to say.

"The game turned out really good. It sucks that you had to cut stuff."

Gage kind of grunted and nodded. The way he was holding his drink, I started to think he might throw it at me.

"For what it's worth, an old teacher of mine used to say, 'A story is only as good as what you cut out of it,' and a lot of great stuff got taken out."

Something about that must have struck a chord, because Gage finally turned and looked me in the eyes. He didn't say thanks or anything like that; he just nodded his head like he was mulling over my words. "I guess that's true."

I should have apologized, should have said, "I know things didn't fully pan out the way you wanted, but you got close. You tried to make something amazing, and people fought you. I'm sorry I was one of them. I see now what you were trying to do. It was smart. It was good."

That's what I should have said.

"Anyway, I just wanted to say congrats."

"Thanks."

We didn't speak again for a very long time.

9

SIGNIFICANT ZERO

was visiting family a few years back. I can't remember why. Christmas, funeral; one of those events that brings the whole clan together. Work was draining the life out of me. I needed an escape. This trip home was the closest I was going to get.

My cousin Doug was in the living room, playing *Grand Theft Auto V* on the big screen. Since he was occupied by the game, I knew he wouldn't want to talk, which was a good thing. He was playing as Franklin, one of the game's main characters. As Franklin, Doug drove a Nagasaki Blazer around the desert town of Sandy Shores. *This is the place*, I thought. *This is where I can let go.* I sat on the couch, not to watch but to listen. I closed my eyes and drifted off to the sound of a four-wheeler ramping off sand dunes.

The first time I visited Sandy Shores, I was Michael De Santa, another one of *GTA V*'s main characters. Michael and I were both in crisis. He was an aging criminal who hated his life; I was a video-game writer who would rather gouge out my eyes than make another game. I wanted to run away—a recurring theme at the time—but it wasn't an option. So, I took control of Michael and made him run away instead. Together, we stole a car and headed north, toward that squalid paradise on the south shore of the Alamo Sea.

Sandy Shores is a malignant tumor in the armpit of a desiccated corpse. The land is dead and dry. You can practically feel the heat radiating off of your television screen. Nothing can take root except dollar stores, trailer parks, and bars where you're more likely to get stabbed than served. Sandy Shores is not a place people choose to live; it's just where they end up. It might be my favorite town in video-game history.

Standing on the side of the road, Michael and I shared a moment of beautiful synchronicity. We both wore a T-shirt and shorts, our faces covered in unkempt beards. I felt numb, as if my emotions had been boiled away by the desert sun. If Michael had been a real person capable of thought, something tells me he'd have felt the same way.

"How long would it take your sister to make a game like this?"

The question came from my dad. He'd wandered into the room while I dozed. Apparently Doug had given him the full Los Santos tour, strip clubs and all.

I honestly wasn't sure how to answer him. The question bordered on nonsensical. My sister is smart; far smarter than me. She already had something like four bachelor's and two master's degrees. Unsatisfied with that level of accomplishment, she'd recently reenrolled to learn programming. My dad understood programming was key to game development. But he might as well have been asking how long it would take for a kid with finger paints to establish Christianity, build Vatican City, and construct the Sistine Chapel, all for the purpose of painting a masterpiece on its ceiling.

I said, "You have to understand, just because she's learning to code doesn't mean she's learning to program games. There are different programming languages, all of which are used for different things."

"Hold on a minute. What is a programming language?"

"Beyond a series of numbers and commands, I don't know."

"So, a programmer types numbers into a computer and it makes pictures in the game?"

"Yes and no. The pictures are called graphics. A programmer writes the code that makes graphics visible in the game. At least, I think that's how it works. Honestly, this is kind of outside my wheelhouse.

"The graphics are made by artists. Literally everything you see in a game—the car, the road, the dust kicked up by the tires—it's all made from scratch by an artist. That's why we have artists for every-thing: characters, environments, lighting, visual effects, indoor stuff, outdoor stuff; it's crazy. And before they can make anything, we hire concept artists to produce reference art so the other artists can remake it in the game.

"Outside of artists and programmers, we have different types of animators, audio people who record sounds and music, different audio people who put the sound and music into the game, designers who stitch all the pieces together into something coherent and playable, pro-ducers who are basically professional cat herders, testers who are just kids chained to a radiator forced to play a game over and over trying to break it, and probably a whole mess of others I'm forgetting or just don't know about."

"That many people?" My dad raised his eyebrows and stuck out his lips. When surprised or impressed, he pulls a duckface, not that he knows it. "Of all the stuff you just listed off, what do you do?"

"Oh, I don't do any of that. I'm a writer."

Imagine you're a Hollywood screenwriter and a director calls you up to say, "I want you to write a movie for me. The story can be whatever you want, so long as it's about soldiers fighting terrorists in a posh Monaco hotel and is tonally similar to the first season of *True Detective,* only with less talking and more explosive headshots. We've been filming for six months and will wrap in two weeks. When can you start?"

That's what it's like to write video games.

Unlike film, where a script is usually written before a single frame is shot, most video-game stories are written during production, when the major details have already been defined. It is writing in reverse; a reactionary process driven by design and gameplay rather than story or reason. There are times when you walk onto a project to find something that looks less like a game and more like the contents of someone's junk drawer, held together by chewing gum and duct tape. Some of the pieces might fit; many of them won't. It's the writer's job to contextualize these disparate pieces in a way that makes the game seem like a cohesive, consciously designed piece of entertainment—preferably using nothing but words. Words are cheap; changing the game is not.

John Carmack, first-person shooter pioneer and lead programmer on games like *Doom* and *Quake*, famously said, "Story in a game is like story in a porn movie. It's expected to be there, but it's not that important." He's technically right. We are willing to forgive a game's badly written and forgettable story if the game itself is fun to play. What Carmack gets wrong is his assertion that story is nothing more than plot and dialogue.

Video games are like rock bands. They have three key parts: art, design, and programming. All parts are essential, but they are not equal.

Art is the lead vocalist. It embodies the theme and tone of your game. That first sight tells players exactly what to expect without ever having to play the game. That's why art will always be the band's front person. Their name, voice, and sexy face are what sells out stadiums.

Design is on guitar. System designers create tools and content. They design weapons, player abilities, progression systems, even AI, the artificial intelligence that determines how enemies react in-game. Level designers use these tools to create a game's moment-to-moment experience, weaving gameplay scenarios like song structure. Exploring an environment is the verse. Fighting enemies is the chorus. The weapons you use, and how they make you feel, is the hook. Design is the music that keeps your audience coming back after the superficial attraction of art has worn off.

Programming plays bass. Computers are only good for executing instructions. Those instructions, known as code, are written by programmers. Artists can create 3-D models, designers can build environments and rules, but without code, it all amounts to nothing but noise. Code is the rhythm and root chords everything else is built upon. It tells the computer how to use data created by the dev team and organizes it into an actual video game.

When art, design, and programming come together, they create a world for players to experience. That experience is its own story, one that is told through the actions of the player. A writer can guide that story, elevate it, but they can't create it. Without art, design, and programming, story can't exist. It has no value, and yet alters the value of everything it touches.

Story has no place in the band, because story is the song.

10

CHARACTER FLAWS

The types of games I make are what we call AAA games, or triple-A. These aren't the games you play on your cell phone. AAA games are considered the best of the best, if only because they cost so much to make. Between development and marketing, an average AAA game will cost between twenty and fifty million dollars to produce, but it's not uncommon for budgets to stretch well past one hundred million. When you've got that much scratch on the line, you stick to what sells—guns and glory. Each game has a different name, but they're all just variations on a theme. Bad people do bad things, but you can stop them, and that's good. The story, no matter what shape it takes, is just spin, a tool to help explain who you're fighting and why it's okay to shoot them, burn them, and blow them into bits. I am the minister of propaganda to the game's one true ruler, that person-shaped void we call "the player." And all of us—writers, designers, artists, and programmers—serve at its pleasure.

Video games require external input or else they cannot function. That input comes from the player. For that reason, the player will always be the game's protagonist. They will experience the events firsthand and resolve them through the use of the game's core mechanics.

The most popular core mechanics are shooting and hand-to-hand fighting, as evidenced by their having genres named after them. Games that emphasize both ranged and melee mechanics fall under the action-adventure genre. These games contextualize their combat through the narrative. The Uncharted series, a present-day spin on the globe-trotting treasure-hunter concept, utilizes modern firearms and brawling, whereas The Elder Scrolls has players wield medieval weaponry and magic spells found in traditional fantasy worlds. My personal favorite context is what I call "video-game science," which is indistinguishable from magic. If games are to be believed, science and its many fields can grant you the ability to throw fireballs (drinkable science, *BioShock*), create localized black holes (biotic science, *Mass Effect*), levitate heavy objects and use them as giant bullets (gravity science meets gun science, *Half-Life 2*), and breathe through your bikini-clad skin (sexy military science, *Metal Gear Solid V*).

Core mechanics are the tools players are given to complete a game and the method by which they interact with the world. When your core mechanic is combat, that says something about your protagonist.

In the case of Rocksteady's Batman: Arkham series, that violent force is conveniently nonlethal. I say "convenient" because there is no visible proof Batman's opponents are dying from repeated blows to the head. When enemies go down, they stay down until their bodies eventually just vanish. Since the character of Batman is known for not killing, we're left to assume these superstitious, cowardly criminals simply woke up and ran away.

Most games don't bother establishing a nonlethal context for their violence. It's cleaner and simpler to kill your enemies and be done with it. This only confounds the issues surrounding the player. Your protagonist will never be more righteous than the core mechanic allows. No matter how heroic or well intentioned, this is a person who uses lethal force to resolve conflicts.

IN GAMES, THERE ARE two types of protagonists—a character and an avatar.

A character is a protagonist who possesses their own voice, name, and predefined personality. You may control a character, but you will never be them. The best character examples in recent years are Joel and Ellie from Naughty Dog's *The Last of Us*.

Twenty years in the future, the United States has been devastated by a fungal plague that turns people into mindless, cannibalistic monsters we're meant to believe are not zombies even though that's exactly what they are. Joel, a smuggler living in Boston, is recruited by a militia group called the Fireflies. They need him to escort a young girl, Ellie, from Boston to Salt Lake City. Somehow, Ellie is immune to the not-a-zombie infection, and the Fireflies believe she is the key to creating a cure.

Over the course of their journey, Joel and Ellie develop a deep bond, which is tested when he finally delivers her to the militia. As Ellie is prepped for surgery, Joel learns the procedure necessary to create a cure will kill her. Unable to let her go, Joel makes the decision to rescue her. Controlled by the player, he kills nearly everyone in the hospital, takes an unconscious Ellie off the operating table, and escapes.

"Turns out, there's a whole lot more like you," he says, when Ellie finally wakes up. "Ain't done a damn bit of good, neither. They've stopped looking for a cure."

Ellie doesn't believe him, and in the game's final moments demands to know the truth. "Swear to me. Swear to me that everything that you said about the Fireflies is true."

Joel looks her straight in the eyes and doesn't flinch. "I swear."

Joel's final acts of selfishness go against what we expect from a video-game protagonist. Although you play as Joel for most of the game, you can't call him the hero. The game's climax deletes that word completely from the conversation. Ellie didn't know the procedure would result in her death, but she still volunteered for it. When Joel decides to kill the Fireflies, he robs both Ellie and the player of their agency. It's a powerful, unexpected moment that tells the player, "This is Joel and Ellie's story, not yours."

I love characters. The characters I create can be heroic, flawed, or whatever I wish, because they don't have to fit the player's ideals or expectations. The opposite is true of an avatar.

Avatars are meant to be the player's physical representation within a game. They are blank slates, designed with no real personality of their own. Our industry has this idea that a player needs to project him- or herself onto a character in order to be fully immersed, which can be difficult to do if the character expresses thoughts and opinions different from those of the player. It's an argument I don't really buy into. People have never had difficulty relating and connecting to characters in stories. It's shockingly narcissistic to assume controlling a character in a game somehow diminishes your ability to empathize with someone else.

When I'm told to write a vague protagonist, what I hear is, "Make them boring." If a player needs a boring avatar in order to feel immersed in a game, then that player is not projecting onto the character. Instead, they are relating to someone who is boring because they, too, are boring. The boring avatar isn't pulling them deeper into the game; it's just helping the player's boring brain imagine what it would be like to live in a world where boring people are also powerful and important. That's why you rarely see overweight, unattractive avatars. Players aren't projecting themselves onto their avatars; it's actually the other way around. By taking control of an avatar, players project its superior qualities back onto themselves. It's not projection at all, really. It's just wish fulfillment.

One of the most famous avatars is Gordon Freeman, the protagonist of Valve's celebrated Half-Life series. Gordon is a white male with glasses and a goatee. He is thin, but not too skinny. He is tall and has no trace of a slouch. Gordon has a PhD in theoretical physics, so you can assume he's always the smartest guy in the room. As far as we know, Gordon does not play sports or exercise, but he is still in perfect physical shape. He is also a weapons expert, despite only receiving minor training once in his whole life, because dumb rednecks shoot guns all the time, so there's no reason someone of Gordon's caliber couldn't figure them out in a single afternoon.

Gordon Freeman is from Seattle.

Gordon does not speak. His genius brain, which is housed inside a perfectly symmetrical head that has neither a double chin nor a receding hairline, doesn't have time to talk; it's too busy contemplating supraquantum structures. Besides, words are for plebeians and should be used only to praise the great Gordon Freeman, never to nag him about taking out the trash or cleaning up his room. This sounds like a joke, but it's true—almost everyone Gordon meets gushes over how amazing he is. Even the villains do it.

It is ridiculous to think Gordon Freeman is considered one of the greatest video-game characters of all time. This is not a character; it's a pile of insecurities molded into the shape of a man. Gordon is the most blatant, half-assed Mary Sue our industry has ever created. We are lucky *Half-Life 2* wasn't good enough to warrant a sequel, or else we'd still be subjected to this mute asshole on a regular basis.

If your protagonist is a fully developed character, it's easy to write around your game's violent gameplay. A character can be flawed, hypocritical, or just plain evil. An avatar has to be a blank slate, so that its personality doesn't conflict with that of the player. The only thing your avatar will have in common with its player is importance. As game designers, we assume players want to be the hero, so that means their avatar must also be the hero.

It is very hard to write a hero who does nothing but kill people, but it can be done. That being said, I'm not the best person to explain how. Most of my characters have been deranged psychopaths, broken souls devoid of hope and humanity—the kind of people you're dying to fuck in your twenties and desperate to escape in your thirties.

Instead, I'm going to turn things over to two of the smartest, most talented writers I've ever had the pleasure to work with—Greg Kasavin and Anthony Burch. I'm not just saying that to be nice; Greg and Anthony produce masterful work. It also amuses me to know these compliments will make them both somewhat uncomfortable.

Anthony Burch was lead writer on *Borderlands 2*, the second game in a first-person shooter franchise built around the simple promise of more guns, more loot.

In *Borderlands 2*, you play an interplanetary treasure hunter/mercenary who travels to the desolate yet inhabited planet of Pandora to locate the legendary Vault, an ancient alien structure believed to contain vast wealth.

"I've played games since I was a kid," says Burch. "The more I play them, the more I respect games that are honest about how shitty games can be morally. It's kinda fucked-up that we enjoy slaughtering millions of people in a game. Not that it'll make you a bad person, but it's kinda fucked-up.

"I love *Destiny*. I play *Destiny* all the time. But *Destiny* keeps calling you a guardian of the galaxy for literally going from planet to planet and wiping out entire civilizations because you had a quest that said, 'Kill fifty Vex.' Why? Because they belong to one particular race, I should kill them? I literally have a quota of what race I should eliminate today? That's fucking weird.

"What really upsets me is in games like *Call of Duty* you'll kill millions of people, and they'll be like, 'You saved the world. You're a good person. You're the chosen one.' I find that so revolting and dishonest. It doesn't respect the player or allow the player to properly contextualize what they're doing."

These feelings were somewhat at odds with the task of writing *Borderlands 2*, the sequel to a game that holds the Guinness World Record for the most guns in a video game—17.75 million guns.

"A lot of people wanted the Vault Hunters to be really badass, heroic figures who save the world. And I, as subtly and sharply as I could, along with Paul Hellquist, the director, tried to refute that at any possible turn in the game's story, because what the player is actually doing is worse than just killing things. They're killing things solely so they can loot their corpses and pick up their stuff and then use it to kill larger things. You're the worst person in the world in this game."

Borderlands presents players with a world taken to its extreme limits of absurdity. This is a game that includes a gun called the Bane, which shoots flesh-dissolving acid bullets while a mad chorus of high-pitched, squealing voices shout "Rat-tat-tat-tat! Bang! Bang! BOOM!!!" It's no wonder Pandora's inhabitants are literally gun-crazy. Bullets, blood, explosions—these are what they live for, and they are all loving life.

By playing into that absurdity, Anthony was able to create a narrative experience that embraced the game's over-the-top-violence and satirized our industry's obsession with bullet-porn.

"The way we tried to make that okay was to acknowledge it and kinda have fun with it . . . You make jokes about everything. You make jokes where the punch line is 'You're a piece of shit.' You make jokes where the guns are the punch line . . . It was way more fun for us to go 'Yeah, you're a badass, but you're also kind of a bad person. It certainly lessens the ludonarrative dissonance [the conflict between a video game's narrative and its gameplay] to be able to say, 'Yeah, you're being a piece of shit, but what would you have us do?' "

Greg Kasavin went a different direction when writing *Bastion*, the first game developed by Supergiant Games.

Bastion is an action role-playing game that takes place in what remains of Caelondia, a city destroyed by a cataclysmic event known only as the Calamity. You play the Kid, a young boy who wakes to find his city has been destroyed. With nowhere else to go, he travels to the Bastion, where everyone was meant to go if things went bad. From there, he begins to rebuild Caelondia.

Greg and I worked together at 2K Games on *Spec Ops: The Line* before he left to make some absolutely stunning indie games, of which *Bastion* was the first. When it comes to interesting characters, Greg agrees that using a blank-slate avatar can lead to boring characterization, but he still believes there is value in the convention.

Greg says, "Part of why we wanted a silent protagonist was that you get those games where the main character is voiced and you get those moments where the character will say something or act in a certain way where you, the player, really disagree. You're like, 'Oh man, what an idiot. I never would have said this.' And those moments are really dissonant because you're supposed to be playing that character."

To avoid this, Supergiant developed a secondary character for *Bastion* that would serve as the game's narrator, providing running commentary on everything the player did. The narrator added depth to the world and also gave players a different way to emotionally connect with what was happening on their screen.

It's sort of the magic of someone interpreting your actions, so it's okay for him to be wrong and for you to think he's wrong, and having that lead to very interesting moments where the player can sort of feel betrayed or weird about it. We wanted these characters to provide both context and an emotional connection. They were all about speaking to things the player couldn't necessarily discern on their own, and speaking to the subtext of the situation.

As an early example in *Bastion*, you go into a little bar and have a little fight in there right at the beginning of the game. And there's an ashen statue of a guy there, and you go in and the narrator says, "Caelondia's most famous watering hole. There's ol' Rondy the bartender. The Calamity got him before his drinking did." . . . So you already feel something, like "Man, that's kind of heavy."

All you can do is hit stuff with a hammer, so if you destroy him with a hammer and he bursts into a cloud of dust, the narrator says, "Rondy always wanted his ashes scattered here." And you're like, "Oh shit." You're just walking about and hitting stuff, just like any action RPG, but in this game we're gonna make you think about it. You're going to stop and have a moment to consider what you're doing.

We found that when people destroyed Rondy's statue, some of them would feel really bad. But the narrator is kind of reassuring you: "No, that's what Rondy wanted." And suddenly it's putting intentionality into the character where there might have been none.

Intent is the thin line between good and bad. Without it, your protagonist is just a force of nature, a tornado destroying anything in its path. A noble goal won't count for much in the real world, but in fiction it's much easier to suspend disbelief. If we're making a shooter, people are going to die. The genre asks for death and shall receive it in abundance. We can't change what the player does, but we can change their target.

There are enemies so universally evil, all it takes is one glance to know they should die a bullet-riddled death. Nazis, zombies, demons, and aliens: these are perfect villains. Years of pop-culture refinement (or recorded history, in the case of Nazis) have defined these villains as the embodiment of destruction. If the player is a tornado, then these monsters are wildfire. They live only to consume and will not stop until you put them down.

If all our games were built around killing fascist hell zombies from outer space, we'd never feel a single ounce of regret or stab of guilt. Sometimes, though, you want a kill that means something. You want to look someone in the face, really size them up as an individual, and then shoot them. That was Anthony's goal when creating Handsome Jack:

"Jack *is Borderlands 2*, in terms of my narrative philosophy for that game. I just really like villain-centric video-game stories, because I tend to feel like those really work in terms of game-space violence. You should be looking for something you emotionally care about fighting."

At the end of the first *Borderlands* game, the Vault is opened to reveal it was actually a prison for a giant alien known as the Destroyer. After it was killed, a strange new mineral called Eridium began springing up all across Pandora, drawing even more people to the planet, including Handsome Jack, president of the laughably evil Hyperion Corporation.

For me, Handsome Jack is one of gaming's great villains. Part of that is thanks to Dameon Clarke, the actor who gave Jack his voice. It's also because Jack is probably the most unrepentant asshole in game history. He's not an asshole because he's uncaring or mean; this is a man capable of wringing pure bliss from something as simple as fucking up a stranger's day.

"The goal was always to make this guy someone you thought was kind of funny and you wanted to listen to, but then specifically have you move to 'Oh, I fucking hate this guy and I want to take him down'—to have your hatred accelerate to the point where the only thing you care about isn't the loot or fighting a big monster, it's putting one bullet in this guy's head. We want them gripping their controllers in anger and hatred. I want them to strike him down with all their vengeance and embrace the dark side. It's fucking creepy," says Burch, "but that's what the gameplay is."

It paid off. Handsome Jack was such a great villain that, as *Borderlands 2* neared completion, Gearbox, the developer, began questioning whether or not he should be left alive at the end of the game.

"It's amazingly flattering that someone would like the character enough to bring him back for a couple of games. I felt really good, but also like an asshole, because at the end of the game people were saying, 'We should let Handsome Jack live because people really like him.' And I shouted and stamped my feet. 'No! He is a bad person! I don't want him continuing! Stop this—he stays dead!' And he did.

"And then we brought him back two more times anyway."

That's the problem of creating a great villain, especially in a game with an avatar for a protagonist. Like I said, people are drawn to a well-developed character. In the absence of a great hero, they will readily accept a great villain to be raised upon a pedestal. This is an important lesson for life and game design. We are attracted to charisma, regardless of who has it and what they use it for.

"When people come away saying, 'You know, Jack's not such a bad guy. He's an anti-hero in his heart,' I kind of feel like that means I failed in some way. Because the goal was for him to feel like an asshole who is worse than you. You, as the player, are an asshole, but he's a bigger asshole. Every single time we had an opportunity to have him do something awful, we took it. He met Helena Pierce, from the first game, then shot her in the head offscreen and laughed about how her head exploded. He imprisoned his daughter since childhood . . . he's an abusive father . . . and we still had people going, 'Nah, I mean, he was doing the right thing.' I just don't know what I could have done to make him more awful."

Anthony worries that he's encouraging the audience to forgive a person's asshole tendencies if they're charming enough. Even if they're an abusive monster like Jack.

"I just don't know what to do with that," he says. "I wanted it to be fun because it's a comedy game, but I didn't want it to be so fun that you're okay with abusive people."

I think what bothers Anthony about the reaction to Handsome Jack is proof of how well the character is written. In the eyes of some, he was a person, not a monster. The way Greg Kasavin views villains sheds some light on that.

"I just don't do villains," says Greg. "Period."

"I make the distinction between villains and antagonists. Antagonists are all around us in life. Your antagonist can be your wife for a few days a week, or something like that, when you're just trying to decide where to go to dinner. You want to eat Mexican food, but she ain't having it. She's the antagonist in your life in that moment. So, antagonism is constant throughout life, and it's a real force. But villainy, I think, is very rare. Usually, it's a lack of empathy that leads people to perceive one another as villains, because in our own minds we're doing the thing we think is best. I really, truly believe that."

In *Transistor*, Supergiant's second game, the futuristic city of Cloudbank comes under attack from the Process, a robotic presence slowly assimilating the city and everyone in it. The Process is controlled, and was possibly created, by a mysterious group of high-ranking officials known as the Camerata. Through its use, Cloudbank would be ever changing, shifting to fit the whims of its people. At least, that was the plan . . .

That was the thing with *Transistor.* I wanted to set up the seemingly cool band of supervillains and then just sort of watch these characters unravel and discover they had these more tragic, potentially more noble intentions in mind that maybe fell apart.

I also think it leads to better characters when characters have motivations you can relate to. Those are the most compelling antagonists, when you're like, "I guess if I was in your position, I would do that, too." I think that leads to interesting characters and interesting stories and interesting twists. I'm really interested in the gap between intentions and reality. I think people typically act with good intentions in mind, but their actions can be deeply misconstrued or have terrible consequences they didn't really anticipate.

We've all been there when we tried to do something good or nice and it just blew up in our face, or situations where we've been really angry with someone, and we realized we were angry on a false premise. Maybe if we had a little more information we wouldn't have reacted the way that we did. I really like taking those kinds of stories and spinning them in a really fantastical context. That stuff is just deeply humane to me.

Humane.

That's not a word we usually associate with AAA games. It's strange, since we strive to create these deeply immersive experiences. Our graphical capabilities have been pushed to the brink as we try to claw our way up the far side of the uncanny valley. Released in 2015, *Fallout 4* went so far as to build a realistic world in which every lootable item has purpose. There is no junk; everything is useable. Players can tear down buildings and use the parts to build their own settlements. Even electricity is made available by building a generator, scavenging circuity and copper wire, and then connecting all the necessary bits in the game's workshop.

Video games have now brought us full circle from where we started. We wanted to escape this world, so we built digital worlds where we could hide, and then we packed them full of everything we were trying to escape.

The player is the only human element in a game as it is being played, and yet they bring no humanity to it. They are limited to the systems we build. And a system, no matter how deep, is a poor replacement for humanity. Gameplay is a cold, incorporeal skeleton kept in motion by the organs and muscles of the game's systems. It will never create the immersive experience we're all looking for. The humanity necessary to ignite our empathy can only come from story.

When I think about story in games, my brain keeps coming back to a quote by Leo Tolstoy: "All great literature is one of two stories; a man goes on a journey or a stranger comes to town." There is a lot of truth hidden in this statement; the first bit being that writers love to simplify complex issues into catchy quotes. But look closely at Leo's choice of words. The quote is like a perspective puzzle; it changes shape depending on the angle from which it is viewed. Look at it straight on and it appears to be two different stories. To see the complete image, you have to turn it over in your hands and study it from every angle. A man goes on a journey. To those he meets, he is a stranger come to town. If he returns home, he will not be the man he once was; he will be a stranger. One story becomes many, all by changing your point of view.

Our story is never going to change. We need the player as much as the player needs us. To grow, we need to change our point of view.

Long live character.

11

WALKING THE LINE

When you think of the great military shooter franchises, Spec Ops does not come to mind. Created by Zombie Studios, the series was a budget franchise, the kind of game you'd find in the discount bin at Kmart. From 1998 to 2002, the franchise released nine installments. The first two games in the franchise, *Spec Ops: Rangers Lead the Way* and *Spec Ops: Ranger Team Bravo*, were well received. The following seven, not so much. I can't tell you why, because I've never played them. But if I had to guess, it had something to do with releasing seven games in just three years. Maybe the quick development schedule caused a drop in quality, or maybe players became burnt out on the franchise. Too much too fast is never a good thing. Whatever the reason, after 2002, Spec Ops games disappeared from the shelves. After that, the franchise somehow ended up at Rockstar—yes, the same Rockstar that makes *Grand Theft Auto*—where a new installment sat in development for two years before it was canceled for unknown reasons.

Finally, in 2006, it came to us.

"Do you play a lot of military shooters?" asked the Fox.

"Not really." I grimaced, hoping my honesty wasn't about to kill my chances of working on the game. "I played some *Counter-Strike* back in the day, but aside from that, the genre just never appealed to me." This was mostly true. My dislike for military shooters actually stemmed from my field training at Lackland Air Force Base back in 2002.

One evening, all the trainees gathered in the auditorium to listen to an AC-130 gunner discuss his tours in the Middle East. To accompany his talk, he showed a video from one of his missions. Through the grainy lens of the targeting camera, we watched little white dots sprint for cover as they tried to avoid the death from above. In the background, we could hear the gunner cracking jokes as the dots fell, one by one, and went still.

The gunner's casual attitude didn't bother me. I don't know what it's like to kill someone, but from all accounts it sticks with you. This guy killed people for a living. It made sense he would develop an emotional distance between himself and his work. What I found unnerving, though, was the reaction from my fellow trainees. They were laughing and cheering like we were at the movies. There were many reasons for everyone to feel okay about what we were watching. The footage bore no resemblance to reality. It was grainy, black and white, shot from high in the sky. The people dying on-screen were dots, blips. Even if you could muster empathy for them, they were still enemy combatants. Their deaths had been sanctioned for the greater good. So why couldn't I shake the feeling we had just watched a snuff film?

I'd always felt a little out of place in the military because I naturally bristle at legally mandated conformity and an institutionalized class system, but those were temporary constraints I accepted when I signed away four years of my life; I'd have to deal. But this was something different. This was the celebration of death. The loss of life is tragic—any life. War happens; I accept that. When it does, death is inevitable. But it is still tragic.

That was the moment I realized the military wasn't for me. Afterward, whenever I played military shooters like *Call of Duty* or *Battlefield*, they made me feel the same as I did in that auditorium.

I didn't say any of this to the Fox. There's a belief in this industry that in order to make a great game you must love the genre or franchise you're working on, as if only a foaming-at-the-mouth fanatic can understand what players want. If you've ever wondered why so many video games feel like microwaved leftovers, this is why. Fans are wonderful and should always be embraced, but their opinions can be deadly to the creative process. Fandom is an organized religion whose holy laws are handed down by people who get angry on the Internet. By defining what something should and should not be, fans secure ownership over that which they love. When their passion informs rather than inspires, it becomes a millstone around a creator's neck.

You don't get into game development if you don't love and play games. That shared passion blurs the line between creator and player. When we see ourselves as players, we design to our audience, believing we are designing for ourselves. By doing this, we forget that our job is not to give players what they want; our job is to show them things they never imagined.

As a writer and designer, I would much rather work on a project for which I have no affinity. I don't need to make something I like; those things already exist. The pleasure they provide me comes from experiencing them as part of the audience. The pleasure I get from writing and design comes from the challenge. For me, there is no greater challenge than taking something I couldn't care less about and finding a way to approach it that sparks my interest.

I told myself this was the reason I said yes when the Fox asked if I wanted to work on *Spec Ops*, despite my opinion on military shooters.

As my mother has always said, "That's a great excuse, but it's not a very good reason." The truth is, I wanted to make *Spec Ops* because I'm a hypocrite. As a military shooter, it would embody a lot of what turned me away from the military. It would also be a full-blown AAA game with a focus on narrative. This was an opportunity to help build a game from the ground up. If it did well, it would potentially open a lot of doors. Could I honestly ignore my beliefs for the sake of furthering my career?

Yes—absolutely and without hesitation.

To MAKE THIS GAME, we needed a development partner. We found one in Yager, an independent studio located in Berlin, Germany. They were new, having only released two games, both of which were combat flight simulators. They lacked AAA experience, but 2K did not. By working together, the Fox knew we could create something special.

Our competition was fierce. We were up against fan-favorite franchises Rainbow Six, Ghost Recon, Battlefield, and Call of Duty. Each of them had carved their own niche into the genre.

Originally developed by Red Storm Entertainment, Ubisoft's Rainbow Six and Ghost Recon franchises were both inspired by Tom Clancy novels. As tactical shooters, they aim for realistic combat, requiring players to focus on caution and tactics rather than fast reflexes. Often, a single bullet is enough to get the player killed. While the two franchises have a lot in common, their core gameplay is very different. Rainbow Six focuses on heavily planned infiltration tactics, whereas Ghost Recon is designed for on-the-fly battlefield tactics. If we were to pick two verbs to describe each game, Rainbow Six would be breach and clear; Ghost Recon would be outmaneuver and progress.

The Battlefield franchise, developed by Visceral Games and EA DICE, built its name on large multiplayer battles, which can include up to sixty-four players at once. These matches take place on large maps designed to simulate the widespread chaos of real war. To further that design, players are not limited to the normal run-and-gun gameplay associated with FPS multiplayer; they can expand their combat arsenal by commandeering vehicles such as tanks and planes.

Activision's Call of Duty is a franchise so big it's developed by three studios—Infinity Ward, Treyarch, and Sledgehammer Games. By excelling in both single-player and multiplayer design, Call of Duty has earned its place as the king of military shooters. Its narrative campaigns are nonstop, action-packed affairs, probably the closest video games have come to distilling summer-movie blockbusters into an interactive experience. Its multiplayer mode matches the stellar gameplay with a progression system that rewards player skill by unlocking gameplay options, both during a match and afterward. It's a perfectly designed addiction loop built around the smoothest, most responsive gameplay in the genre. Play unlocks new features, which lead to more play, which increases your skill, which unlocks new features, and so on.

These were all time-tested franchises, with formulas refined over multiple installments. We weren't foolish enough to think *Spec Ops* could make a run at any of them. All we wanted was to carve out our own niche so we could stand beside the greats and hopefully enjoy a reasonable piece of the market share.

YAGER'S PITCH FOR *SPEC OPS* was exactly what you'd expect from a military shooter: Dubai is taken over by terrorists, and three Delta operators are sent in to rescue the city's captive billionaires. The military shooter genre was already packed with games about duty-driven Caucasian soldiers fighting terrorists of unidentifiable nationality. If *Spec Ops* was going to succeed, we needed to offer players something different, so we threw out the guts and kept the skin.

The location, time period, and setup remained the same—three soldiers fighting in present-day Dubai. That was the box we had to work within. As far as creative constraints go, these were spectacular. They were loose enough that we could essentially write any story we wanted. At the same time, they were defined just enough that we were able to bypass the initial brainstorming and not get lost in the weeds of preproduction.

Trying to decide the who, where, and when can be an enjoyable part of the brainstorming process. It's fun to sit around spitballing ideas, to feel that rush of adrenaline when a concept ignites the possibilities in your brain. But it can also be very treacherous to navigate. A new idea is like a new relationship. It's exciting, electrifying. Everything about it seems perfect and unspoiled. Dwell on it for too long, however, and suddenly the new idea becomes an old idea. The initial excitement wears off, and its cracks begin to show. You wonder how you could have ever been so blind. This idea was never good. You can do better than this. So you begin to brainstorm again, and soon a new idea catches your eye, and that familiar chill runs down your spine as your scalp tingles with elation. *This is it*, you think. *This is a brilliant idea*. And the cycle begins anew. Everyone gets caught in this trap. Coming up with an idea is easy; the pleasure is almost instantaneous. It's instant gratification that requires zero follow-through. Good stuff, but deadly to the creative process. A great idea can get you high, but the process of actually bringing it to life will lay you low. If you get addicted to that new-idea buzz, then every time you hit a creative wall, you'll go back for another hit, and you'll never move forward.

Coming off the success of *BioShock*, the Fox wanted to double down on dark and gritty. "We need something with a story," he said. "Something thought-provoking that makes people scream, 'What the fuck did I just play?'"

Yager's art director, Mathias Wiese, ran with the idea and drew concept art showing Dubai half buried beneath the desert. There was no reason behind it; he simply thought it looked cool. Normally, that would be enough to make me hate it. Cool is one of those meaningless terms that get tossed around during development. It is nothing and everything— cultural dark matter. Its parameters are subjective. You could almost argue it doesn't exist, except for the fact its proof is all around us: the clothes we wear, the games we play, the music we love. Coolness is the lifeblood of mainstream entertainment. As pop-culture artists, we live and die on our cool. That's why cool is the most dangerous word in video games. We chase a concept that cannot be defined, terrified it will elude us, and in the grip of our fear, we are easily controlled.

In this case, however, I had to admit, a sand-covered Dubai looked pretty cool.

Taking that image and the Fox's directive, I wrote a one-page story proposal riffing on *Apocalypse Now*, a film that military shooters had somehow not yet ripped off. The concept was centered on a US Army colonel who goes rogue and seizes control of an abandoned, sand-covered Dubai. A trio of Delta operators is sent into the ruined city to find the Colonel and take him down.

When writing one-pagers, I never come up with characters' names. At that point in the process, there's no guarantee what you're writing will make it to the final product. Anything and everything could end up on the chopping block, usually sooner than later. It's like working at a cattle ranch—you don't name the cow you're eating for dinner. This being a military story, it was easy to explain the plot without naming my characters. Everyone was referred to by rank. We had the player's character—the Captain—the two Squadmates, the Lieutenant, the Sergeant, and finally the villain, the Colonel. That would have been the end of it, except for one problem: I am a fucking glutton. I love to eat, and not well—the junkier, the better. Fried chicken is a particular passion of mine. If I see it on TV or on someone else's plate at a restaurant, I have no choice but to get my own or else spiral into seething jealousy. This made it difficult for me to type "the Colonel" over and over. The further I got into the document, the more my mouth began to water. Instead of finishing it, all I could think about was driving to the nearest KFC and sacrificing my digestive tract on the altar of that white-suited Kentuckian. My story proposal would be completely lost on the reader, if they happened to love fried chicken nearly as much as I did. The Colonel needed a name change, or else my efforts would amount to nothing more than fast-food propaganda.

When it comes to naming things, I'm a devout follower of the "I Spy" method. If I can see it from where I'm sitting, it will eventually show up in one of my stories. That day, it just so happened, my copy of *Heart of Darkness* was sitting beside my keyboard. I glanced at the author's name—Joseph Conrad. It seemed too on the nose. I needed to make it less obvious, so I swapped the C for a K and voila! Problem solved.

I said a silent prayer to our *Mortal Kombat*, whose victories art flawless, toasty be its name, and thanked it for teaching us K would always be cooler than C.

I emailed the proposal to the Fox and headed home.

"Hey," he called out as I walked to the door. "This is brilliant."

The shock must have been clear on my face, because he quickly backpedaled. "I mean, it's good. It's not bad. I think it's workable." His praise grew fainter with every sentence, but none of it registered. In his enthusiasm, the Fox had fucked up. My proposal was brilliant, ergo so was I. He sent the one-pager to Yager. I went home, confident they would love it. I was going to write this fucking game, and no one would be able to deny me.

A FEW WEEKS LATER, I sat in Yager's conference room, staring across the table at the writer they had hired to turn my idea into a script. We'll call him Mr. Sunshine.

I was rambling, as I always do when I first meet someone alone. Socially, I am a naturally shy person. I have to meet someone a few times before I'm comfortable enough to be myself. Professionally, I don't have that problem. If I'm talking to someone because of my job, all of my insecurities disappear. It doesn't matter if someone dislikes me; we're there to work, not make friends. To get these conversations going, I developed a form of rambling that would help break the ice.

I'd start with a comment about being tired, which I always was, and then slide into a series of self-effacing anecdotes about food, film, and guilty pleasures. When the conversation inevitably stalled, I would return to an earlier topic and use it to segue into a personal story about one of my many irrational fears. It was all nonsense, which was the point. The other person felt comfortable because I was clearly an idiot, and I felt comfortable because after going on like that for twenty minutes, there was little I could do that would embarrass me.

Mr. Sunshine smiled politely as I went through my routine.

"I did the math, and it turns out I spend almost thirty hours a month floating over the Atlantic in a giant hunk of metal. It sounds crazy when you say it out loud. Flying used to be so amazing to me. I'd wake up in one place, and a few hours later I'm on the other side of the world. Now, I feel like I'm living on borrowed time. Tempting fate, you know? Anytime the plane hits turbulence, my brain says, 'Guess this is it!' Then I pull out my iPod and find a suitable song to die to."

"What song?" he asked.

I feigned hesitation. ". . . 'For Crying Out Loud,' by Meat Loaf." That wasn't a lie. Track seven on *Bat Out of Hell* was my go-to dying song. The only reason I feigned hesitation was because I'd noticed the admission landed better if I came across as slightly embarrassed. I don't know why, since the musical stylings of Mr. Loaf and Jim Steinman are a goddamn national treasure, but whatever. You have to play to your audience.

"I think it's good that you accept it so calmly," said Mr. Sunshine. "It means you're at peace with death."

"You know what's funny, though? I think my plane is about to crash, and I'm fine. But if a spider ran across this table right now, I'd lose my shit. What's up with that? It's like I'd rather die in a fiery crash than look at an itsy-bitsy eight-legged abomination."

With no trace of humor or sarcasm, Mr. Sunshine looked me in the eyes and asked, "Have you considered the possibility your fear of spiders comes from a genetic memory sent back through time by your descendants who live in a future where arachnids have evolved into mankind's primary predator?"

That shut me up.

I couldn't get a read on this guy. He had those blank, empty eyes shared by sociopaths and idiots. It's possible he realized I was rambling by design and decided to throw a verbal wrench in my spokes.

Or, he was crazy. I don't mean that in the ablest sense. Genuine mental illness and self-destructive tendencies—I understand these. But there is a type of crazy that can only be described as a willful denial of the world around us. I had no idea what Mr. Sunshine was trying to do, and it scared me to death.

THAT AFTERNOON, I CALLED a meeting with Mr. Sunshine and some of the team leads. I thought it would be good for us to kick-start the week by defining who our main characters would be. It was the first meeting I had ever organized at Yager, so I started off by rallying the troops with a boilerplate pep talk.

"We have an opportunity to make a game unlike anything else. If we do this right, *Spec Ops* could be the most important war game ever made." I remember thinking I was nailing it, because one of the leads was smiling and nodding along.

"This is the moment we decide to be different. I think we do that by setting out to make a game about people instead of war. That won't happen if our characters have names like Gunn or Brand. They need real names so we see them as real people. A good name speaks to the nature of a character, like Norm from *Cheers*, the guy at the bar who is always there, in the same seat. If we brainstorm about who we want our characters to be and then find a name that embodies that, it will inspire us even more as we flesh them out.

"Let's start with our player character, the Delta squad leader. Who is this man? What type of person do we want him to be?"

The team said nothing. All they did was stare.

"It's okay to say whatever you're thinking. This is brainstorming. There are no wrong answers here."

Not a goddamn word. Even the nodding guy had forsaken me.

"No one has any ideas about who our main character should be?"

Mr. Sunshine stared at me with those dopey, blank eyes. He had a lot of opinions on spiders, but nothing about the character he'd been hired to write.

I threw my hands in the air. "Well, I guess our main character will do a lot of walking in the game, so how about we call him Walker?" I wrote it down and kept going. We can change it later, I said to myself. We never did.

"Let's move on to the members of Walker's squad."

The blank reactions continued. There were a few Americans working at Yager. If one of them hadn't been in the room, I would have believed my words were getting lost in translation. But no—either the team was too afraid to speak their ideas or they didn't have any yet. Whatever the reason, I was too annoyed to brainstorm new names, so I just began naming my friends from the air force.

"Personally, I feel it's important for our game to have a diverse cast. There's three guys in our Delta squad. I don't see any reason they can't be Caucasian, African American, and Hispanic. The Hispanic guy's name could be . . . oh, let's say John Lugo. And the African American guy could be Alphonso Adams."

"I don't know about that," said Mr. Sunshine. Apparently he did have opinions about names. "It's not realistic for a character's first and last name to start with the same letter."

I leaned forward over the conference table. "What is my name?"

"Oh—"

Before he could continue, I began listing off my coworkers whose first and last names also started with the same letter. Not my best idea, since there were only three of them, but luckily Mr. Sunshine backed down before I had to start naming comic-book characters like Peter Parker and Bruce Banner.

For someone I was inclined to dislike through no fault of his own, this guy was managing to hit all of my buttons. What had started out as petty jealousy was already nearing genuine loathing, and it was only our first day together.

OUR FIRST TASK WAS writing a script for the game's vertical slice. A vertical slice is an internal demo that will serve as a quality benchmark for the rest of the game. The script for the vertical slice mainly would serve as context for the action beats. Aside from that, it was expendable. Once the game's full story was agreed upon, the vertical slice script would be rewritten and integrated with the larger narrative.

Every writing team has disagreements, some more heated than others. That's what happens when you get a bunch of show runners together in one room and ask them all to cede control. Everyone has their own opinion as to how certain things should be written. Over the years, I've become more diplomatic about how I navigate these disagreements. Back then, however, I was young and cocky. I wasn't looking for diplomacy; I was looking for the quickest path to the finish line. If anything got in the way, I'd steamroll it and move on.

Mr. Sunshine didn't want the characters to use vulgarity. He was adamant that professional soldiers wouldn't swear when speaking to one another. It was a silly argument. Of course soldiers swear; the phrase "curse like a sailor" exists for a reason. For a soldier, a bad day at work means getting shot at and possibly killing someone. That is not a job for people who find vulgarity to be unprofessional.

This fight went on for weeks. I couldn't understand why it was such a sticking point. I cussed all the time, and thanks to a contract I signed when I was eighteen, I was technically an ex-soldier. I was living proof of my own correctness. Mr. Sunshine wouldn't budge, though. Finally, I just ignored him. When we wrote a scratch script for the game's demo level, everything I wrote used vulgarity. If Mr. Sunshine wrote something, I added vulgarity to it, usually right before the actors recorded it, and always without telling him. This did not go over well.

On the one hand, what I did was not out of the ordinary. When you have multiple writers on a game, someone has to review all the scripts to ensure the character voices remain consistent. There was no time for feedback and iteration, so I did the rewrites myself. Plus, it's worth mentioning, I was right and he was wrong.

On the other hand, it was a dick move.

When you're in a collaborative industry, everyone must work toward the same vision, or else everything will fall apart. To swear or not to swear may not seem like an important issue, but it directly informs the personality of your characters. The language we use when communicating with other people tells a lot about who we are. This is why dialogue is so important. When thoughtfully crafted, it can reveal untold depths. As the saying goes, "Actions speak louder than words." But the actions we're comfortable performing in front of others do not necessarily reflect the feelings and personality we hide from the world. To know someone, you must hear them speak when they are most vulnerable. It's our accidental words that reveal our true selves.

Here's the thing about swearing—everyone does it. Even if you go out of your way to say "dang" instead of "damn," you are still swearing, just in a family-friendly way. A curse is an emotional exclamation. Your body produces an emotion and in response, your mouth forms a word meant to convey that feeling. The severity of that word will vary based on numerous factors—upbringing, vocabulary, native tongue, age, social norms, and most importantly, the intensity of what you are feeling. Everybody swears, some more crudely than others.

The thematic journey of *Spec Ops* was one of descent and denial. The main characters struggle to maintain control in a situation that is already out of their grasp. Had they maintained a constant level of professionalism by not swearing, they would have exercised superhuman control over their emotions, which would have been in direct opposition to their actions and story.

I could have compromised by writing a vulgar draft and a clean draft and then having the actors record both. The problem is that's not a compromise; it's a deflection. Appeasing both sides would only have prolonged the argument and pushed a resolution to a later date. Even worse, by recording a clean draft of the script, I would have given my opponent the ammo necessary to win. It would have been very easy for Mr. Sunshine to say, "It's already recorded, so let's put it in the game and see how it feels"—at which point it would never have been removed. I wasn't going to let that happen. The game deserved better than that. Also—and I can't stress this enough—I was right.

AROUND THIS TIME, YAGER's development producer went on maternity leave. If you're an American, and therefore unfamiliar with how other civilized nations treat maternity and health care, it might surprise you to learn German maternity leave can last up to three years. This is what's known as quality of life. Germans have it; we don't.

Three years is a long time. We could conceptualize, build, and ship the entire game in that time. The game was already in production. Processes were in place, wheels were spinning. All we needed was a producer, someone who could drop in and take control without missing a beat.

Back in California, there was just such a producer: Bonnie LaFramboise. She had cut her teeth at Looking Glass Studios, the legendary studio that went on to spawn Irrational and many others. When Looking Glass shuttered its doors, rather than move to a new studio, Bonnie chose to leave the industry and build a new life for herself as a baker and midwife. Luckily for us, she'd recently dipped her toe back into the development cesspool.

The way I imagine it, someone took a helicopter south from Novato deep into the business-park jungles of Redwood City, California. There, they would have found Bonnie engaged in a stick fight with some uppity young designer who'd gone over time and budget.

Bonnie would have heard our pitch for old times' sake, but that was no guarantee she'd be willing to take on a job like this.

"This mission's important, Bonnie."

"Do you really think it's gonna make a difference?" she'd have asked. "It didn't before."

"That was another time . . . You said that your war is over. Now, maybe the one out there is, but not the one inside you. I know the reasons you're here, Bonnie, but it doesn't work that way. You may try, but you can't get away from what you really are—a full-blooded development producer."

Basically just like the opening of *Rambo III*.

I don't know what they said to convince her, but it worked. Bonnie LaFramboise arrived in Berlin fully prepared to get production on track. In our first meeting, she asked me to fill her in on where we were with the story. It was just the two of us, alone in a conference room. I launched into a foaming rant about Mr. Sunshine.

Without raising her voice, Bonnie looked me dead in the eyes and said, "You do not yell at me."

I liked her instantly.

AFTER THE VERTICAL SLICE, it was time to create a detailed story summary. Yager wanted Mr. Sunshine to take the lead, so it was up to him. I gave him the one-pager I had written, along with directions for what his summary needed to include—a full story outline, backstory for the game world, character bios, proposals for missions, possible locations, and a list of key moments. It was a substantial amount of work, but it was still a first pass.

"I'll need a month," he said.

"Really? I'd have thought like a week and half."

When making a game, the first idea never survives. It is the sacrificial lamb whose innards will be used to divine the game's future. Think of it as a form of hepatomancy, the art of reading omens in the entrails of animals. Disemboweling a first idea is bloodless, but not painless. The more time spent doting on your first idea, the harder it will be to see it sliced from tail to sternum and flipped inside out.

"I'm not comfortable turning in work that falls below my personal standard of quality."

"I can respect that. If you need a month, that's cool with me."

A month went by, and sure enough, Mr. Sunshine's summary appeared in my email. He'd met his first deadline; always a good sign. I opened the document, expecting to find the usual affair—an overview of the main plot points, characters, and thematic arcs, plus a few proposals for missions, environments, and set pieces. I expected this because my mind was small and limited in what it could imagine. What I found inside that document was nothing short of madness.

The game opened on our heroes scaling a skyscraper and then gunning down a squad of unarmed enemies who were playing volleyball and eating nachos. It only got better from there.

In Mr. Sunshine's story, the game's villain was a soldier turned dictator turned eco-terrorist, whose goal was to turn Dubai into a war-torn hellhole so he could broadcast footage of his atrocities across the globe via cell phone. These terrible images, accompanied by his charismatic speeches, would incite a Third World War that would decimate the earth's population and save the planet from global warming.

Highlights included a spunky young reporter who traveled from New York hoping to snag a one-on-one interview with Konrad; a holographic zoo dedicated to lions, giraffes, and other extinct animals; and an overturned boat that had been converted into a dive bar/memorial where the parents of Konrad's soldiers spent their days getting drunk and lighting candles. Like the cub reporter, these parents all traveled from the United States just to be here, somehow managing to traverse the impassable sandstorm surrounding Dubai.

Nothing in Mr. Sunshine's summary made sense. It defied structure, logic, the game's core design, and any concept of quality I had ever known. The choices he made were so baffling that I began to question whether it might be a work of genius beyond my comprehension.

I needed a fresh pair of eyes, so I sent the summary to Bonnie. Her reaction would tell me whether Mr. Sunshine was a buffoon or I was a lowly gnat incapable of appreciating his majesty.

Three minutes later, I had my answer.

"THEY'RE EATING NACHOS?!?!"

Thank God. It was just a piece of shit.

I'M NOT TRYING TO belittle Mr. Sunshine. His intentions were pure. Idiotic, but pure. The man had a story to tell, one he was very passionate about. That's commendable. It wasn't his fault he had no idea what he was doing. For a video-game story to be powerful and true, it has to grow from the game itself.

Every game has a natural story, which is the expression of its art, design, and gameplay. Everything has a reason; every action has a cause and effect. As video-game writers, we have to take a step back and look at everything that exists and ask, "Why?" The answer to that question is the story of your game.

The natural story of *Spec Ops* was "US soldiers fight one another in a Dubai that has been abandoned to the desert." Our Dubai was covered in sand because we thought it looked cool. It was mostly uninhabited because we couldn't figure out a way to believably populate the city with noncombat NPCs (nonplayer characters, or computer-controlled AI). The player controlled an American soldier because our game was a military shooter, and North America was our largest market. We fought other American soldiers because no other game had done it, and we wanted to be different.

SOMETHING caused Dubai to be abandoned and covered in sand.

SOMETHING brought a US Army battalion to the city. SOMETHING turned those soldiers into despots. Later, SOMETHING would bring three Delta soldiers to Dubai, and SOMETHING ELSE would make them go to war with their fellow Americans. None of these things were defined by the story; they were all caused by external constraints.

Bad stories ignore their constraints. Good stories work within them. Great stories embrace external constraints and repurpose them as the core elements of the narrative.

Mr. Sunshine's summary did the opposite. He saw Dubai covered in sand and asked, "Why?" The answer, he decided, was global warming. He ignored the other pieces because they weren't necessary to *his* vision. His story rang false because he treated the characters, gameplay, and genre as window dressing. As a writer, your loyalty is to the game, not yourself or the player. Betraying that loyalty is the only way you can fail.

I'LL GIVE HIM CREDIT; he stood by what he wrote. His summary wasn't the result of a misunderstanding. He consciously ignored my direction because he felt his story was more important. For him, *Spec Ops* was a platform, an opportunity to speak out against carbon emissions. Not to do so would be borderline criminal.

I explained to Mr. Sunshine that I appreciated his dedication to his beliefs, but we weren't interested in making a game about global warming. He was being paid to write a story based on *Heart of Darkness*, and blatantly ignoring that direction was also borderline criminal. Now that his first idea had been expressed, he needed to rework it into something that resembled the original concept.

No writer enjoys getting contrary feedback. You can tell the difference between a pro and rookie by how they react to it. Mr. Sunshine got huffy. "I see. You want something dark and gritty."

"Yes. But specifically, something inspired by *Apocalypse Now* and *Heart of Darkness*."

If you only take one lesson from this book, let it be this one: never challenge a German to be dark and gritty, because holy shit they will take it all the way to eleven.

"What about a level where the player has to blow up a mosque filled with women and children? Is that more to your taste?"

"No, it is not. It should go without saying, but try to avoid scenes that might spark an international incident. Think you can do that?"

"Fine." He crossed his arms and turned away, like a kid being told to clean his room. "I'll need another month."

"Whatever. Just get it done."

Mr. Sunshine spent the next month poring over his original summary and then sent it back to me, without making a single change.

"Please tell me, because I swear I want to know, what it is about this summary that you think matches the assignment you were given."

"All of it."

"See, that's hard for me to believe, because I asked for a new summary, and what you've given me is the exact same document as before. Even worse, you took an entire month to do it. How is that in any way acceptable?"

"I'm sorry, but I think we have a responsibility to say something important about how we're treating the environment."

"By shooting people in the face."

"I . . . what?"

"We're making a game about shooting people in the fucking face, and you think that is the best venue to start a conversation about global warming."

"You're being purposefully dismissive, but yes. That's what I think."

"Well, okay." I had no more questions. And Mr. Sunshine had no more time. His career as a video-game writer had reached its end.

Au revoir, auf Wiedersehen, and good riddance.

In the end, we built a fantastic writing team for *Spec Ops*. For some reason the game's final credits don't list everyone, but the team consisted of myself, Chad Rocco, Georg Struck, Jack Scalici, Richard Pearsey, and Shawn Frison. Remember those names, because the game would not have been the same without them. Mr. Sunshine could have been a part of that team, if he had just learned to let go. But writers who cannot take feedback are not writers; they are children playing make-believe. All they want to do is bang on a keyboard, hear that fun clickity-clack sound, and be told how special they are.

Game development is not a day care; it's a job.

Video games may be art, but not all of us are artists whose personal visions must be allowed to blossom like a delicate flower. Our value is measured not in ideas but in our ability to execute. A team needs to know you have their back. We ride together, die together, and for God's sake, learn our fucking place. Doing so will not make you a soulless wage slave. It will grant you immortality. Don't like the task you've been given? Let go of your ego, find an angle that interests you, and then bring it to life like it's the last thing you'll ever create. I guarantee it will be unforgettable.

12

WE ARE NOT HEROES

At least once a year, usually during an industry trade show, I tend to look at what we're creating and ask myself, "Why are games so violent? How did we reach this point?"

There's a simple answer—violence is entertaining, easy to dramatize, and sells like cold beer on a hot afternoon. Violence is not a "video-game problem." Just take a step back and look at your life. You are a person whose body requires the continual murder and consumption of living matter in order to survive. Not forever, but long enough for something—be it drugs, the sun, your liver—to kill you in an equally violent, possibly unnoticeable way.

Existence has a violence problem. Video games, like all art, are just expressing the world around them. The reason games face more scrutiny is because they are the latest mass-market art form, they are interactive, and most are built around some form of violent game mechanic. Anything that brings joy to children by letting them pretend to kill people will of course get prudes and politicians up in arms. What many people don't realize is that video-game violence doesn't belong to the game industry. We stole it from film, along with most of what we know about tone, theme, and story.

It all began in 1990 when John Carmack, John Romero, Tom Hall, and Adrian Carmack gathered at a lake house in Shreveport, Louisiana, to create *Commander Keen*, a side-scrolling platformer about an eight-year-old genius defending the earth from an alien invasion. Its success led to the founding of id Software, where Romero, Hall, and the two unrelated Carmacks chose to abandon the family-friendly platformer in favor of focusing on 3-D action games. In just three years, id Software released four games: *Wolfenstein 3D, Spear of Destiny, Doom*, and *Doom II.* These first-person shooters were fast, frantic, and violent in a way many gamers had never seen because they were too young to watch films like *Evil Dead II.*

If violence was the only thing worth remembering about *Wolfenstein 3D* and *Doom*, we wouldn't be talking about id Software right now. There are plenty of forgotten developers who tried to ride a wave of mutilation all the way to the bank. id Software understood there had to be more underneath the blood; something new. Their games brought people together through LAN connections and dial-up modems, allowing people to play together in the same game. Modular data files and level editors made it easy for fans to create their own levels and share them with one another. These games created communities and popularized the first-person shooter. The violence was just curb appeal.

In 2001, gaming took another leap forward in the form of *Grand Theft Auto III.* Published by Rockstar Games, *GTA 3* diverged from the early games in the series by presenting a fully three-dimensional world for players to move through and explore. The innovation of an open game world came out of nowhere, but that's not the reason *Grand Theft Auto* became a household name.

Described as a "crime simulation game" by its producer, Leslie Benzies, *GTA 3* was an immersive American satire and homage to crime films *Scarface* and *Goodfellas*. The player took on the role of Claude, a criminal betrayed by his girlfriend, who works his way through the criminal underbelly of Liberty City, the franchise's version of New York. The open-world nature of the game allowed players to do all manner of terrible things—run over civilians with a car, shoot police officers, sleep with prostitutes and then kill them to get their money back. There was nothing in the game that could not conceivably be found in an R-rated crime film, but the interactive component transformed players from voyeurs to participants, giving the game a forbidden edge.

Grand Theft Auto III was the highest-selling game of 2001 and sold more than two million units in its first five months. As with *Doom*, its success and innovation created a new video-game genre—the open-world 3-D action-adventure game. It was arguably the last earth-shattering leap made by the AAA industry, and the genre is still going strong. When *Grand Theft Auto V* was released in 2013, it made more than one billion dollars in just three days. That never would have happened if *Grand Theft Auto* was an open-world game about living in a city, working a nine-to-five job, and obeying traffic laws.

As a gameplay mechanic, violence is the most dramatic and empowering form of conflict resolution. It's flashy, it's familiar, and it sticks with you, which is important, because we need people to notice, remember, and purchase these games. With every new generation of video-game console, our games cost more to make. It took five people less than five months to create *Wolfenstein 3D*. *Grand Theft Auto V* took a team of around one thousand people over four years to complete.

Violence sells. If it didn't, we'd be bankrupt within a year.

The problem is, constant exposure to imaginary violence can lead to desensitization. Our job is to keep pushing the envelope and make killing great again. Do you need realistic hit reactions? Okay, enemies now grab their crotches when you shoot them in the dick. Too tame? Fine, here's an X-ray camera that shows your opponent's organs being liquefied by your punches. Whatever it takes to make you feel something, we'll do it. But that's not always enough. Sometimes, to get your blood pumping, we have to let you decide how far you're willing to go.

"PEOPLE LOVED THE MORAL choice in *BioShock*," said the Fox. "It was controversial and thought-provoking. I think *Spec Ops* can do it better."

The Fox and I were in Berlin, presenting his latest idea to Yager. He was adamant we follow in *BioShock*'s footsteps by presenting players with a moral choice, but he wanted to take it a step further. Where *Bio-*

Shock offered a choice between good and evil, he wanted ours to be a choice between bad and worse. To explain the idea, he came up with a concept he called "the Wailing Virgin."

"Imagine you're behind enemy lines, wounded and low on ammo. Konrad's men are patrolling nearby. If you're not careful, they will find you. You try to sneak through the area but are spotted by a woman, a wounded refugee. She knows you're one of the good guys and begins crying out for your help. Her voice rings out like a siren. Every soldier within earshot is now headed your direction. What do you do?"

The project leads stared at the Fox with blank expressions, as if he were a schoolteacher who had asked if someone would volunteer to complete a math equation on the chalkboard.

"Anyone?" asked the Fox.

Kurt—lead level designer, bird watcher, scarf aficionado—raised his hand. He was an interesting guy. What I liked about Kurt was his tell. I always knew when he disagreed with me, and it made my job much easier.

"You don't have to raise your hand," I said.

"Yes," said the Fox. "You are all free to speak. The virgin is wailing, soldiers are coming, what do you do?"

"I leave the area," said Kurt.

"Very smart. To your horror, the woman follows, continuing to scream. What to do you?"

Kurt shrugged. "I do not know. What am I allowed to do?"

"Anything," said the Fox.

"Hmm, yes." Kurt pursed his lips, crossed his arms, and nodded his head. "I see, I see." That was the tell. Kurt knew where this conversation was going, and he did not approve.

I knew Kurt was done playing, so I jumped in. "I hit her with a melee attack." There were two basic attacks in *Spec Ops*, ranged and melee. Ranged attacks were throwing a grenade or firing a weapon.

A melee attack was a close-range attack in which you struck someone with the butt of your weapon. It dealt less damage than a ranged attack, and was conceivably nonlethal.

The Fox turned his attention to me. "You hit the virgin with your rifle. She screams even louder. What do you do?"

Kurt leaned forward and rested on his elbows. "There is nothing else you can do." I'd only seen him like this once before. For Kurt, this was the equivalent of flipping the table.

The Fox looked at Kurt, then at me. "Yes, there is." He was a little put off. If I had to guess, he probably thought we were ganging up on him.

"I can't shoot her," said Kurt.

"Why not? You have a gun."

"Because she's an innocent woman."

"Not anymore," said the Fox. "Right now, she's a homing beacon, and both of your lives are in danger because she can't take a hint. Your pistol only holds six bullets. If you think that's enough to survive, then you can let the virgin wail and wait for Konrad's men to arrive. You might survive, but she is a very loud and hysterical target and will definitely die in the crossfire. Or, you could shoot her and slink away to fight another day. No one will ever know. What do you do?"

The room was quiet as Yager pondered the question. Kurt spoke first.

"I see, I see," said Kurt. "You want us to make a war-crime game."

"Whoa! No, no, no! Who said anything about war crimes? I want you to make a game about soldiers trying to do their best in a bad situation."

"What you just described is a war crime."

"That was an example to illustrate what I meant by bad or worse. The player doesn't have to shoot the woman. It's only an option."

"The option to commit a war crime."

The Fox threw up his hands. "Do you hear this guy? I know you Germans have a history with this sort of thing, but come on. You're the one who called it a war crime, not me."

Timo, one of the company founders, leaned in. "I think what Kurt is saying is this might be too extreme for some players. It is worth asking ourselves if people want to play a game that makes them feel bad."

The Fox raised his eyebrows in my direction. We'd been fielding this exact question back in California, so I had an answer locked and loaded. "I think they do. People use art as a way to safely explore emotions they might not want to feel in their normal, day-to-day lives. Think of the different movies, books, and songs we consume. They can make us feel sad, scared, angry. Music is especially bad about this. Think of how many sad songs you've listened to over the course of your life. I don't think people are afraid to be emotionally challenged by their games. I think they're waiting for it. Gamers are ready for a deeper, more emotional experience. They want to play games that matter."

"That's right," added the Fox. "*Spec Ops* is a game that matters. But it is also dark and gritty and thought-provoking."

One of the art leads said, "I think dark and gritty is good." He had been drawing during this entire conversation and turned his pad around so everyone could see. "This is an idea I had. What if Konrad flew a helicopter above Captain Walker and then tilted it so dead refugees fell out the side and rained down on the player? We could zoom the camera in very close and watch the bodies fall in slow motion. I think it would be very reminiscent of people jumping out of the towers on 9/11."

Oh. Oh God, no. "That might be taking it too far," I said.

Straight to eleven, every time.

JEAN-PAUL SARTRE COINED THE phrase "Hell is other people" in his play *No Exit* (translated from the French *Huis Clos*). In the play, three damned souls are brought to a locked room in hell by a mysterious valet. Through conversation, they are each forced to see themselves through the eyes of others and to learn for the first time who they truly are.

That is the crux of Sartre's point—we can never be truly individualized beings, for we cannot know ourselves without the views of others.

Video games solve this philosophical dilemma by removing other people entirely. We design choices that clearly state the player's options and outcomes so they can decide who they are and how the world will see them. Do you want to play pretend hero or pretend villain? Make your choice; the game will reinforce your personal fantasy. Moral choices offer players validation instead of revelation, because in games, choice is synonymous with player agency.

Agency is the player's ability to control their experience through a branching narrative, gameplay, or a moral choice. There are other methods, but these are probably the most popular and widely used.

A branching narrative is a split in the road. The player comes to a point in the story where they must decide which way to go. It can be as simple as choosing which of your crewmates will sacrifice their life to disable a bomb. The player moves forward in the game, having lost a member of their crew, and the dev team moves forward by designing two slightly different branches of the story in which only one of those characters survived.

With gameplay agency, the player is given a goal and must accomplish it in order to continue the game. Goal-driven progress is mostly linear. Let's say the player needs to find the red key and open the red door. Nothing is going change that goal—if the player wants to continue, they have to find that key. To give the player more agency, you can design multiple ways of accomplishing their key-focused goal. For example, they could sneak into the key office and steal the red key without killing anyone, or they could locate the key master, shoot him in the face, and then loot the red key from his corpse. Choices like these usually don't affect the larger game, but there are exceptions.

Dishonored is an FPS stealth action-adventure game, meaning the player can accomplish their goals through nonlethal stealth or wholesale slaughter. It takes place in the steampunk city of Dunwall, where a plague is turning the city's poorer citizens into Not-Zombies. If the player chooses the lethal path, it will increase the number of rats in the city. More rats mean more plague. As the plague spreads, the city falls more into chaos.

There is a vague moral-choice aspect to this, but it's ultimately undercut by the game's narrative. You play as Corvo, a royal bodyguard turned assassin who is framed for murdering the Empress. After he is broken out of prison by the Loyalists, Corvo is tasked with "eliminating" the conspirators who overthrew the government. There is a nonlethal option for disposing of each conspirator, but they all make assassination seem like a mercy. One man is branded and left to live in poverty, where the plague turns him into a Not-Zombie. Twins have their heads shaved and tongues cut out before being sent to work in the mines for the rest of their lives. One woman is kidnapped and handed over to her stalker. Finally, the man who orchestrated the entire plot is arrested and sent to be executed.

To summarize, after the player is sold on being an assassin, the game tells them it's bad to kill people, so if they want the "good ending," they must doom four people to lives of torture and misery and then have someone else kill the fifth person. Nothing says "clean hands" like facilitating the inevitable deaths of five people but refusing to deliver the killing blows. *Dishonored* is video-game morality at its most technical.

A real moral choice is like the one from *BioShock*, which we discussed earlier. To acquire ADAM and purchase new Plasmids (aka "science magic"), the player must choose to "Rescue" or "Harvest" a Little Sister. Harvesting kills the Little Sister, grants a large amount of ADAM, and brands the player as a bad person. Rescuing a Little Sister will free her of servitude and give the player a tiny bit of ADAM. However, for every three Little Sisters the player rescues, they will be gifted a large amount. If the player sticks to one path or another, without wavering, they will receive roughly the same amount of ADAM during the course of the game. This creates a choice that is purely moral. It exists solely within you, the player, and depends on how you feel about killing a helpless girl. However, if the end result had been unbalanced, players would have been forced to choose between killing girls and growing more powerful or rescuing them and remaining weak as the game's difficulty increased. Had this been the case, the *BioShock* choice would have challenged the player's morality, and therefore been more engaging.

I don't know how I feel about moral choices.

On one hand, moral choices feed my hunger for complex, emotionally driven situations while also satisfying my desire for audacious trash. I also enjoy audacious trash. They straddle the line between good and bad taste more than any other gameplay mechanic.

On the other hand, moral choices normalize violence by setting morality apart from the killing that takes place in moment-to-moment gameplay. In *BioShock*, only Little Sisters fall under the game's moral rubric. You only have to kill one to be ineligible for the game's "good" ending. The hundreds of Splicers you kill don't factor into it. Their deaths are amoral. We could argue their deaths don't matter because the player was just defending him- or herself, but that's a paper-thin rationalization. The only reason it's okay to kill a Splicer is because killing them is the point of the game. First-person shooters exist because people want to shoot things. A thought-provoking, well-written shooter is not exempt from this truth. In these games, a moral choice positively reinforces the idea that might equals right; making the good choice lets a player feel heroic despite his or her violent actions.

On the third hand (my secret hand that no one knows about), I think moral choices conveniently shift the burden of morality from the designer to the player. Unlike other artistic media, games are treated as a form of audience expression rather than the artist's. We've spent years telling players, "This is about what *you* want to do."

If you Google "PlayStation Greatness Awaits," you'll find an advertisement in which a grinning man walks through a ruined city while extoling the virtues of you, the player. "Who are you not to be great?" he asks. "Who are you to be afraid? You, who can serve as judge and jury while hoarding infinite lives?"

In PlayStation's "Michael" commercial, video-game characters gather in a bar to share stories about the player who saved their lives and did the impossible. It wasn't Kratos who killed Hades or those American soldiers who stormed Normandy Beach. It was Michael. "For all he does," says the bartender, "for all of us."

"To Michael!" they shout. "To Michael!"

Only a kid or a very sad adult would take these commercials to heart. Most people will see them for what they are—pandering. That doesn't change the fact they are an extreme echo of our design methodology, Player First.

What will the player want?

What will they think?

What will they do?

We've been asking ourselves these questions for so long that we've forgotten how to ask our own questions. "What do I want? What am I doing? What does this mean?" We've removed ourselves from the equation. Nothing makes that more obvious than the rhetoric we spew in support of moral choices.

"It's the player's choice."

No, it's not. We conceived it and built it. The choice is ours. Forcing it onto someone else does not excuse us from moral obligation. If we believe games can establish and reinforce social norms, then our obligation is to the future, not the player. We are the architects of these digital worlds; the power to design a better future is in our hands.

Like I said, I'm very conflicted when it comes to moral choices. The one thing I'm certain of is you should strive to make your game as engaging as possible. Moral choices can do that, but only if you can resist the pathological need to validate the player.

Validation is for assholes.

Good people—by which I mean genuinely compassionate, caring, and empathetic people—don't need validation. They have chosen an outward-facing worldview that focuses on other people. For them, validation is unnecessary.

But take me, for example. I'm vain, insecure, and mildly narcissistic; in other words, an asshole. Validation is all I crave. Without it, the precariously constructed illusion that is my self-image would collapse, leaving me exposed as the fraud I secretly believe myself to be.

I'm convinced nothing good comes from validating assholes who are not me.

For *Spec Ops*, we decided the moral choices couldn't just be dark and gritty. To do that would have been exploitation, shock for shock's sake. If we wanted our game to truly be compelling, the underlying question of our choices couldn't be, "What is right and what is wrong?" We needed to attack the core of our own game by asking the player, "What are you going to do with the gun in your hand?"

The Wailing Virgin was thrown out almost immediately. It would have been a difficult choice for the player to make, but one that would have played off their annoyance. It would have been too cheap. Instead, we created a new example called "the Hanging Men."

The player finds two men hanging from a street sign by their wrists. Snipers line the street, guns pointed at the player. It's all a tableau designed by Konrad to prove a point.

KONRAD

The civilian on the right stole water—a capital offense.

The soldier on the left was sent to apprehend him. Which he did,

killing the man's family in the process. Five innocent people are dead,

because these two animals couldn't control themselves. They are guilty.

But what is justice? And how would you see it dealt? Who lives? Who dies?

Judge these men, or pay the price of insubordination.

The idea was to present the player with a binary choice that actually had more than two options. The player was told to kill the refugee or the soldier, which they could do. But they could also walk away, attack the snipers, free both men by shooting the ropes from which they hang, or stand there and do nothing. Again, it all came down to the question "What are you going to do with the gun in your hand?" In the case of the Hanging Men, the possible answers were "Exactly what the game tells me to do" or "Whatever the hell I want."

The twist was that none of the outcomes would play out the way you might expect. Walk away and refuse to play Konrad's game? The snipers kill both prisoners. Attack the snipers and it will trigger combat, killing both prisoners in the crossfire. If you free the prisoners by shooting their ropes, Konrad's snipers will execute them both. We gave the player every option we could think of, but none of them would lead to success. In fact, the only way the player could save anyone was to do as Konrad ordered by executing either the soldier or the refugee. The snipers would then free whoever was still alive and let them escape.

The Hanging Men were a message from us to the player—you are not in charge here. This world will not bend to your wishes.

From there, we designed six more choices, each contextually different but thematically the same. Only the Hanging Men were presented as a literal choice. The others were just moments that arose in the story. For example, the first American soldier you meet in the game is Lt. McPherson, who you witness killing a CIA operative in cold blood. Stunned by your arrival, he raises his gun above his head as a sign of nonaggression and then slowly backs away. You, the player, decide what to do with the gun in your hand. You can shoot the Lieutenant or not, because those are the only two things you can do with a gun. If you let McPherson leave, he'll come back with more soldiers and try to kill you. At that point, the choice is taken from you: one of you has to die. If you want to keep playing the game, it'll have to be McPherson.

Later, another CIA agent named Riggs convinces you to help him steal the city's water supply from Konrad's men. When you do, he betrays you and destroys it, dooming everyone in the city to die of thirst. The act leaves him pinned underneath a water truck that is slowly being engulfed in flames. He asks you to shoot him. "Please, Walker. Don't let me burn." Do you pull the trigger or leave it be?

Any other game would have added these choices together to calculate whether the player deserved the good or bad ending. I've never liked that system; it's unrealistic. Humans are flawed. We all make mistakes. Our only salvation is that we're able to learn from them and hopefully become better people. When a game assigns a particular ending based on the player's earlier choices, it is saying, "Only your past is important. There can be no change of heart, no lessons learned. The person you are now does not matter." Fuck that noise.

With *Spec Ops*, we kept the choices coming all the way to the very end. In the game's final moments, the player looks back on everything they've done—none of it good—and is told to judge him- or herself while holding a pistol to their own head.

"What are you going to do with the gun in your hand?"

A well-designed moral choice should sear itself into the player's brain, like a hand burnt on a hot stove. Will it cause outrage? Yes. It should. Your gut will tell you to tone it down; make it more palatable so players won't be too put off. Your gut is wrong. You created something monstrous; let that mother roar.

I can hear your sad little cries all the way from the future. "B-b-but it's just a game!" No. This stopped being a game the moment we all decided it was cool to be transgressive. If we're going to present players with deplorable choices, then by God, we have to stand by them. Games are art, but sometimes they barely rise to the level of a Thomas Kinkade painting. Art doesn't embrace the viewer; it grabs them by the arm and drags them out back into an alley filled with shit and needles.

A moral choice should be dirty and dangerous and frightening. It needs to make players look over their shoulders just to be sure no one is watching. Repulse your players. *Seduce* them. Leave them so ashamed they want to vomit and touch themselves at the same time. They shouldn't be spared the memory of what they've done. They shouldn't be spared at all.

13

DEVELOPMENT NEVER CHANGES

Production on *Spec Ops: The Line* began in 2007, with a plan to release in 2009. That didn't happen. All we got was an announcement. On December 12, 2009, we unveiled our first trailer at the Spike Video Game Awards. That was a victory of sorts. We had managed to release *something* in 2009, just under the wire. Instead of releasing our game, we announced it to the world for the first time. It wasn't the original plan, but it gave us a desperately needed morale boost. People were excited. We entered 2010 fully convinced we could rally our efforts and ship *Spec Ops* by the end of the year. All we had to do was get on track to reach alpha.

In game development, you have many phases: alpha, beta, gold master, just to name a few. Gold, as we've already discussed, is software that's been released to the manufacturer. Beta software is feature complete, meaning everything that should be in the game is now in the game, albeit in a very buggy, unpolished form. Alpha is the validation phase, where you try different approaches and systems to see if they'll work. This is a broad definition of alpha. To be honest, every studio defines it differently. That's in part due to our terrible naming convention.

There is pre-alpha, which is any development activity that occurs prior to alpha. Then, there is the alpha phase, as described above. Being *in* alpha doesn't mean you *are* alpha, it means you're striving to *become* alpha. When you believe your game has reached alpha, you prepare an alpha candidate, which is a version of your game meant for review. You'll send it over to your publisher, who will review against the alpha definition put forth in your milestone agreement. If the build is alpha certified, then your game has reached alpha, at which point you are instantly thrown into the beta phase.

At this point in the production of *Spec Ops*, we were trying to reach alpha. It wasn't going well. There were a myriad of factors involving both publishing and development, but the most prominent was the Fox. He had begun suggesting new features to Yager, random ideas he thought would transform the game into something unique and sellable. Some were good, others were ludicrous. What they had in common was that they were all outside the game's scope.

When it came time for alpha approval, the game met the milestone requirements, but the Fox still wanted more features. Rather than proceed to beta, it was decided *Spec Ops* would move into alpha 2.0. Then, alpha 3.0. And so on. The longer we stayed in alpha, the more hesitant Yager became toward the Fox's suggestions. A good idea isn't worth anything if you don't have the time to implement it and polish it. We were already behind schedule, so in Yager's eyes, every new suggestion was just another delay.

"Don't they understand I'm trying to help them?" he asked me one day. "I want to make the game better."

"They get that, but you're working against the production schedule. They're trying to meet their deliverables, and you keep adding to their to-do list."

"We're not going to ship a game that isn't good. I don't care if it meets the milestones."

"You and Bonnie need to speak to Yager together. Because right now, they're getting mixed messages. They're like a kid trying to finish their chores, and you keep showing up and offering them candy.

"You say, 'Want some candy?' and Yager says, 'Bonnie told us to finish our chores. She'll get mad if we stop to eat candy.' But you won't let up. You're like, 'It's really good candy, though. Bonnie will understand if you stop to have some.'

"You push and you push until finally Yager gives in. They reach out to take the candy from your hand, at which point Bonnie steps out from behind you and punches Yager in the face. 'What are you doing?' she screams. 'You don't have time to eat candy! Get back to work!'

"And then, as soon as Bonnie's gone, you reach back into your pocket and pull out another piece of candy."

The Fox thought about it for a moment and then nodded. "That's a pretty accurate metaphor."

"I know. That's why you pay me to write things."

My visits to Berlin, once only two weeks long, soon stretched to months at a time. My apartment in San Rafael, California, became nothing but an expensive storage room. My true home was an apartment in East Berlin, located in the neighborhood of Friedrichshain, one block from the Karl-Marx-Allee. It contained none of the amenities you might find in a hotel: no cooked meals, fresh sheets, Internet, television, phone—the things which made working on-site tolerable. Internet, that most basic of modern human rights, was limited to my time at Yager's office during work hours. Since I was the publisher, they felt it was inappropriate for me to have free access to their office when no one was around. Aside from my work-issued BlackBerry, the Internet was my only access to my life back in the States. And I could only use it Monday through Friday, barring holidays, of course. During this time, I received a call from our corporate office in New York, informing me that I'd rung up the second largest phone bill in Take-Two history. I don't know the amount, but it was bad. I apologized and explained that I was in Germany, having to use my BlackBerry for regular Internet access. This got passed down the line, through the Fox and on to Yager, who finally gifted me with a key to the office. Unlimited Internet access was mine, seven days a week, so long as I was willing to walk the mile and a half from my apartment to the office.

With full-time access, work became my only priority. If I worked harder and longer, I could single-handedly drag *Spec Ops*, kicking and screaming, across the finish line. It wasn't ego that drove me; it was desperation. No matter how long the project dragged on, at the end of the day, everyone got to go home. Everyone except me. I couldn't leave until it was over.

To hurry things along, I wrote all the time—at home, on the plane, during meetings. I'd print out script pages and design documents and take them with me wherever I went, along with a collection of colored pens. Someone once commented that you could always tell whether a page had been edited by me, because it looked like someone had stabbed a hobo to death on top of it. Ever since, I've used an array of colors— red, green, blue, pink, burgundy, teal—to help track my different notes. Burgundy was, and still is, the best. It straddles red and black in a way I find visually delectable.

It didn't matter if we were out to lunch or in a meeting, I was editing. While in California, during a brief return from Berlin, the Fox volunteered me for an in-house playtest of the *Spec Ops* multiplayer mode. Next to my monitor was my script. Whenever I died in the game, I'd have to wait before my character would respawn in the match. The respawn timer was just long enough that I could edit two or three lines before having to continue playing.

The Fox looked over from his on-screen killing spree. "Are you editing scripts?"

I checked the timer. "For another thirteen seconds, I am."

"I love you."

"No you don't. You just love how I crunch."

CRUNCH. ONE OF THE most loathed words in our industry. It's that period of time in which a team must tighten their belts, buckle down, and work more than the standard forty-hour work week. During crunch, it's not uncommon to work ten- to twelve-hour days, seven days a week. Crunch can last a week. It can last six months. It drains you, literally sucks your life away. Time flies by, and you have no idea where it went because you were locked in a dim room for a month, surviving on lattes and Cheetos, the pale glow of your monitor mirroring the fading light in your eyes.

Yes, Crunch is that fun. And yeah, I'm going to capitalize Crunch as if it were a proper noun, because Crunch is not some idle concept or a construct of the human mind; Crunch is a demon lord, hiding behind the no-charge Coke machine, laughing as you guzzle down those free sodas, knowing that each delicious slurp sells off tiny pieces of your soul, and that soon—so very soon—that bill's gonna come due and Crunch'll step out into the light and there will be weeping and gnashing of teeth as the hope vanishes from your overly caffeinated eyes because you know this is all your fault; it was you who allowed this foul demon into your midst and now your ass belongs to Him.

When I think about Crunch, my heart races. It only takes an instant for my eyes to drift off into that thousand-yard stare, and then it all comes rushing back. My head goes all swimmy, like I haven't slept in forty-eight hours. My tongue dries up, aching for the disgustingly sweet taste of Red Bull. My mouth wants to rage and howl and spit until designers and directors alike bow to my creative will.

All hail Crunch.

There are many arguments against Crunch. Crunch is exploitive (true). Employees feel their jobs are at risk if they resist the will of Crunch (also true). And, most damning of all, Crunch isn't necessary (so true it hurts).

Opponents of Crunch claim it is avoidable. If our industry learned basic time-management skills and exercised restraint, we could ship games on time and on budget without Crunch's shadow ever crossing our door. It's true; all of it. Conveniently so. That tends to be the case with demons, even metaphorical ones. It's why they make such easy villains—you never have to give them a second thought. But nothing's ever as clear-cut as it seems. There is another side to Crunch you can rarely hear over the sound of righteous indignation. Luckily, it's just you and me right now, all by our lonesome—no message boards or comment posts to get in our way. So, let's turn down the lights and get to cuddling, because I'm about to whisper sweet truths in your ear.

"IT'S ONLY CRUNCH IF YOU DON'T WANT TO DO IT."

Crunch isn't a pandemic or a death march. It's not even exclusive to the games industry. If anything, Crunch is a natural occurrence brought on by the creative process. Driven by passion, artists give themselves entirely to their art. When art exists in a collaborative medium, Crunch will always deal collateral damage. How much damage you personally sustain will always be inversely related to your investment in the project.

Listen: someday you will find yourself Crunching on someone else's project, hating every wasted second. You will rant and rage and pray to gods in which you don't believe, begging them to strike down this corrupt system so that something pure and good may grow in its place. Your prayers will go unheard, but take heart—you have not been forsaken. The system is not broken; it is, in fact, working exactly as designed.

When you choose to enter a collaborative field, you become a cog in a machine. It is inevitable you will work on a project you do not like, under terrible conditions, for miserable pay. When it happens, take comfort in the knowledge that you are not being melodramatic. Your situation is truly as bad as it seems. Afterward, once you've stopped feeling sorry for yourself, be happy with the fact that your sacrifice is helping bring someone else's vision to life. You may think the vision is terrible—and I'm sure it is—but even shitty ideas mean something to someone. If you find no pleasure in helping others achieve their shitty dreams, then you can always quit. Or, you can Crunch hard, keep your wits about you, and try not to lose your head. If you manage that, someday you may get to be the asshole building their dreams on the backs of those less fortunate.

Ooooh, shivers. What's that? You want more? Well, okay then.

"WE ONLY CARE ABOUT CRUNCH WHEN IT DOESN'T WORK."

It's easy to hate Crunch when you don't like the end result. However, when Crunch results in a game people love, then it wasn't Crunch at all—it was Passion. That's the lie we tell ourselves, because it's the one you let us believe. Polish and innovation come at a cost. Not to you, of course. You'll only pay sixty bucks and not a dollar more, because you lack the ability to measure the value of digital goods either through cost or effort. If we try to sell you five-dollar downloadable content, you'll attack us with negative reviews, claiming we're trying to nickel-and-dime you. But if we package our game with a plastic figure and book of concept art, you'll shell out an easy hundred because it's "limited." It's this same mentality that allows you to say Crunch is plaguing our industry while shouting, "Masterpiece!" at games that laid waste to the hearts and minds of their developers. You're a bunch of fucking hypocrites, but it's okay—so are we. We're happy to Crunch when we believe it will pay off for us individually. There's a reason studio owners, creative directors, and people who drive Lamborghinis never complain about working too hard. It's only when the payout is less than the wager that we get pissy.

Just saying it makes me feel dirty. Still not there yet? No worries; I have one more.

"SOME OF US ACTUALLY LIKE IT."

Here's a secret about growing up that no one tells you. When you're young, your body is basically a meth lab, bubbling over with all sorts of hormones and strange chemical reactions. You don't realize it, but you're getting high on your own supply twenty-four-seven. Everything you feel is vivid and intense and seems like it'll never end. But it does. In time, the hormones stop bubbling, the chemicals even out, and you become a more-or-less sane human being. The problem is, you never forget the high. Without it, you'll always feel less than you once were, as if you lost a vital part of your soul. You're going to chase that high for a long time. Booze, drugs, sex, love, work, art—anything that allows you to let go and give yourself completely—that's where you'll find it. There's nothing wrong with the high. The high is natural. The high is *good*. It's the chase that kills you.

Crunch is my chase, and it leads me to a high that's like Vegas, Amsterdam, and Bangkok rolled into one. See, there are few things I love more than being in a fight. It fills my need for power, pain, and righteous indignation. If I win, I'm a god. If I lose, I'm a martyr. Both feel fucking stellar. No sir, there's nothing bad about a fight. And Crunch is a fight from start to finish. It's the entire development process condensed into a never-ending string of dustups, like in *Game of Death*, starring Bruce Lee. Except instead of Kareem Abdul-Jabbar, you're fighting tech, memory, art, design, publishers, players, reviewers, budgets, schedules, weekends, egos, studio closures, unpaid royalties, cultural relevance—the list goes on and on.

When I worship at the unholy altar of Crunch, everything outside of the work fades away. By design, my world is reduced to where I sleep and where I work. Every day must be fast, focused, and above all else, homogenized. Give myself too much downtime, too much room to think, and I start asking questions, like "Why am I doing this to myself?" So, I lose myself in the routine. When every day is a rehash of what has been, and a preview of what will be, they blend into one another. This creates an out-of-body effect, not unlike highway hypnosis. Soon, who I am becomes an abstract concept—a loose collection of character flaws and neurotic tendencies. Only then can my body become the vessel through which an impossible amount of work will be accomplished in a short amount of time.

I love it, except for when I hate it, but I can't hate it if I never stop. Even when I'm not crunching, I work too much. I've edited scripts in ICU rooms, responded to emails while begging lovers not to walk out the door, sent brainstorming lists during the birth of my child. I held my grandfather's hand while he passed away, then went into his office and wrote text for mission descriptions. None of this was expected of me, and no one would have dared to ask. I did all these things for me. Work brings order to my world. When things get tough, I slide down into my job and disappear. I let my health, relationships, and responsibilities fall to the wayside. When I finally come up for air, there's a smoking crater where my life used to be. Instead of picking up the pieces to start again, I slip back down into the thick of it. This is how I cope.

My muscles ache for no reason. Sleep eludes me. I sit in my living room with the lights off and stare at the wall. When I manage to doze off, I am plagued by recurring dreams in which I'm trapped in a plummeting elevator, or buried alive, unable to move. It may sound like torture, but it fills me with a sense of purpose and potency. This is what God must feel like when he's on a bender.

This isn't an endorsement, by the way. It's the confession of an addict. Some people will say it shouldn't be like this, that making games shouldn't come with so high a price. And in a perfect world, maybe they'd be right. It's clear what kind of world we wish for; its design has repeatedly appeared in our games for decades.

Our perfect world is not devoid of struggle or opposition, but the path to victory is much more certain. Hard work always results in positive growth, a growth measured in strength and power. What once held us back can easily be overcome if we just put in the grind. So long as we keep working, we will continue to grow stronger. Our bodies will never flag or waver. We are forever young, and there is no obstacle we cannot overcome.

That's not our world. In this plane of existence, we are limited. We can accomplish almost anything, but only if we're willing to pay the price. It may not be fair, and it definitely won't be the same price quoted to someone else, but it will still need to be paid. In this industry, we all make sacrifices: love, life, health—those things we're told we cannot live without. It's natural to wish things weren't this way, but it won't change anything. You either agree to the cost or move on with your life. Those who rail against it are either naïve or bitter—they paid the price and didn't go as far as they had hoped. That's the risk you take. Being an artist is not easy. Selling your soul will not always bear a profit.

I've paid the price more than once. In return, I more or less got exactly what I wanted—I shouted into the void and the void shouted back, "We hear you." That puts me in a unique position to look back on the past ten years and ask, "Was it honestly worth it?"

I don't know. But I know the price was fair.

14

AIRPLANES

As 2010 ticked away, it became clear we wouldn't make our deadline.

"I want to push alpha 3.0 back another six months," said the Fox. "Think you can handle that?"

"Yeah, but only six. If you delay it again, I'm done." It was meant as a threat. I wanted to motivate everyone to band together so we could hurry up and ship the game. The problem is, a threat is only effective if people believe you'll follow through on it. I didn't know it then, but I was weak. No matter what I said or felt, I'd never be strong enough to walk away.

The Fox knew. He always knew.

To stay focused, I developed a routine. I woke every morning with the sunrise. Next to my bed was a wooden chair I used as a nightstand. On it, you'd find Adderall, a bottle of water, and the half-eaten remains of a large bag of Peanut M&M's and can of paprika-flavored Pringles. This was my breakfast, seven days a week.

On my way to the office each morning, I bought and drank a one-and-a-half-liter bottle of soda. Upon arriving at work, I'd chase the soda with two lattes. For the next hour, I would surf the Internet. This was the most essential part of my day.

By the time everyone else arrived at work, I'd be awake enough to communicate like a normal human being. I would make my rounds, doing quick reviews with individuals but never as a team. Group reviews felt clunky and disruptive. A one-on-one discussion was what you wanted. In ten minutes or less, you could cut straight to the important bits: What are you working on? Can you show it to me? Are you happy with it? Is there anything I can do to help? How much longer until it's done? That was all I needed to know.

When the team broke for lunch, I began to write. Fewer people meant fewer distractions. My own meal wouldn't come until my blood sugar dropped low enough that I had no choice. From there, it was afternoon meetings and end-of-day reviews. Then, as the others began to head home, I'd tuck in for another round of writing.

Work would carry me past the time when restaurants and bars would stop serving food. My only option for dinner was a convenience store next to my apartment. Every night, I bought a large bag of Peanut M&M's and a can of paprika Pringles. And every night, the same old man was working the register. For the seven or eight months I did this, we never said more than one word to each other.

"Cheers."

Back in my room, I'd eat half the candy and chips and then crawl into bed, where I'd lie awake for hours, trying to ignore the people fucking upstairs. There is nothing worse than the sound of people having sex when you are not. I know this because whoever lived above me had a libido so insatiable that it had to be fed at least once every two hours. Every squeak, gasp, and cry made me an unwitting participant in their coupling and only served to amplify my loneliness. When it got to be too much, I'd walk—night after night, for hours at a time, until my body felt tired enough to fall asleep and stay asleep no matter how loud they were.

Somehow, my dreams were always worse.

I remember dreaming of fire. My apartment burned and I ran into the street, where a crowd had gathered. I watched the crowd. They watched the fire. One man in the crowd watched me. He walked across the street to reach me and then stabbed me in the neck.

I awoke in Berlin, pain in my neck. I checked for blood, but my throat was unmarred. Was it scissors, a pen, what? I couldn't remember. Either it had happened too fast for me to see or the dream was already fading. Only the sensation remained. I tried to rub it away, but my left hand was numb. I'd heard your left arm goes numb right before a heart attack. I knew from experience that it also goes numb if you sleep on it or if you have a pinched nerve. I felt a slight pain in my chest. Was it real, or was I imagining it into existence? It occurred to me that I might be dying.

I had two choices: I could get out of bed, put on pants, and go outside. If I were about to have a heart attack, someone would see me and be able to help. Or, I could stay in bed. Not move. With cardiac arrest, I'd be dead within minutes. All of this would finally be over.

I stayed in bed for half an hour. Still not dead, I got up and went to work.

"YOU LOOK TERRIBLE," SAID the Fox. "Like you've been covering an actual war from the front lines."

I said, "I'm not sleeping very well," as if that would explain my appearance.

I leaned against the wall in the Fox's office in Novato. My eyes had sunk into deep, dark circles. I hadn't shaved or cut my hair in months. Some dev teams do this as a sign of solidarity—no one shaves until the game ships. My unkempt appearance was born from a complete disregard for my physical well-being that went beyond overgrown hair. What had started as a sore neck a few weeks prior had spread down to my hands. Once it reached my fingers, I lost all feeling in my extremities; the only sensation was a vague numbness, like I'd fallen asleep on my arms. When not writing, my hands would make fists, trying to feel something.

"How's the game going?" he asked.

My response was involuntary: a short, shrill laugh that made the Fox pull back.

"Sorry. It's going. The game is going. It goes."

I saw the Fox's eyes light up, the way they did when he thought of something clever. "You might be the first writer to have PTSD without ever having gone to war. *Pre*-traumatic stress disorder!"

Instead of a laugh, this got a blank stare. He seemed disappointed. "Anyway . . . I've been playing this week's build, and the game isn't where I expected it to be. What do you say to another six months?"

I didn't say anything; I just walked out. I'd reached the far side of a crowded room before the Fox called after me.

"Where are you going?"

"Home. Call me when you decide you want to make a fucking game."

It was only 10:00 a.m. I'd been at work all of forty-five minutes. The Fox did not fire me.

Out of options, I persevered. I convinced myself that this was it. This time we would get it right. Finish the game. Win my freedom.

"If you delay it again, I'm done." I swear, I meant it every time I said it.

SPEND ENOUGH TIME WORKING on a game, and you begin second-guessing yourself. An idea that seemed great at the beginning will grow old and stale as time goes on. It feels boring to you, so you convince yourself that the player will feel the same. This happens on every game. If you're not careful, it can lead you to question your entire design, down to the smallest detail. By *Spec Ops*'s third year of development, we'd fallen into this trap a few times, and it was beginning to wear on the team.

Back in Berlin, I was having lunch with Xander, one of Yager's visual-effects designers.

"I've been thinking of making a comic strip about game development," he said. "I'd call it 'What if We Made Airplanes?' Every strip would be a single panel of people gathered around a whiteboard, trying to design an airplane the way we design video games.

" 'There's nothing special about flying. Any plane can do that. What if—just hear me out—what if we put the wings on the *inside*?'

" 'I'm telling you, once passengers see how much work we put into our tray tables, they won't care that the plane doesn't have any seats.'

" 'Of course they're going to crash. These things are really hard to build.' "

Every joke was spot-on, but I was finding it hard to laugh. My arms had been numb for weeks. I was starting to get worried. Xander believed the numbness was probably due to stress and tight muscles. It seemed plausible; I hadn't taken a day off since I started living there.

"Everyone needs to rest sometime," he said. "And you'll be no good to us if you're dead."

On Xander's advice, I scheduled a massage for that Saturday. It worked, to an extent. Afterward, my arms were still numb, but feeling was beginning to return to my hands. Maybe my friend had been right about the tight muscles.

The sky that day was overcast. As I walked home to my apartment, the clouds finally opened and began to rain. Having left my umbrella at home, I ducked into an archway to wait it out. From there, I watched rain fall on an empty street and felt more alone than I ever had. I began to cry so hard, I had to sit down. As I bawled into my hands, I realized that that massage had been my first physical contact with another person in almost three months.

"MAYBE I'M DEAD."

I was back in California, catching up with my normal coworkers, who I hadn't seen in months. Some of them, I'd never seen at all. "My plane probably crashed in the ocean, or maybe my heart gave out. Whatever happened, I'm dead, this is hell, and you're all a bunch of fucking demons."

Everyone laughed, like I knew they would.

"It's the only explanation I can think of for this endless string of delays. I am Sisyphus, and *Spec Ops* is the stone I'll be rolling uphill for all eternity, six months at a time. Hell isn't war or pain or other people. Hell is hope. Everything exists in a perpetual state of decay, and yet we honestly believe things will get better? That's not denial; it's insanity.

"I'm worried that since I've figured it out, hell will have to change. If I know *Spec Ops* will never ship, then hope dies, and my punishment becomes ineffective. Hell will have to convince me I'm still alive, which means now the game *will* ship. Then I'll go about my life thinking everything is fine, until someday I'm dying in a hospital bed and someone shows up—maybe a janitor or a nurse—and as the light fades from my eyes, they'll lean in and whisper in my ear, 'You were right.' Then it'll start all over again."

I'd told the story just right; smiled and winked in the appropriate places. You can't tell a story like that if it's not funny, and this one needed telling. It had gripped my mind, and I could feel its words on my tongue.

There is something about the tangible nature of speech that makes even the darkest thoughts manageable. Once spoken, they lose power. Not all of it, but enough that you want to keep repeating it, chipping away with every repetition until the words no longer hold sway.

"Maybe I'm dead, and this is all a lie."

ONE MONDAY, IN OCTOBER of 2011, something clicked inside my head. Being in Berlin wasn't helping. Nothing I did would ship the game any faster. I don't know if it was true or if the thought just made me feel better, but I decided to act on it. I sent an email to my travel agent, requesting a one-way ticket home. The next day, I went around to the team and said, "If there's anything you need from me by the end of the week, let me know, because I'm leaving and I will not be returning." By Thursday, I was gone.

By December, I was back.

In the time between, the Fox had called me into his office to discuss the game's story.

"It's good," he said. "Honestly, it's very good. It's just not good enough." He was concerned the game had missed its window. Had it been released in 2009, as originally planned, *Spec Ops* would have been cutting-edge. However, since then, military shooters had embraced the dark tone and morally gray narrative we believed would set us apart. For the project to succeed, we needed something new. It couldn't be related to gameplay; production was too far along for us to innovate and include a show-stopping feature. Story was the only avenue left.

"I need you to rework your story so that it can carry an entire AAA game." He didn't ask if I was willing to do six more months. It was understood. "Can you do that?"

"Give me a week, and I'll come up with some ideas."

THE FIRST DRAFT OF a story is like a new relationship. If you keep things moving and focus on emotions rather than details, then a first draft can be a fun, exciting experience. A rewrite is like a marriage on the rocks. It's a long, seemingly endless slog. The initial rush is long gone. Every fault of the other party is magnified, leaving you to wonder how you were drawn here in the first place. Part of you blames the "other," but deep down, you know the flaws you see are your own, reflected back at you. Your instincts tell you to run, to leave it all behind and start over. Or, you could stick it out, put in the time and effort necessary to make it work. That's rewriting.

This is important, so grab a penknife and carve it into the back of your hand—your first idea is your worst idea. Just because you had it, liked it, and wrote it down doesn't mean it's good. Real writing happens in the rewrite.

Every writer has his or her own method of dealing with a rewrite.

Some rewrite constantly. Others procrastinate, waiting until the last minute to start working. With a deadline looming, your body kicks into overdrive. Adrenaline pumps through your veins, causing your neurons to fire more quickly and make more cognitive leaps. A similar effect can be achieved through the use of numerous chemicals, some less legal than others. However, none of these "supplements" can provide you with the main benefit of procrastination—a lack of time. Writing at the eleventh hour leaves no time for self-doubt. Is the writing good, or do you just not have time to care? There's no way of knowing. It's probably good, and that's what matters. At the last minute, probably good is good enough. To work this way, you must be profoundly confident and equally stupid.

I use both methods. Throughout a project, I will rewrite constantly, often from scratch. The goal is to immerse myself completely in the story while giving myself as many options as possible. This is not so much a method as it is a result of my most stringent belief:

Everything I write is garbage.

This is the guiding principal and North Star of all my work. For me, a completed draft is not something to be edited. It is an expanded outline for the next draft, which I will write from scratch. There are no breaks in my process, no time to think and debate with myself. If I finish a draft on Tuesday, I start the next on Wednesday. Any hesitation is an opportunity to do something—literally anything—else. Writing does not happen in outlines or summaries or group discussions. It happens when you sit your ass in a chair and put letters in order. That's where the real decisions are made. You can't know if a story is worth telling until you start telling it.

I may rewrite constantly, but I do not start a final draft until the last possible minute. Procrastination galvanizes my mind, causing it to see the work in a new light, specifically through a lens of terror brought on by looming deadlines. Like plunging hot iron into cold water, my ideas coalesce into whatever shape will be their last.

I'd already gone through this process multiple times on *Spec Ops*.

Now, the Fox was asking me to wind it back to the brainstorming phase.

Upstairs in my office, I shut the door and moved a cabinet in front of the window. I could neither see nor be seen. There was a whiteboard on the wall. I grabbed a dry-erase marker and drew fifteen columns, one for each chapter. At the top, I wrote the location. In the column, I wrote two to three key words representing that chapter's events. Once that was done, I sat down in my chair and stared at it. This is how I brainstorm. That's all there is to it.

It sounds like bullshit, but ask any writer how they come up with their ideas, and they'll feed you a similar load. They take a shower, walk through the woods, or look out the window of a moving train. If you're looking for a concrete answer, you won't find one. To find the answer, you have to look for the pattern.

People get bored. When bored, people think about things to help pass the time. Sometimes, they will daydream. For creative people, daydreaming is research and development.

This is where my blackboard comes into play. By writing down key words and staring at them in silence, I focus my boredom on the task at hand. The words influence my dreaming. As ideas occur to me, I add them to the whiteboard, and the influence grows. All I need is one idea. I can grow an entire story from a single idea, simply by following the path of action and reaction. But I have to be honest with the progression of events. Sometimes I have a few ideas but can see no narrative line that pierces them all. This means some of the ideas aren't good for the story. If I refuse to let them go, then I'm being dishonest about the story's progression. This is where I can get hung up, because I like my bad ideas. I gave birth to them, and it was really exciting when I did. And, oh, I know they don't work right now, but they're going to be so good in the end, you just have to wait and see!

That's not writing a story—that's forcing a plot point. It is bad and it is wrong.

Kill the bad ideas. Burn them. Let them bleed out in a ditch. This is better than the alternative of locking them away in a notebook and promising you'll visit them, and when you do, telling them you're looking for a better story where they can live out their lives not feeling unloved and abandoned. That's a lie, the same one your children will one day tell you when they put you away in a nursing home. They say they'll visit, but deep down, you know you won't see them as much as you'd like. And when they do show up, they'll always be checking their phones to see what time it is. They still have a life to live, while you're just hanging on.

Sometimes, you just have to let go.

In *Spec Ops*, Walker's problem was that he couldn't let go. Instead of cutting his losses, he kept doubling down, hoping the risk would pay off. Our current story—the one the Fox wanted me to rewrite—played out in the most obvious way. The further the player progressed in his or her quest to find Konrad, the more damage Walker caused to the world and people around him. At the end, Walker confronts Konrad atop the tallest skyscraper in Dubai. As a final statement on his own brutality, the villain throws himself off the building. Walker wins, but only technically. There is no satisfaction, no joy in his victory. He is a broken man whose sacrifices didn't even earn him the chance to put a bullet between Konrad's eyes.

Staring at that board, I began to wonder if it was worth the effort. We'd gone back and forth on the game so many times, and here we were doing it all again. Maybe rewriting the story would finally move things forward, but there was no way to know.

What if we were doomed to fail and we just refused to let it go?

Forty-five minutes after telling the Fox I'd need a week to come up with a new story, I walked back into his office and presented the final version of *Spec Ops: The Line.*

"Konrad is dead."

The Fox sat up straight in his chair. "What do you mean he's dead?" I could see in his eyes the idea was already resonating before I even had the chance to explain it. It was the same reaction I had had when the idea first hit me.

"Walker fights his way across Dubai in search of Konrad. He tears the city apart, tears his men apart, all so he can find Konrad. And when he does, Konrad is dead. Everything Walker went through was for nothing."

"So Konrad kills himself before Walker reaches the top of his tower?"

"Uh-uh. Konrad killed himself before you even started the game."

The Fox sighed. "When I said change the story, I didn't mean rewrite the entire thing. Konrad is a major presence for half of the game. He's constantly talking to Walker over the radio. And now you want to cut all that out?"

The wickedest of grins spread across my face. "No. I want to keep it all in."

"Then who's Walker talking to?"

"Nobody. Walker is fucking crazy."

Ding! The lights clicked on behind the Fox's eyes. This was what we'd been looking for.

If this was going to work, Walker couldn't start off unstable. That would be cheating. When a player starts a game, they become their character. At that moment, they need to understand the character's state of mind. You don't need to tell the player much—who they are, why they're here, and what they're doing—but it's still vital information. Anything that doesn't relate to the character's immediate motivation is irrelevant. For example, is Walker married? I don't know, and neither does the player, because it doesn't matter. Walker being married has no bearing on him or the game; therefore it has nothing to do with his state of mind.

Mental instability is different, because it is a literal state of mind. When the player inhabits Walker, they step into his head. At that moment, they would need to be told of Walker's instability; otherwise they are playing the character under false pretense. Basically, they'd be living a lie. A lie we forced upon them for the sake of a surprising twist.

To earn Walker's insanity, we needed to break him emotionally and psychologically. There had to be a moment when Walker, under the player's control, committed an act so terrible it could conceivably shatter his mind. If it took place during a cinematic, it would again be cheating. Walker can only do what the player wants him to do. They are the same person inhabiting two different bodies, one real and one digital. If Walker's mental breakdown was caused by a moment outside of the player's control, then they would no longer be in sync, and the twist would not work.

In chapter 8, Walker and his team stumble upon an encampment of Konrad's men. They are hopelessly outnumbered. To engage the enemy in a firefight would be suicide. The only way for them to progress is to use a white phosphorus mortar taken from Konrad's soldiers.

If you don't know what white phosphorus is, I recommend you don't Google it. White phosphorus is an allotrope that burns extremely hot and is capable of igniting cloth, fuel, munitions, and flesh. Once ignited, white phosphorus will burn until it is deprived of oxygen or completely consumed. This is especially bad for people, because phosphorus sticks to skin. If it lands on you, you can't brush it off. The allotrope will burn deep into your tissue until it has run its course. If you survive the fire, there's a good chance the phosphorus has now entered your blood through the wounds it created, meaning you can look forward to multiple organ failure. White phosphorus is a terrible weapon, and it is 100 percent legal.

Walker orders Adams to set up the mortar. Lugo disagrees.

LUGO
You've seen what this shit does. You know we can't use it.

ADAMS

We might not have a choice, Lugo.

LUGO

There's always a choice.

WALKER

No, there's really not.

Adams does as he's told.

The mortar launches a camera into the air. As it slowly descends on a parachute, it broadcasts its view in black and white to a targeting computer manned by Walker. It is an image evocative of the AC-130 footage I watched during my field training. The enemies are reduced to white dots running around a black screen. The player, as Walker, shouts targeting coordinates to Adams, who launches white phosphorus onto the soldiers below.

It's a one-sided battle that ends quickly, but before it does the camera catches sight of a large group of soldiers attempting to retreat through a trench. The player tells Adams to fire. No one survives. It's only afterward, when the player moves through the carnage, that they realize the truth of what they've done. The soldiers' deaths were terrible, but they were your enemy. The people in the trench were not. They were civilians—men, women, and children—trying to escape the combat zone. You didn't know, because you couldn't see them. The targeting system had reduced them to white dots on a screen. All you cared was that the dots stopped moving.

This is the moment Walker breaks. He wasn't the only one.

I was in Berlin when I got an email from the Fox. They'd focus-tested the scene for the first time. Immediately following it, many of the testers paused the game and left the room. They couldn't continue playing without having time to comprehend what they'd just done.

It was the best news I'd had in months.

Walker was unable to accept what he'd done, and it broke him. To protect his sanity, he projected his guilt onto Konrad, unaware the man was already dead. As the rest of Walker's mind unraveled, he hallucinated himself having conversations with Konrad through a walkie-talkie Walker believed had been left for him to find.

The haunting didn't stop there. I wanted the player to come under attack even when they weren't playing. When a game has to load a new level or location, it will bring up a loading screen, usually a black screen or a static image. Normally, loading screens will also display a small bit of text, giving the player helpful hints or gameplay tips. They're innocuous and mostly forgettable. That's why we decided to use them as a weapon of psychological assault; the player would never see it coming.

At the start of the game, our loading screen text was normal:

> "Remember, you can sprint by pressing down on the Left
> Thumb Stick."
> "Captain Walker is a member of Delta Force, an elite unit of
> the US Army."

As the story progressed, the tone of our loading screen text began to shift. Instead of discussing the game, it educated the player on thematic, real-world topics:

> "Cognitive dissonance is an uncomfortable feeling caused by
> holding two conflicting ideas simultaneously."
> "The US military does not condone the killing of unarmed
> combatants. But this isn't real, so why should you care?"

Finally, near the end of the game, the loading screens began addressing players directly, calling them out for the atrocities they and Walker had committed since starting the game:

"If you were a better person, you wouldn't be here."

"This is all your fault."

"Do you feel like a hero yet?"

Not everyone was comfortable with the new direction. Whereas before, we were often asked if people would play a game that made them feel bad, we were now asked a new question.

"What if people stop playing?"

My response was always the same. "If the game makes them uncomfortable, they *should* stop playing." I could say this because I knew people wouldn't stop. They'd keep going because we had trained them to believe they were the good guys. No matter how bad things got, everything would work out in the end, because that's what happens when you're the hero. All they'd need to do is reach the end and defeat Konrad, then their guilt would be washed away.

This is what I meant when I said the player and Walker are the same person. They really are. Every motivation Walker has in the game is designed to mirror the motivation of someone playing a video game. That's why at the end of the game, when Walker learns the truth of what's happening, he's asked to accept blame for what he's done. Standing face-to-face with a hallucination of Konrad, the player holds a gun to their own head and must decide if they can live with what they've done. The choice is simple: Shoot Konrad or shoot yourself.

When the game was released, some players found this choice to be unfair. They felt we, the developers, had forced them to do terrible things and were casting the blame onto them. These people missed the point.

If Walker was the player, then Konrad was the developer. John Konrad wasn't ordered to evacuate people from Dubai; he volunteered, just as Yager had originally offered their services to 2K. They all became trapped in the storm. The Colonel and the studio were desperate to bring order to their worlds, but as time went on, the game and development only grew darker. In the end, they both built the same thing—a city of rules and horror, locked in constant opposition. Faced with this knowledge, Konrad chose to end his life. He took leave of his creation and left it for someone else to sort out. This is what developers do when their game finally ships. We build a world and then walk away so players can clean it up.

Spec Ops: The Line wasn't a war story. It was the story of you and me.

I MADE IT CLEAR to the Fox that I wouldn't stay in Berlin for more than two weeks at a time. He agreed, and my East Berlin apartment was traded in for a hotel that had TVs mounted to the wall at the end of every hallway, endlessly playing *The Big Lebowski* on repeat. My theory that I had died and gone to hell was only gaining more traction.

In December, when we were both in Berlin, I told the Fox I wanted to relocate to Dallas. My grandfather had been in and out of the hospital. My mother, having torn a ligament, had lost the use of her right arm. The rest of my family was old, and getting older. I wanted to be near them so I could help, but also because I felt as if I were losing valuable time.

I knew this was asking a lot, which is why I suggested Dallas rather than my hometown. Instead of a six-hour flight, I would be a three-hour drive away from my family. From there, I could use DFW airport to travel anywhere the Fox needed me to go. It was the perfect compromise.

"Let's talk about it after the new year," he said. It seemed like a fair request, so I agreed.

When I brought it up again in January, he said, "Finish the script first, then we'll talk." He wasn't comfortable letting me leave until the work was done. Again, I understood.

By February, the script was done. We traveled to Berlin and delivered it to Yager. After a week of meetings, everything was approved for implementation. As we were preparing to leave, I broached the topic once more.

"This isn't a great time," he said. "Maybe we can revisit the idea in June or July."

I said, "Okay. I understand." And I did. This was how the Fox dealt with unwanted situations. He didn't like to say no. Instead, he repeatedly pushed off making a decision until the other person took the hint and stopped asking.

It's hard to tell when you've reached the end of a road, because the end looks a lot like a rough patch. Smooth asphalt gives way to uneven dirt and stone. You keep driving, waiting for that smoothness to reappear, but it's not until the blacktop has long since vanished from your rearview that you realize it is truly gone. You keep driving, because to stop would be to accept that you have wasted many, many miles. So you drive on, desperately looking for another road. If you can find it, everything will be all right. You'll be back on track. You won't get lost; not this time. Not ever again.

"Now that the script is finished, I think I'll take some time off. If that's all right with you."

"That's a good idea," said the Fox. "You look burnt out. How long do you want?"

"Is three weeks possible?"

"Yeah, we can do three weeks. It'll be good for you."

When I got home from Berlin the next day, I packed up everything I owned, then called a moving company. Forty-eight hours later, I was on a plane headed to Dallas. By the end of the week, I had signed a lease on a new apartment.

It would have been easier to quit, but even then I couldn't bring myself to do it. Quitting felt like failure. I needed the Fox to fire me. It would be my only saving grace, a lie I could hold on to in the future when I looked back and wondered where I'd gone wrong.

He didn't.

15

INTO DARKNESS

In Dallas, I had a one-bedroom apartment where I rarely left the living room. A card table and folding chair were my office, a couch was my bed. Every day from eight until eleven in the morning, I was online with Germany. Starting at noon, I was with California.

When we started production on *Spec Ops*, 2K was still located in New York. That put us only six hours behind Yager, meaning our office hours overlapped. If there was a disagreement or concern on either side, we could get on a conference call and talk it out. This all changed when our office moved to California. Those three extra hours were literally the difference between night and day.

When I was still living in Novato, Yager and I were out of sync. I'd arrive to work in the morning as they were heading home for the evening. The ability to converse in real time became limited. Most issues were discussed over email, which changed the dynamic. Instead of talking through issues together, we were responding to one another hours later. This only led to increased frustration between the publisher and the dev team.

It was unexpected, but my relocation to Dallas helped production during the final months of development. Moving two time zones to the east made me the bridge between developer and publisher I was always meant to be. This was great for them, but I was still spiraling. Even though the *Spec Ops* script was finished, my work wasn't done. There were new cinematics to storyboard, music to license, a final voice-over session to direct, and DLC to write.

DLC stands for downloadable content. It's an expansion to the original game and can be something like additional character costumes, a new multiplayer map, or a narrative expansion that tells a new story within the same world. Sometimes DLC will be given away for free, but usually the player has to pay for it.

The more DLC a game has, the more players tend to see it as an attempt to nickel-and-dime them. Make no mistake, that's exactly what DLC is, but as I've said before, wanting to make money off your work is not evil or wrong. You see, the production cost of AAA games has steadily increased while the consumer cost has remained at sixty dollars for around eleven years. If AAA games were appropriately priced, you'd pay more than a hundred dollars for them. Since that won't fly, we've turned to DLC to cover the difference.

Over the past few years, we've made DLC a major part of a AAA game's release by preselling season passes. A season pass guarantees a certain amount of downloadable content to be released over the course of a year. This shows we won't abandon the game upon release, which in turn earns a bit of loyalty from you. That's enough, though. We also hook you by selling the season pass at a slightly discounted price, in the hopes that by purchasing it you will hold on to your game for at least a year and not sell it back to a retail store, which means there are fewer used games for sale.

Used games are bad for the industry. When players buy used games, all the money goes to the retailer. If someone buys a new game on Tuesday for sixty dollars, then sells it back three days later, the store can resell it for fifty-eight dollars. That afternoon, someone else buys the used copy because two dollars off is better than nothing. In four days, that game technically made two sales, but only one of them earned money for its creators. DLC, especially season passes, helps prolong the amount of time between purchase and resale, meaning more money ends up where it belongs—with us.

DLC isn't going anywhere; it is now an essential part of a AAA game's life cycle. If that seems wrong to you, as a gamer, I'm sorry to say I don't care. You're already paying less for our work than you should be. I'm far more concerned with what it means for us, as creators. The financial necessity of downloadable content means narrative-driven games can no longer stand on their own. Even if the core experience doesn't need a narrative expansion, it will get one at some point within the next year.

With some games, this is easy to pull off. The Borderlands franchise has amazing DLC that continues the main game's story in an organic way, including the greatest piece of DLC I've ever seen, *Tiny Tina's Assault on Dragon Keep*. In *TTAoDK*, you play a character in an FPS representation of a pen-and-pencil role-playing game (think *Dungeons & Dragons*). With Tiny Tina serving as Dungeon Master, you play a game within the game and set out to save the Queen, who happens to be a pony made of diamonds named Butt Stallion. I mean, holy shit. Layers upon layers, and all for a six-hour expansion pack.

Other games, like *Spec Ops*, weren't designed for narrative expansion. In fact, one of the reasons all the characters die is because I was worried we might try to make a direct sequel, which to me felt untrue to the characters and what they endured. I was naïve. In video games, only death and DLC are certain, and the former will not stop the latter.

YOU HEAR STORIES ABOUT method actors who attempt to inhabit their characters so completely that they never stop acting, even between takes. Daniel Day-Lewis is a great example. He's notorious for staying in character for the entire duration of a film's production. While filming *The Last of the Mohicans*, he didn't go anywhere without his twelve-pound flintlock. During *The Crucible*, he only traveled on horseback. As Bill the Butcher in *Gangs of New York*, Lewis made things very difficult for the catering department, as he refused to eat meat he did not personally butcher. A lot of people don't know that. Mostly because I made it up. But it sounds like something he'd do, and that's my point. Creating and inhabiting a character can lead you to do some crazy things.

There has always been concern that violent video games create violent people. It's nonsense. All you need do is look around to see the truth of that. No matter how violent a game or extreme the carnage, players are rarely required to take part in a malicious act of violence. The most common combat scenario for a video game is one of survival: the player comes under threat of deadly force and must respond in kind. This won't put them in the mindset of a desperate victim struggling to survive, unless that's what we want them to feel. It's more likely the situation will be designed toward fun and adrenaline, but that is a different emotional space than what is required to kill someone.

Even when there are exceptions, players are still physically separated from the actions of the character they're controlling. They can inhabit a character for a time and walk in their blood-soaked shoes, but it is a superficial connection. Violent actions are as physically close as the television or monitor and yet still a million miles away. Even though players control a character, they are still separate from the actions occurring in the game. The physical effort required to kill a person is replaced with the press of a button. Shoot someone? Press a button. Hit them with a stick? Press a button. Summon forth a swarm of man-eating rats? Press a button. The player's physical interaction is minimal; it carries none of the literal or figurative weight of a real act of violence. Any connection between the player and character ends the moment they put down their controller.

The same cannot be said for a character's creators. We have to live with these creations for the rest of our lives. The main characters of *Spec Ops*—Captain Walker, John Konrad, and the rest—were not plucked fully formed from the ether. They grew from the darker side of our minds. Their brutality did not exist until we gave them name and verb.

Spec Ops had left me in an emotional state that was me and yet not me. It was the Lizard Brain—a mind capable of creating a hundred maniacs who in turn create a mind capable of birthing them. My mind was eating itself, like some kind of bastard *ouroboros*, that ancient symbol of a snake devouring its own tail.

The last thing I wanted was to return to Dubai, but it was out of my hands. Someone had to write the DLC. Over the course of two weeks, Yager and I hashed out a plan for a narrative expansion. We considered doing a prequel about Konrad and the Damned 33rd going to war against the CIA Grey Fox squad, but the idea had no meat to it. Most prequels are pointless; anything worth seeing was already in the original story. That left a sequel story, or a narrative coda. What happened to our characters after the game had ended?

Unfortunately, *Spec Ops* had already answered that question. Lugo was lynched, Adams was killed by a falling helicopter, and Walker was . . . well, depending on what ending the player chose, he was either dead or insane or on his way back to America. That didn't leave us much wiggle room. The only thing we had going for us was that we don't see Adams's death. The player, as Walker, is sprinting across a bridge. Adams is behind you, shooting a helicopter with a mounted .50 caliber machine gun. We don't see the chopper crash, but we feel it. Its explosion knocks us off our feet. Walker face-plants into the concrete and blacks out. When he comes to, there's no sign of Adams; only smoldering wreckage.

Adams's final act in the game was a purposeful one: he wanted to ensure his own death. But what if Adams didn't die? What if the chopper crash missed him by just enough that the explosion blew him off the roof into the nearby water? Even after all he'd been through, would waking up scarred and alive be the worst thing that ever happened to him? That was the premise of our DLC expansion, *Long Way Home*.

This five-mission story was never produced, but the script exists. In it, Adams wakes up to find Dubai in a state of relative calm. The carnage caused by the player during the main game has brought a semblance of peace, if only because afterward, so few are left alive. The survivors are making their way out of the city. They know the sandstorms might kill them, but death is certain if they don't try.

Adams, his face burnt enough to be unrecognizable, attempts to leave Dubai by pretending to be one of Konrad's men. Along the way, he meets Sgt. Pozza, a young member of the Damned 33rd. Adams can't help but see echoes of Lugo in Sgt. Pozza; somehow, the horrors of Dubai have not touched his youthful optimism. Adams came to Dubai to save people, but instead brought pain and suffering to everyone he met. Rescuing Pozza is his last chance to do something good.

The DLC ends with Adams and Pozza passing safely through the sandstorm surrounding Dubai. For Adams, his mission is finally over. He uses his radio to call for an evacuation. As Adams talks, Lieutenant Pozza realizes this man, his savior, is not who he claimed to be.

Pozza raises his pistol. Adams turns to face him, weapon already drawn. They lock eyes. Adams shakes his head, as if to say "Not yet."

Adams finishes his report. Help is on its way. He shuts off the radio and lets it fall from his hand, almost thoughtlessly. It lands in the sand at his feet.

POZZA
You lied to me.

ADAMS
Yeah, I did. So what?

POZZA
So *what*? You ruined everything. This is your fault.

ADAMS
It's everyone's fault.

POZZA

We were trying to help.

ADAMS

So were we. Things got outta hand.

POZZA cocks his gun.

POZZA

You destroyed the water. You killed those people at the Gate.

ADAMS

Not arguing that.

ADAMS lowers his gun and throws it away. His shoulders sag.
He is weak, tired. His eyes stare at the ground.

ADAMS

Go home to your family. Be better than what happened here.

POZZA

The hell are you doing? This some kinda trick?

ADAMS

No trick. Just calling in your debts.

ADAMS pulls LUGO's dog tags out of his pocket. He tosses them
in the sand between him and POZZA.

ADAMS

Those belonged to Staff Sgt. John Lugo. Make sure they get to his family.

That's number one. Number two . . .

ADAMS lifts his head just enough to look POZZA in the eyes.

He points to the left side of his chest, below his heart but near his lung.

ADAMS

Aim here. It won't be fast, but that's all right.

I'll bleed out before the medevac arrives.

Tell them I was injured during our escape.

You tried to revive me, but I was too far gone.

POZZA

. . . Why?

ADAMS

'Cuz I can't do this anymore.

Subtlety has never been my strong suit. This was my cry for help. I couldn't write *Spec Ops* anymore. My characters had to die so I could get them out of my head.

THE FOX MANDATED I spend one week a month in California. Since I had relocated without his permission, he would not allow me to expense these trips. That's what he said, but I later found out the real reason I couldn't expense anything was because no one knew I was in Dallas. Everyone at the office believed I was still living in Berlin full time. The Fox was afraid that if word got out he'd have no choice but to fire me, and that's not something he wanted to do.

Flying to the Bay Area for a week is not cheap. I did the math, and each trip would eat up an entire paycheck. I couldn't afford that, so I picked up a sleeping bag and cot from an army surplus store and hid them in my office. Whenever I was in town, I slept there. My office was secluded enough that I could disappear inside it and most people wouldn't know I was there. There was a window by the door, which I blocked with a bookcase. At night, after everyone had gone home, I'd set up my cot, put on my jammies, and watch TV on the free Wi-Fi until I fell asleep. In the morning, I'd wake up early and rush downstairs to shower in the men's room before anyone else arrived.

Look, I've been pretty honest with you about my unhealthy relationship with work, so it shouldn't come as a surprise when I tell you that living in my office felt natural. This was where I'd been heading all along, and you know what? I kinda liked it.

One night, after I thought everyone had left, I went for a stroll around the office. I've always enjoyed being alone in a place usually filled with activity. The stillness feels alien, the silence expansive. Both have a way of seeping into your skin.

This particular night, I wasn't as alone as I thought. There was a light coming from the back of the hangar. By sheer chance of luck, I had not yet changed into my pajamas, so I decided to check it out.

The light was coming from Carlito's office. I hadn't seen him since I'd moved to Dallas.

I stuck my head in. "You're here late."

He grunted. "Going over animations for *Darkness II*."

Based on the comic book of the same name, *The Darkness II* is an FPS in which you play Jackie Estacado, don of the Franchetti crime family and host to the Darkness, the supernatural embodiment of all things evil. What this means for the player is that you're not limited to killing people with just guns; you can also tear them apart with twin demon heads sprouting from your shoulders, crush them inside localized black holes, or use your giant tentacle to whip them around like a squirrel caught by its tail. It's quite fun. In the game, Jackie comes under attack from the Brotherhood, an ancient order once sworn to fight the Darkness that now seeks to harness its power to rule the world. The Brotherhood is comprised of some truly sick fuckers, as is required by the game's main conceit. When your hero is an amoral mob boss literally possessed by the Devil, then your villains have to work overtime to convince you they're not actually the good guys.

Before this moment, I'd had only a brief involvement with *The Darkness II*. When coming up with the game's story, someone had sent me a summary outlining the Brotherhood's evil plan. It read: "Jackie's gang is selling drugs throughout the city. As part of their evil plan, the Brotherhood hijacks those drugs and adds a chemical to them, causing drug users to spiral into paranoia and despair."

To which I responded: "Drugs already do that."

It was a humorous oversight that was quickly corrected, but no one sent me another summary after that. Having enjoyed the first game in The Darkness franchise, I was excited to see how the second one was shaping up.

I watched over Carlito's shoulder as the Darkling crawled up the mobster's shirt and proceeded to claw his eyes out. Lizard Brain punched me hard in the gut. Words oozed out of my subconscious, coating my mind in a rancid, oily film. Anyone with nails can claw someone's eyes out, I thought. There's no style in it. No flair.

My mouth said, "It'd be better if he face-fucked that guy to death." Would it, Mouth? Would it really?

"I think they want the British Darkling to do that."

"There's a British one? If he doesn't fuck that guy's face while screaming 'I call this one the Margaret Thatcher,' then this game is bullshit."

Lizard Brain smiled, and I smiled with him.

"You about to head to your hotel?" asked Carlito. He was busy. This conversation may have been a brief respite, but I could tell he was ready to get back to work.

"Technically, I'm at my hotel. The Fox won't let me expense my trips out here, so I've been sleeping on a cot in my office. Don't tell anyone."

Telling Carlito was a little risky. I knew that if the Fox learned I was sleeping in the office, he'd make sure to kick me out every night. But honestly, I'd been dying to tell someone. If there was anyone I could trust to keep it a secret, it was Carlito.

He sniffed at the air. "Have you been showering?"

"Don't worry; I'm clean. I wake up at five a.m. and use the shower downstairs before anyone else shows up. If you've noticed a pair of flip-flops in the hall drying over an air vent, those are mine. I've been thinking about getting a hot plate. Then I can invite people over for dinner. Honestly, I don't even know why he has me fly out here. I'm not working on anything."

Carlito looked up. "You know, we need someone to write lore for *Darkness II*—"

"I'll do it." My answer came out a little too fast. Carlito could see I was jonesing. With nothing of substance to write, my depression had been steadily growing. I didn't need a long-term fix; I was still holding out for a new project I could shepherd from start to finish. Until that came around, I needed something to fill the hours and make the keyboard go clickity-clack. I needed to save the day.

"Are you sure you want to work on this?" asked Carlito.

"Listen," I said. "I don't want to join up for the rest of the project. All I want is to help out." I was pumping myself up as I spoke. "Tell me what you need, and I'll send you a script. After that, you and the team can do whatever you want with it. We saved *Spec Ops*, man. We can save this, too. Let's do it. Let's slay the fucking dragon!"

Carlito was not the sort of person to be moved by a motivational speech. He arched an eyebrow in my direction. "Do you *actually* want to help, or are you just bored?"

"Seriously, I want to help."

"Okay. I'll send you the stuff." He turned back to his wall of computer screens. "Now, fuck off. I got shit to do."

WHAT IS LORE?

If you play video games, you already know about lore. For the un-initiated, I'll try to explain it to you in a way that gives you the fullest picture.

Imagine you are a level-one associate at the latest installment of a derivative yet beloved fast-food franchise. You lead a life of grand adventure, undertaking such quests as "Fetch Ten Hamburgers" and "Defeat the Clogged Toilet," and yet it all feels so arbitrary. Why am I fetching hamburgers? you wonder. Who's eating them? Where did they come from? Is there some ancient, mystical significance to the number ten? If you could answer these questions, it would strengthen your re-solve and renew your sense of purpose. Lucky for you, the franchise managers have hidden a complete set of the *Encyclopedia Britannica* around the restaurant. During your legally mandated break, you track down a few volumes and learn how your fast-food franchise got its start in Southern California, a state whose name was derived from an early-sixteenth-century Spanish novel, *Las Sergas de Esplandián*, the fifth book in a series of chivalric romance novels, which was a literary genre of high culture famously burlesqued in *Don Quixote*, which served as the source material for the film *Man of La Mancha* starring Sophia Loren and Peter O'Toole, an actor who received eight Academy Award nominations for Best Actor in a Leading Role, making him the most nominated actor to never win the award, a fact many people consider a travesty since his body of work includes such beloved films as *Lawrence of Arabia*, *High Spirits*, and *King Ralph*, many of which were once available on VHS, an ancient video-playback device you've seen gather-ing dust in a dark corner of the break room. Wow! You had no idea you were fetching hamburgers in a world with such a rich, vibrant history.

That's lore—an encyclopedic brain dump of nonnecessary exposi-tion injected into a video game by way of audio logs, notepads, books, and actual encyclopedias. These textual diversions exist to make digital worlds appear larger by padding them out with useless trivia. Lore is great, and I love it dearly.

Not everyone feels this way about lore. If a game's lore is too detailed, it runs the risk of committing the one true cardinal sin of game design—infringing on the self-indulgence of the player. By expanding a game's world through backstory, we create a prison of words and meaning. Our authorial intent destroys the player's narrative agency, turning a subjective story into an objective one. But lore isn't just for the player; it's also for the writer. I may write a game's story, but it doesn't belong to me. I bend and twist my words to fit the player's dreams, not my own. Lore is mine. The player can't have it. Even if they could, it would never give them the same thing it gives me—the sweet release of artistic freedom.

Everyone who works on a AAA game will find some way to leave their personal mark. Audio designers secretly implement their own sounds, audibly immortalizing their cat, car, or child. Designers build hidden rooms into their levels, never intending for them to be found. Artists create signs for stores and products, naming them after friends, family, and teammates. These are fingerprints—small, human touches added to huge AAA games. Each smudge is a moment of self-indulgence through which we claim ownership of our work. For writers, this can be hard to accomplish. So much of what we write for a game is directional. "Go here." "Shoot them." "Find the thing." It's only with lore that we're free to just be writers. For us, lore is the easiest way to leave our mark.

"I made this," we shout into the digital void. "I was here. I mattered."

DIGITAL EXTREMES, THE DEVELOPER of *The Darkness II*, needed me to write lore for thirty Relics scattered throughout the game. The art assets had already been created; they were random things like an old metal box, a human skull engraved with runes, and a Nazi dagger.

JOHNNY POWELL
Oh, man . . . This takes me back. It was the year I turned twenty-one.
I scrawled my first pentagram that summer. Talked to my first dead person.
Slept with my first succub—uh, you know what? Forget that.
I'm rambling. It's this knife. Nazi paraphernalia always makes me nostalgic,
and *wow*, that sounds really bad when I say it out loud. I should explain . . .

It was my job to provide narrative and historical context to each Relic. The information would be explained by the character Johnny Powell, the player's in-house occultist. When the player brought Johnny a Relic, he would rattle off the description, giving the player some lore. When strung together, these bits of backstory would tell a semi-coherent tale of the war between good and evil spanning all of human history.

JOHNNY POWELL
What you got here is "The First." As you can guess by its name,
this thing goes back. Like, way back. To the beginning. You're a good
Catholic boy, so I know you remember the story of Cain and Abel.
How Abel was like, "Oh, God loves me," and Cain was all, "Jealousy!
Wham!" and killed him. With this. That's right—you're now the proud
owner of Murder Stick #1. So, congrats, I guess.

Carlito sent me the spreadsheet on a Friday. As usual, he needed the lore by Monday. There were no reasonable schedules with this man. That was fine. A weekend was more than enough time, and it's not like I was doing anything with my life. I hadn't cracked a copy of the Bible in ten years, but it all came rushing back to me.

JOHNNY POWELL
Ah, the Lantern of St. Anthony. Possibly the most misidentified
item ever created. I don't mean people look at this lamp and say, "That is

a very luminescent club sandwich." I mean most people see this lantern as a symbol of hope, but really it's a symbol of soul-crushing despair.

I wasn't filling in cells on a spreadsheet; I was exorcising demons.

JOHNNY POWELL

This is the Reliquary of the Blessed Blood, said to contain a relic of untold worth. An object of unfathomable holiness. A preserved piece of flesh from the Messiah himself. Yes. That's right. We're talking about the foreskin of Jesus Christ.

Over the next two days, I channeled all my years of Bible schooling into that lore. When Monday rolled around, I proudly delivered thirty Relics to Digital Extremes. I had no idea how they were going to react, and I didn't care.

JOHNNY POWELL

This is, well . . . it's a thumb screw. Don't really know what else to tell you.

What? You want more? Ugh. Sure. Just gimme a second . . . Ummmmm, ah! Okay, I got something . . . This is the infamous Black Thumb. In 1631, it single-handedly ripped its way across the English countryside, leaving behind a trail of bloody bastards and broken dreams. Never has the world seen such carnage. Pray it never will again. Yes, I'm being sarcastic. No, I don't want you to kill me. Okay, I'll shut up now.

Turns out they loved it. After that, Digital Extremes sent me everything that had managed to slip through the cracks. I wrote barks for the game's four-player multiplayer mode in which a samurai, a Mossad agent, a voodoo doctor, and a Scotsman who's drunk enough to realize he's a video-game character team up to find the Spear of Destiny.

I churned out a Glenn Beck–inspired radio show decrying the socialist underpinnings of a beloved character whose name "starts with an M and ends with an Ario." I created hours of fake public-access programming and delivered commercials for such fine establishments as Dave's Drive-Thru Daiquiris & Discount Divorces and Itty Bitty Bang Bang, New York's premier—and only—little-person gentlemen's club, a callout to the *Rope* article I wrote in college that set me on the path to game development.

Writing lore for *The Darkness II* was my fucking vacation, a chance to free myself from the brutal self-loathing of *Spec Ops* and go full tilt into the Lizard Brain. If you get a chance, you should really pick up a copy. It's the only game in existence that includes the shrunken head of Pope John XII and a PSA for a failed Planned Parenthood drive asking college students to not use the condoms that came stapled to their safe-sex brochures.

LIKE ANY VACATION, MY time with *The Darkness II* came to an end far too soon. The downside to being a fast writer is that you reach the finish line long before everyone else. With my work finished, I returned to my normal life of waiting to die or for *Spec Ops* to ship, whichever came first.

Spec Ops: The Line was finally released on June 26, 2012, three years later than we had hoped. By then, my life was back in boxes. It had been that way for months. My brain was ready to run again, but my body didn't know where to. Working remotely had made me realize I could do my job from anywhere so long as I had an Internet connection. Five years after D. T. had spiraled out of control, I was contemplating the same thing he once had. I could put my belongings into storage and then leave to wander the world, living from paycheck to paycheck, sending dispatches from wherever I happened to be at the time. There were so many places I'd never seen, so many vacation days unused. If I was going to work too hard, it was only logical that I do it in a way that showed me the world.

Mainly, I just wanted to run away. My depression had returned with the release of *Spec Ops*. It would be easy to say I was affected by the game's performance. While *Spec Ops* found critical success, it didn't fly off the shelves. According to Strauss Zelnick, Take-Two's chairman and CEO, sales of *Spec Ops* were disappointing and "lower than expected," which helped contribute to a net loss of more than $110 million during Take-Two's first-quarter. Believe it or not, that didn't bother me one bit. It's not like it was my money. I could appreciate why Take-Two wouldn't be excited, but the lack of sales certainly wasn't a reflection on me. The only thing I cared about was the story, which seemed to be resonating with people. For the most part, reviews praised it. We were nominated for some awards, and even won a few. Some people didn't like it, but honestly, that didn't bug me, either. The way I saw it, if you played through the entire game and didn't like it, your opinion was as valid as anyone else's. So why was I depressed?

If you give yourself completely to a project, when it eventually ends, you'll find part of you is gone. Your mind will linger in the mental space you created for that game, but only as a sense memory. The game itself is no longer in your grasp. You brought it into existence, and now that it has left you behind, your purpose has been served. I was depressed because *Spec Ops* was over.

It had been eight years since I told my parents "Don't worry. I'm going to be a writer." Everything had worked out fine, just as I said it would. I had found success. Why, then, did I feel like such a failure?

It took me a long time to figure it out. It didn't even come to me until I was writing this book. Success is an oasis in the middle of the desert. Is it real or a mirage? There's no way to know, but we pursue it anyway. Some of us never reach it, but those who do are met with a surprising realization: an oasis is not paradise; it's just shade and water. If that's not what you're looking for, then it has nothing to offer.

I thought success would be a transformative experience. Once I found it, I would be content knowing that I had accomplished what so many had failed to achieve. There would be this warm, fuzzy glow in my chest, kind of like what I assumed the Prize felt like in the film *Highlander.* I'd stand up straighter and carry myself sexier, and when I looked in the mirror I'd see the person I had always wanted to be.

None of that happened. Writing didn't get easier. My confidence decreased rather than soared. And the only things that gave me a warm, fuzzy glow were watching porn and eating half a jar of peanut butter in one sitting.

Success didn't make me happy, because I wasn't looking for success. I was looking for a new me, and that asshole never showed up.

16

NOT THE FALL BUT
THE STOP

was eating dinner at a Chili's in Frisco, Texas, when I got the email.

FROM: The Fox
SUBJECT: Hey

When it comes to work emails, "Hey" is one of the worst subject lines you'll ever see. "Hey" is not a greeting; it is the textual equivalent of sitting you down, taking your hand, and saying, "We need to talk."

The email read, "I hope you are having a great Thanksgiving. We should have a call after the holiday."

The Fox once told me, "You can always tell when someone is about to quit. If they poke their head into your office and ask if you've got fifteen minutes, they just want to talk. But if they ask, 'You free?' they're quitting." The brevity is what gives it away. People tend to use fewer words when they're setting someone up for bad news. It's a trick we all use when we need to be serious but don't wish to cause alarm. I'm not sure it's ever worked. Instead you immediately know something terrible is coming. Your brain kicks into overdrive as it runs through the possibilities. That's the worst part; the not knowing.

My mind immediately jumped to its standard foregone conclusion. Surprisingly, I felt no panic; my heart didn't race. I looked at my family gathered around me—my grandparents, mother, aunt, cousin, and her three sons. I had a plate of chicken crispers with a side of honey mustard *and* ranch for optimal dipping. There was still queso in the skillet, waiting to be eaten. After dinner, we'd head back to my cousin's house and play rummy around the kitchen table.

It was nice.

Whenever I was out with people, I'd place my BlackBerry face-down on the table. The idea was that if I couldn't see the flashing red light, I wouldn't be constantly checking it—which of course made me check it more often because I couldn't see if the light was flashing. It was terrible manners, but my friends and family had come to accept it. I think that's why they noticed when I shut off the BlackBerry and shoved it in my pocket.

"Is something wrong?" my mom asked.

"Nope. I just got an email from the Fox, but it's no big deal."

"What'd it say?"

I smiled and reached for the tortilla chips. "Either I'm getting fired or the Fox is."

MY GUESS HAD BEEN close to the truth—the Fox was leaving, by choice. He'd been at it for ten years and was ready to move on. He wanted to try something new, work on a smaller scale than big-budget AAA games. But that was down the line. For now, he was going to take time off, spend it with his family, get in as much kitesurfing as possible.

I flew to San Francisco to meet my new boss, the Owl. With me, he inherited a strange situation, so it was important to introduce myself: "Hi. I'm the guy who works for you but never comes to work. Please keep giving me money." He agreed to let me keep my job, but only if I moved back. I said I needed to think about it.

That night, I met the Fox for dinner in San Francisco. We ate sushi and spent most of the meal quietly judging an exceptionally fit man in his late forties. The Fox swore he knew the man. "I see him on the weekend at the soccer fields. He likes to hit on the fifteen-year-old girls." Looking at him, it wasn't hard to believe. He wore a Lycra shirt and shorts, in December. While perusing the menu, he commented aloud so no one in the restaurant would miss out on his very important opinion. He was a joke, and made for an easy distraction from our uncomfortable conversation.

Maybe eight years is too long to work with the same person. The closer your relationship, the harder it is to separate that person from the job. Just the sight of their face can trigger an emotional response, ingrained through years of shared stress. The Fox and I had our ups and downs. Through the years, our relationship had been paternal, empowering, toxic, or any combination of the three. We'd never been afraid to speak openly with each other, so you might think our dinner conversation would have been an honest reflection of our time together. In my experience, that's not how endings work in the games industry.

There is relief that comes with the completion of a project. It is an opiate, numbing you to the pain you've felt for months, even years. You can't deny the bad times, but in the high of the moment, you'd rather focus on the good. Talk of terrible schedules, overblown egos, unreasonable demands, and never-ending dumpster fires can wait until later. Later almost always means never. If an unsolved problem didn't ruin a project, then was it really a problem? The theoretical answer is yes; obviously this issue needs to be addressed. The practical answer is what you'd expect—Eh?

Who knows? Maybe every job is like that. For all we know, on April 16, CPAs across the country pop bottles of champagne, pass around plastic cups, and do their best to leave the last four months behind them.

"Yvonne, about what I said—"

"Forget it, Jillian. We can hate each other tomorrow. Today, we're alive."

The Fox and I reminisced, listed off regrets, and were generous with our compliments and apologies, but we never touched the sore spots. The bruises had formed during the last two years, as we fought to get *Spec Ops* out the door. There was no reason to sully our good memories with the bad. This was the end.

After a few hours, we stepped out into the cold, foggy San Francisco night. I appreciated the ambiance. The best good-byes always come with a little drama, and the weather was definitely giving off a *Casablanca* vibe.

The Fox unchained his bike and rolled it toward me. "Do you think you'll move back?"

"Who knows? They want me to, but I feel like I've done San Francisco. The idea of moving back feels like going in reverse. I guess we'll see."

He leaned across his bike and gave me a hug. "It was good to see you," he said. "Good luck with everything."

"You, too."

The Fox climbed onto his bike and steadied himself with one foot on a pedal and the other on the sidewalk. He looked back at me and said, "If I could give you one piece of advice, it would be this—work on your people skills. I've always believed you would be someone in this industry, and I'm not just saying that. People like what you do, but they think you're difficult. So far, every developer you've worked with has said they never want to work with you again. You won't go very far if you can't get along with anyone."

"In my defense, no one wants to work with me because you always made me deliver your bad news. You made me play the bad guy so you wouldn't have to."

The Fox's eyes sparkled. His grin was wide and smug. "It's true; I did. Thanks for that."

With that, the Fox pushed off and peddled away. He raised a hand above his head and waved, never looking back.

"Ciao."

IN THE END, I came back.

I like making things, and my job allowed me to do that. It never occurred to me that I wasn't ready. There were a lot of new faces in the office. Even people I'd known for years looked like strangers. Between my time in Berlin and Dallas, I'd been gone too long. During my occasional visits, my constant negativity had pushed them away. Instead of trying to reach out and rebuild relationships, I did what I always do—sought comfort in my work.

Trying to find a new project was like going through my closet only to learn I had outgrown all my clothes. The places I'd been, creatively, had left me in a particular state of mind. To call it dark would be dishonest, because to me it never seemed that way. The people I worked with probably would disagree.

I joined the *Mafia III* writers' room for a few weeks. The game was set in a facsimile of New Orleans during the sixties. It seemed like a good fit since I was from Louisiana. It was somewhat late in the project; the writers had already worked out most of the story and characters. I was just there to help iron out the kinks, one of the biggest being the third act. The plan was for Frank, the player's character, to take advantage of a gang war and use it to wipe out his rivals. They just didn't know how to kick things off.

"What if," I said, "Frank's rivals kill Sam, but they do it in a normal, mundane way, like shooting him in the chest? Frank knows Sam's gang will be pissed, but not enough to fight back. So what if Frank secretly desecrates Sam's corpse and makes it look like he was tortured? Then, when Sam's gang finds out, they lose their shit and launch a full-on gang war that Frank uses to wipe out his enemies and take over the city."

The room was silent. I thought they were letting the weight of my genius settle in, but then I noticed their uncomfortable looks.

"I dunno," said one of the writers. "That kind of makes Frank seem like a bad guy."

"Frank is a heroin dealer and a cop killer. He *is* a bad guy."

"Right, but we're not making a game about a heroin dealer. This game is about the *fantasy* of being a heroin dealer."

Clearly, it wasn't meant to be. I wasn't upset. *Mafia III* was their game, and they'd been working on it for a very long time. They didn't need my hang-ups thrown into the mix. Besides, the idea of writing another violent game wasn't enticing. There are only so many ways you can justify shooting people in the face; I'd pretty well exhausted all of them. It was time I took a break from shooters and tried something new.

Firaxis had a game in the works—*Civilization: Beyond Earth*, the latest in a franchise of 4X strategy games. In the Civilization franchise, players grow an empire from prehistory all the way to the near future, and they do it by eXploring, eXpanding, eXploiting, and eXterminating. Hence the genre name, 4X.

As *BioShock* was a spiritual successor to *System Shock 2*, *Beyond Earth* succeeded another beloved PC game, *Alpha Centauri*. In both *BE* and *AC*, players colonized alien worlds and built new human civilizations among the stars. The game had violence, but it wasn't necessary. *Beyond Earth* and the other Civilization games pride themselves on giving players multiple paths to victory. Even if you chose the path of military conquest, it wasn't AAA violence. No one would be gored by a giant drill or orally violated by a tiny demon. At most, you'd be looking at an animated version of the board game *Risk*. It was exactly what I was looking for.

There were no story meetings for *Beyond Earth*. Firaxis would send me a list of prompts, and I would generate text for them. Simple, straightforward. I liked that.

The first prompt they sent was for a quest. A spaceship crashes near the player's outpost. Upon inspection, the player discovers the ship's inhabitants have survived thanks to technological modifications they made to their bodies. These people are cyborgs, and they need the player's help to survive.

The quest plays out one of two ways. The player can aid the cyborgs by inviting them into their community, causing technological body modification to spread among the player's citizens. Or, the player can kill the cyborgs to ensure their citizens remain fully human.

"We like what you sent," said a voice on my phone. "It's well written, but it's too dark."

"I mean, it's kind of a dark choice," I said. "We're giving players the option to kill refugees to protect the genetic purity of their people. I hate to play the Hitler card, but it's a little Third Reich, don't you think?"

"We hear what you're saying, and in the real world that would be true. But in a video game, the player is always good. Whatever choice the player makes is always the right choice. The script needs to reflect that."

Whatever choice the player makes is always the right choice.

It was the most insightful and damning description of video games I had ever heard.

Despite this book being evidence to the contrary, I consider myself a professional. If you pay me to write something, I will write it regardless of my own feelings. That's how jobs work. Careers are not magical wish fulfillment where you are paid a constant living wage for only doing what you want to do, when you want to do it. This understanding has served me well in the video-game industry. Working in AAA, I never had a problem writing and designing terrible things for players to do, because it was always presented with a degree of honesty. At its core, art is emotional manipulation. If you're inclined toward that sort of work, there's a good chance you already inhabit a philosophical gray area. Even in *BioShock*, when we downplayed killing Little Sisters by keeping the death off camera and referring to it as "Harvesting," the player was still labeled a "bad" person. If you killed a Little Sister, you could not receive the game's happy ending. To this day, I'm still fine with it.

So, I rewrote the quest and sent it back, expecting that to be the end of it.

There was no call this time; just an email. "The text was still too dark," said the words on my computer screen. The developer would write it themselves.

That night, I couldn't sleep. Rewriting the mission felt like I had normalized genetic cleansing. Even worse, I apparently did a piss-poor job of it. It would be wrong to say it compromised my integrity, because I did it willingly, but I definitely felt like I'd crossed a personal line.

I wasn't angry at Firaxis, though. During game development, there's no such thing as a bad idea. An idea becomes bad only once it has shipped. Prior to that, it's just an idea. During development, it can be expanded, removed, or altered in such a way that it barely resembles the original concept. For this reason, a potentially bad idea can go unnoticed for longer than you might expect, and that's okay. What matters is catching the bad idea before you ship. Firaxis did that. The quest to save your people's genetic purity from a bunch of filthy cyborgs never made it into the final game. The only person who failed was me. I rewrote a quest that made me extremely uncomfortable, but not so uncomfortable that I stopped writing the game.

If you want be angry at someone, look no further. I will always be your guy.

MONTHS LATER, I WAS still looking for a full-time project. *Beyond Earth* was behind me. I was at a new developer, which will remain nameless. The studio's in-house writer was explaining their game's opening sequence. I looked across the table to Carlito. His face echoed what I was feeling: so much of the opening sequence was wrong.

I don't mean it was bad or trite; I wasn't looking at it subjectively. I mean the sequence accomplished the opposite of what the developer intended. They wanted the player to feel powerful and in control but had designed a scenario in which the player is forced to run for their life. My instinct was to stop the writer's presentation and explain the misstep so the team could go about fixing it.

There was a familiar excitement in the team's eyes. I could see they were in love with the idea. They thought it was stage-ready, and nothing would convince them otherwise.

I already knew what came next. I would point out the mistake; they would get defensive and reject our feedback. Their rejection would offend me on some primal level, and I would write them off as incompetent. We would struggle for power until the end. They would despise me, and I would lose another year inside a hotel room, trying to move the needle a few centimeters for a game I didn't even care that much about.

Wait. This isn't right. We've done this already.

Yes, I had. And I was so very tired.

I picked up my BlackBerry and sent an email to Carlito. "I don't want to fight anymore. Let them do what they want."

NINE YEARS AFTER WALKING through its door in an ill-advised suit, I said good-bye to 2K Games. When the familiar faces are outnumbered by the new, it's time to go.

Geekjock left for WB, where he now produces some of the best AAA games I've ever played. Bruce, the Persian goat snake of PR, stayed in New York instead of following us to California. He left the industry after that, choosing to pursue a law degree and learn circus gymnastics. Lily also jumped ship and moved back east. These days, she's a VP at a popular Internet company and couldn't be happier. Bonnie quit after she got married and realized being a mom is actually fun when you're raising a kid instead of a dev team. She came back four years later and is now director of development for an indie studio that focuses on experimental, sustainable development. Young Philippe left 2K Publishing to fulfill his dream of being a game designer. He worked on *Mafia III* for a bit before spinning off to join Jordan Thomas's indie studio, Question

LLC. I've heard from mutual friends that D. T. is doing well. We haven't spoken in years. I reached out, but never heard back.

Carlito is still Carlito, for the most part. His body has been worked to the brink so many times that it now requires routine maintenance for things like staph infections, nerve damage, and the occasional spinal surgery. He's more machine now than man, which is why I'm sure he'll outlive us all. Carlito will never get the recognition he deserves, but the games we play are better because he's still out there doing what has to be done.

The last time I saw the Fox was at my apartment in Oakland, a month after my daughter was born. It was awkward and a little bittersweet. I didn't know what to say to this man who gave me a chance when I was just twenty-three and was now meeting my daughter before I packed up my entire life and moved back to Louisiana. I still don't know what to say.

You might think a video-game company is defined by its games, but really it comes down to the people who create them. A company is just an idea whose boundaries are defined by paperwork and red tape. Its heart and mind are the people who work there. A great company is not a well-oiled machine; rather, it is a collection of seemingly incompatible pieces, soldered together to create something better, stronger, and faster than the sum of its parts. It may be a little messy, but so are video games. Like all art, games are an expression of the people who make them; people who are unique, derivative, functional, broken, and above all, messy.

These people were my coworkers and my family. Good and bad, I owe them everything.

Epilogue

NEW GAME PLUS

Looking back, I can see where I began to pull away from the games industry. While living in Dallas, I'd reconnected with Katie, whom I had dated in college. Katie wasn't interested in video games. She respected them and understood their importance in my life, but that was the extent of it. When I talked about games with her, it wasn't a hobby or a passion, it was just my job. It may not seem like much, but it was enough to make me engage with the real world. Katie encouraged me to disconnect from work and interact with new people. It started slow; just leaving the apartment once a day for lunch. After a couple weeks, I was taking daily walks to grocery stores and coffee shops. Soon, I was visiting family, bowling with friends, attending plays, taking vacations. She reminded me what it meant to have a life, and to actually live it. I think that was the most important part. For a long time, the people closest to me were those who loved work as much as I did. Spending Saturday or Sunday in the office didn't seem strange when your friends were there, too.

It would have been easy to slip back into my old routine when I returned to working full time in 2K's California office. But with Katie there, I had an anchor to the outside world. Instead of obsessing over projects, she and I were making new friends, spending weekends in Napa, attending all-day board-game parties, getting married, honeymooning on Kauai, gorging ourselves on chicken wings, hiking in Big Sur, riding party trains to Reno, tracking down lobster rolls, watching the sun set over Oakland. Turns out the Bay Area is an amazing place when you can enjoy it with the right person.

After all that good living, work just wasn't fun anymore. I left 2K and went to work for a start-up, but it wasn't any better. I was simply tired of making games. When Katie and I found out she was pregnant, we packed our bags and headed south. Back home in Louisiana, I'd write this book; my final contribution to the game industry. Then, I would open a sandwich shop. There's a small piece of undeveloped commercial property on the side of a road in Monroe, Louisiana. No more than a hundred feet all around, just enough room for a shack and a picnic table. There would be no designers, no players; just hungry people looking for a brief moment of happiness, one sandwich at a time. That would have been a good life, but it wouldn't have been mine.

As we were preparing to leave San Francisco, I received a call from Mark Thompson and J-F Poirier, the game director and executive producer at EA Motive in Montreal. I thought there was nothing they could offer that would pull me back in.

"We're curious if you'd be interested in writing *Star Wars*."

I was an idiot to think I could give this up.

Ten months later, after a brief stop in a galaxy far, far away, I'm in Louisiana, hard at work on the next chapter of my life. There's a concept in video games called New Game Plus. Sometimes, after you beat a game, you can choose to start over from the beginning. You'll keep the skills you gained during your first play-through, but the game's difficulty will be greatly increased. That's what I'm working on now—my New Game Plus.

I'm starting a new studio with James Stewart, a brilliant programmer and engineer from my hometown of Bossier City–Shreveport. We both worked at 2K for years but didn't meet until my final day at the company. Now, we've both come home to build a Louisiana studio inspired by the filmmaker Roger Corman. Corman is known for shooting entire films in just a few days with almost no budget. He works fast, sometimes producing up to nine films a year. If he rented a film set for seven days but finished filming in five, he'd use the last two days to make a second movie. Sets, props, actors, all carried over from one film to the next. His method is fast, focused, and straight from the hip. Having spent years on AAA games, fretting over every decision, James and I think Roger Corman is a goddamn hero.

It's time the video-game industry had a solid, trash-pop, B-grade developer churning out games that are cheap and strange. We'd love to be that for you; that is, if we don't fail gloriously. I'd be lying if I said that didn't worry me. But if there's one thing I learned as a twenty-three-year-old kid who moved to New York with nothing but a suitcase, it's that anything is possible when you're too naïve to realize you're screwed.

I still work too much; usually seven days a week. There's no helping that. If I go longer than two days without writing, depression sets in. There's something about making these keys go clickity-clack that's better than any drug or drink. I love it, except for when I hate it, which is a lot less often than it used to be. As I write this, I can hear my wife eating dinner in the kitchen, her fork scraping against a plate. My daughter is crying, probably because she tried to grab the dog's ears and he ran away. Life is waiting for me at the end of this book, and I try to not stay gone for too long.

There are thirty-five games lined up on a shelf next to my desk, the result of ten years of work by me and at least a thousand other developers. Eleven of those games are unplayable on modern consoles. In another decade, who knows how many more? Video games are technologically dependent. If the bombs ever drop, they'll be completely wiped out. There will be nothing left for archeologists to discover. We video-game developers will not share the grand stage of human history. Even if our medium persists until the stars die out, the games we make now won't be around to see it. They are temporary, like us. It's their impermanence that makes them truly unique. Games, as an art form, reflect humanity by embodying our mortality, self-indulgence, and delusions. They are digital performance art, capable of imprinting messages onto our memories as easily as they're received from real-life experiences. In this way, games are more than entertainment. Even though you and I may never meet, our lives have already overlapped. We've known the fear and isolation of *Metroid*'s alien planet, Zebes. In *Call of Duty 4: Modern Warfare*, we hid in the grass of Pripyat and held our breath as enemy soldiers passed by not ten feet away. We have felt our fingers begin to slip as we clung to the wing of a giant bird in *Shadow of the Colossus*. Games let us transcend our subjective points of view and come together in a life of shared moments.

Now that I'm free to create anything I want, it's more important than ever that I make something worthwhile. When an idea grips me and won't let go, I ask myself one question. *Is it worth abandoning my real world to create this fake one?* The question I've stopped asking is, *What does the player want?* There are seven billion people on this planet, all of whom are potentially the Player. I'm not masochistic enough to lump the entire spectrum of humanity into a singular entity—the Player—just so I can spend my life trying to please it. Player interaction and gameplay are important, but on their own, they don't create meaningful experiences. Gameplay requires context and consequence beyond simply beating the game. Without them, the player's actions carry no emotional weight.

As developers, we have to abandon the idea that an action is just a tool. It's easy to think that way when you distill a game to its most basic elements. An enemy is just an obstacle. Jumping, punching, running, shooting—those are tools the player can use to overcome that obstacle. But viewing a game this way robs the work, and the players, of their humanity. To shoot, stab, or punch is a choice. And our choices define us. They reveal who we are, what we stand for, and how far we're willing to go. Why should it be any different for the characters we play in our video games? In *Spec Ops: The Line*, Captain Walker doesn't shoot people because he wants to defeat Konrad, just as I don't write video games solely to make money. Walker uses lethal force because he wants to be a good man. In his head, every bullet he fires makes the world a little safer. I write games because I want to be someone else. When I work, I can inhabit a character and forget all about my fears and insecurities. These flaws make us human. To keep games fresh and feeling new, we need to embrace that humanity, to pour every ounce of pride, jealousy, and insecurity into our work, to choke the player with honesty until they're gagging for breath.

Many independent games already do this. They don't have the large staff or outrageous budgets of AAA, meaning they're not usually beholden to a larger company. With that comes freedom. *That Dragon, Cancer* is an autobiographical game by Amy and Ryan Green chronicling their son's four-year battle with cancer. Nina Freeman's game *Cibele* is based on her experiences falling in love with someone she met while playing an online video game. In *The Novelist*, by Kent Hudson, you play a writer who must choose between finishing his book and spending time with his neglected family. These types of stories aren't found in AAA games; they're too vulnerable. That's fine. Games shouldn't be forced to fit a single definition. Billion-dollar franchises like Call of Duty and Assassin's Creed are built on empowerment, not honesty. It's an easier sell. For that reason, they will only grow more elaborate, beautiful, and expensive. But so long as AAA games continue to focus solely on what the player wants, that growth will amount to nothing but sound and fury.

Forget that noise. We can do better.

Imagine a video game that inspires the best in us rather than the worst. Imagine exploring what it means to be human instead of revisiting how it feels to be powerful. Imagine putting down the controller and being left with a sense of hope, for you and for the world.

Imagine all of these things. Then, get to work.

ACKNOWLEDGMENTS

Writing a book is very different from writing a game. The freedom that comes from a lack of designers peering over your shoulder is terrifying. Thankfully, my amazing editor, Todd Hunter, was there to guide me through the alien process of writing for myself rather than the whims of a player. I never would have made it this far without him.

Of course, none of this would have been possible if not for two people—my fantastic agent, William LoTurco, and my wife, Katie Williams—who convinced me this was a story worth telling. Katie, along with my parents, also deserves special thanks for shouldering the brunt of baby duty while I hammered out the final draft.

A huge thanks to 2K Games for allowing me the freedom to tell this story—in particular Pete Welch, who is honest but fair and wise beyond measure. To my former coworkers, whether you appear in this book or not, thanks for tolerating me throughout the years. I love you all. Yes, even you.

Thanks to Anthony Burch, Greg Kasavin, Hogarth De Le Plante, James Stewart, Jason Bergman, Ken Levine, Michael Kelly, Ryan Mattson, and Tiffany Nagano for helping fill in the blanks. To Russ

Pitts, for being a bridge to all of this. To Mitch Dyer, for constantly talking me off the ledge. And, finally, to Lin-Manuel Miranda, for writing "Non-Stop," which played on repeat as I worked to finish this book and *Star Wars Battlefront II* while moving across the country with a newborn.